TARNISHED HEELS

HOW UNETHICAL ACTIONS AND DELIBERATE DECEIT AT THE UNIVERSITY OF NORTH CAROLINA ENDED "THE CAROLINA WAY"

By:

Rob J. Anderson

"Fantastic and illuminating read. This book is ultimately a modern day tragedy in that it exposes, with excruciating detail and facts, how one of America's best public institutions sold its soul for the perceived benefits of athletic glory at the expense of core values and academic integrity. Despite years of claiming the Carolina Way and doing it right, the University of North Carolina, like so many other institutions before it, has now firmly placed itself amongst the worst offenders of academic integrity in intercollegiate athletic history."

– Dr. B. David Ridpath, Ed.D., Kahandas Nandola Professor of Sport Management at Ohio University and author of Tainted Glory: *Marshall University, The NCAA, and One Man's Fight for Justice*

"Tarnished Heels" documents the efforts to uncover the facts of the worst combined academic and athletic scandal in the history of the University of North Carolina, America's first public university. It is a sad tale of expensive and ineffective efforts at "spin" control preventing the UNC administration from admitting and correcting clear wrongdoing at an early stage in its now four-year effort. The book shows that despite specific, repeated urging of both the Chairman of the UNC-Chapel Hill Trustees and the Chairman of the Consolidated University System's Board of Governors to be quickly forthcoming and transparent, the administration repeatedly withheld facts until ordered by a court to disclose them or they were exposed by the investigative reporting of several news agencies.

"Tarnished Heels" reviews clear, and to date uncontroverted, evidence of many fraudulent no-show "classes" by faculty with the direct involvement of staff, athletic academic advisors to players, tutors and others. It is a sad story for those of us who received degrees from and truly love this great university. It is a reminder of the danger of "big time" athletics corrupting a university's academic mission and demonstrates the vital role of investigative reporting and a free press in America.

– Burley Mitchell, Retired Chief Justice of North Carolina, President, UNC Law Class of 1969

CONTENTS

Requests for permission should be directed to strategicmediabooks@gmail.com, or mailed to Permissions, Strategic Media Inc. 782 Wofford St., Rock Hill, SC 29730.

13 digit ISBN 9781939521224
10 digit ISBN 193952122x

INTRODUCTION

"The Carolina Way." It is a term that has long been used by those associated with the University of North Carolina at Chapel Hill. The connotations have by and large stood for "doing things the right way." Always being honorable. Always making the correct choice. Always doing for group and university, rather than for self.

The following declarations are proudly displayed on the website of the University's Office of Student Council:

> Since the 1875, students at the University of North Carolina have had a tradition of self-governance in matters of student discipline. Our students have pledged themselves not to lie, cheat, or steal. This commitment to academic integrity, ethical behavior, personal responsibility and civil discourse exemplifies the "Carolina Way" and serve as the foundation for our student-led Honor System.

> The Office of Student Conduct supports the fostering and development of students at the University by promoting honor, integrity, and ethical decision making. This philosophy supports the student-led Honor System's promotion of the Carolina Way by education the campus on community expectations and responsibilities. When

the need arises, the student-led Honor System
adjudicates allegations of violations to community
standards. This site is designed to help promote
Honor at Carolina. The Honor Code can be found
as part of the Instrument of Student Judicial
Governance (Instrument). The Instrument outlines
the prohibited conduct, policies and procedures for
adjudicating allegations of student misconduct.

Over the past several decades the phrase has transcended beyond the regular student body, and has been a battle cry of honor for the school's various athletic programs; teams that have enjoyed unparalleled success on the courts and fields, and whose marketing brand has brought millions of dollars to the school in the form of consumer revenue.

Hall of Fame Basketball Coach Dean Smith wrote a book in 2004 titled *The Carolina Way: Leadership Lessons from a Life in Coaching.* He was long viewed as the paradigm of the phrase; his teams won, and his players almost always graduated. The overall graduation rate of his dozens of Carolina basketball teams was a reported 96 percent.

Smith retired in 1997, and for over a decade his (and the school's) image remained spotless. The proud phrase stood strong, and the university continued to be viewed as a top educational university.

Questions would arise, however. And following the questions would come data which would point to solid facts. And with those facts would emerge doubts. Athletes were given preferential treatment, above and beyond the normal scholarship stipulations. Money was paid, at times apparently with coaches' knowledge. Most seriously, however, were the academic misdeeds. Grades were given for classes that athletes never attended, and in many cases those classes never even existed except on paper. Other grades were changed by those associated with academics in the school, without permission. And in certain cases, these fraudulent grades appear to be the only thing that kept some athletes eligible to participate.

Without the money, the grades, and the fraud that benefitted countless star players dating back to the early 1990's, certain players may not have chosen to attend the school, and the various teams surely would not have achieved the same success – on the fields, on the courts, and certainly not in the classrooms. Graduation rates would have been much different, as would the bottom line of marketing revenue. And perhaps most importantly to those who claim to care, the reputation of the school – and the phrase "The Carolina Way" – would also mean something else entirely.

* * *

Mark Emmert, the president of the National Collegiate Athletic Association, stood at the podium on Monday, July 23, 2012. He was before a packed room of reporters in order to address a terrible crime against humanity – which also happened to have a direct tie to athletics. A cover-up had occurred at Penn State University, and Emmert's organization, the NCAA, saw it within their bounds to take strong and swift corrective action.

The events at Penn State were horrific, and nothing else in the history of college sports can compare to the pain that the victims endured. Emmert had a wider message to give on that day, however, which was a warning and guideline to all universities that serve the greater good of its students (and student athletes). It was a message that seemed to indicate why those schools have athletic programs in the first place: to teach honor, fairness, and positive life lessons.

In the midst of passing down Penn State's sanctions, Emmert's message resonated from the podium:

"These events should serve as a call to every single school and athletics department to take an honest look at its campus environment and eradicate the 'sports are king' mindset that can so dramatically cloud the judgment of educators."

It is doubtful that Emmert knew just how prophetic and accurate his words were on that day. There have been many other cases of impermissible benefits in college sports. There have been occasional instances of random teachers giving preferential grades and treatment. But never has there been a case when multiple factions within a university and culture did so much to cover up decades of improprieties – improprieties that did exactly what Emmert's words described.

The University of North Carolina at Chapel Hill, since at least the early 1990's, did just that: It allowed a "sports are king" mindset to cloud the judgment of its educators. Coaches were complicit, as were boosters, fundraisers, tutors, administrative assistants, tenured professors, and even administrators. Collectively, they have allowed a once-proud phrase – and, consequently an entire university – to have its reputation tarnished and compromised. Even worse, many have refused to come forward and speak out against the improprieties. Instead, they have continued to tout those words despite strong public evidence that the phrase has been largely bolstered not through honorable actions, but rather through deliberate academic and social deceit. Sadly, evidence shows that the old "Carolina Way" is no more, with the new version being a far cry from what the school and its alumni once envisioned.

CHAPTER ONE

MARVIN AUSTIN'S TWEET; INITIAL NCAA INTERVIEWS

"1 live In club LIV so I get the tenant rate. bottles comin like its a giveaway"

@ANCHORMANAUSTIN

When the above words (a reference to champagne bottles and a 30,000-square-foot night club at Miami Beach) were sent out across the internet via the social media site Twitter at 3:07 AM on May 29, 2010, they set into motion a domino effect that would threaten to topple the reputation of one of the most storied schools in collegiate history. At the time of that early-morning "tweet," Marvin Austin was a rising senior on UNC's football team. A top prospect out of high school, he was one of several star players on a team that many sports analysts felt was a "sleeping giant," and even a dark horse for the National Championship. Austin's ill-advised boast, however, would ultimately all but assure that the program would not be competing for any legitimate and recognized championships for years to come.

According to sportsillustrated.cnn.com, the tweet was "one of several posts that drew attention to Austin's lavish lifestyle – and which ultimately led to Austin's suspension for his entire senior season due to NCAA violations involving extra benefits from agents, middlemen and marketing representatives." It was the onset of a mass discovery of evidence that pointed to impermissible benefits and academic fraud – but not only for some of Austin's fellow football players, as it was first assumed, but eventually also for the school's more prestigious basketball program.

* * *

In the early months of 2007 Marvin Austin was a top recruit attending Ballou High School in Washington, DC. He was ranked by the Rivals.com recruiting service as the #1 defensive tackle in the nation during his senior year. The Scout.com recruiting service ranked him as the third overall prep prospect in their final rankings, and he was also USA Today's "National Defensive Player of the Year." While at Ballou he played for head coach Moses Ware, but it was another football staff member – assistant coach Todd Amis – who would later play a role in the events that eventually unfolded at UNC.

Austin was considering many top collegiate programs as National Signing Day approached in February of 2007. Throughout his recruitment several schools had been consistently reported at the top of Austin's wish list. These included such powerhouse destinations as Tennessee and the University of Southern California, with yet another top program, Florida State

University, rumored to be the leader. On signing day, however, it was a surprise school which garnered Austin's commitment: the University of North Carolina.

The August 30, 2007, edition of the Fayetteville (NC) *Observer* newspaper contained an article dedicated to UNC football, and how it has been historically difficult for traditional "basketball" schools to succeed on the gridiron – but that the new football head coach, Butch Davis, and the Heels appeared to be turning that stigma around. Amongst a series of segments and storylines penned by staff writer Dan Wiederer, one in particular stood out. It gave an interesting and detailed accounting of a specific moment in Marvin Austin's recruitment, and in hindsight possibly provided some details as to his seemingly quick affinity towards UNC. In a section titled "Mettle of Achievement," Wiederer outlines the first contact:

Strange as it sounds, the revival of UNC football may have received its most significant boost last December at a Metropolitan Police Department awards banquet in Washington, DC. Inside DAR Constitution Hall that night detective Todd Amis, also the top assistant coach at Ballou High School, accepted a medal of achievement. On hand to support him: Ballou's star defensive tackle Marvin Austin, widely considered the top defensive prospect in the country. On hand to introduce himself to Austin: Butch Davis.

The first interaction proved momentous. Firm handshake. Sincere conversation. One grand sales pitch from an eager and proven coach to a five-star 300-pound defensive tackle who previously had as much interest in North Carolina football as he had in skipping dinner. Come to Chapel Hill, Davis implored, and we can build a national power. Austin listened to the fan-

*tastic proposition and envisioned his future. Inspired Saturday
victories. BCS Bowl trips. A paved path to the NFL. They were
the same promises delivered by the coaches at Southern California, Florida State and Tennessee, the schools at the top of
Austin's wish list and programs with more substance with which
to back those claims. Yet somehow, Davis' ambition and energy
won out.*

"I was sold, man," Austin said.

* * *

Paul "Butch" Davis, Jr. was hired as the head football coach
at UNC in mid-November, 2006, replacing Tar Heel alum John
Bunting. Davis arrived on campus with much fanfare, as he
boasted work experience at a number of "big name" college
teams – as well as most recently serving a stint in the NFL as
head coach of the Cleveland Browns.

In the college ranks his most notable tenure came when he
served as the head coach at the University of Miami. He was
hired in January of 1995 and would go on to lead the Hurricanes for six seasons. Prior to gaining the head coaching job at
Miami, Davis worked as a top assistant for the Dallas Cowboys.
It was during his time in Dallas that Davis first worked with
John Blake, who 14 years later would become his UNC coaching mate. Their connection did not begin at that time in Dallas,
however. It goes back more than 30 years to when Davis taught
Blake in high school in Oklahoma in the late 1970's.

In 1993 Davis was the defensive coordinator with the NFL's
Dallas Cowboys and Blake was the defensive line coach. That
arrangement insured that the two worked closely together on
a daily basis for several years in a row. Preceding that job in

Dallas was his first tenure (as an assistant) with the Miami Hurricanes in the mid 80's, and one of Davis's earliest collegiate destinations (beginning in 1979) was with Oklahoma State University.

* * *

It was announced in December of 2006 that John Blake was being hired as the defensive line coach at UNC, and he would also later serve as the program's recruiting coordinator and associate head coach – essentially the second-in-command behind Davis. At the time of Blake's hiring, the intimate past connection between Blake and Davis was quickly made apparent. In an online article posted by cstv.com on December 15, 2006, Butch Davis was quoted as saying, "(Blake) is known throughout the country as a terrific recruiter and teacher. I had the pleasure of working with John when we were both assistants for the Cowboys, and his commitment to excellence both on and off the field is unmatched."

Blake's previous coaching stops included the aforementioned stint with the NFL's Dallas Cowboys (alongside Davis), as well as being an assistant at numerous colleges. These stops included Mississippi State University, the University of Tulsa, the University of Nebraska, and the University of Oklahoma. He also served a brief and tumultuous stint as the head coach at Oklahoma from 1996 to 1998. While Blake would eventually gain national (negative) attention due to his role in the UNC football scandal, his more distant past was not without controversial rumors. He allegedly earned the nickname "Black Santa" during periods of his prior career as being the coach who always had "gifts" for his players. Whether that meant actual money, or simply arrangements to meet with NFL agents, is unknown.

Former collegiate star and Oklahoma player Brian Bosworth stated in a 2010 Associated Press article that Blake set up meetings between Bosworth and NFL agent Gary Wichard.

"You have to understand, John was the eyes inside the locker room," Bosworth told the Yahoo! Sports website. "He was the fisherman and Gary was the cook. You've got to have somebody out there who is going to get the bounty, and Gary's the one who then goes and sells the bounty. I don't understand why they would be trying to skirt the truth on that. That is what it was. It was so blatant. And I know I wasn't the only player who saw it."

As more details regarding UNC's football scandal began to surface in 2010, it became evident that the NCAA was initially focusing on Blake and possible impermissible benefits. Steve Spurrier, the well-known head coach of the University of South Carolina, made a reference to Blake's past when he commented, "When you've been in coaching as long as I have, we know the reputation of almost all the coaches that have been around a long time. We all have a reputation, especially guys who've coached 20 years or so. It's hard to hide whatever your reputation is."

* * *

A name mentioned earlier in the chapter was Todd Amis. As referenced in the Fayetteville Observer news article, Amis was a detective in the Washington, DC, area, but more importantly a top assistant coach at Ballou High School where Marvin Austin played his senior year. Austin also first met and spoke with Butch Davis at an event where Amis was one of the centerpieces. This may seem fortuitous and coincidental at first glance, but the details that would emerge later – details that show that Amis was closely associated with not only UNC assistant coach John Blake, but apparently also with NFL agents who provided impermissible benefits to Austin – would suggest that the meeting might not have been such a coincidence after all.

On June 21, 2010, Chance Miller, a member of the NCAA's enforcement staff, sent an email to UNC to schedule interviews with various football players. This marked the beginning of a probe into Austin's extracurricular activities (such as partying into the late hours in the Miami area), but also indicated that the NCAA would be focusing on other team members as well. As a result, a number of disturbing facts quickly began to surface. Many of these coincided with the release of the phone records of John Blake's UNC-issued cell phone, which were provided by the school in early October, 2010, following an open records request by the Raleigh *News and Observer* newspaper.

From there a three-pronged dissection of the illegal transgressions of Austin, Blake, and others associated with the school would commence. The *News and Observer* did its part. Charles Robinson, a noted reporter with Yahoo! Sports, revealed a number of facts in early August and then again in late September. The third source was a bit unexpected, but would prove time and again to be capable of uncovering damaging revelations related to UNC's improprieties. That source was the message board portion of a collegiate website, PackPride. com. While football and benefits would be the initial focus, the microscope would eventually reveal the much bigger topics of academic fraud and the school's basketball program.

* * *

It would quickly become clear that 2010 was not the beginning of Marvin Austin and John Blake's troubles. Records that were obtained in part by Yahoo! Sports showed an invoice from Altour International, a business and travel company based in California that has 61 offices on three continents. That February 25, 2009, invoice was for a trip that Marvin Austin took to California to train at Proactive Sports Performance, a training facility where the rookie clients of NFL agent Gary Wichard had trained since the mid-2000's. It was shown that Austin was training with NFL player (and former Tar Heel) Kentwan Balmer – a client of Wichard's agency, Pro Tect Management – which is conveniently located less than two miles from the Proactive Sports facility.

Numerous other invoices were obtained, as well as copies of checks – and that is where the web becomes more intricate. A check dated March 1, 2009, was shown from Todd Amis, Austin's former high school assistant coach, covering his travel costs to California. A March 3, 2009, check revealed a payment from Pro Tect Management to Amis. Furthermore, a March 4, 2009, Altour invoice showed that Pro Tect Management paid for changes in Austin's flight itinerary. All of this occurred while Austin was a collegiate player and representing UNC on the field.

March 7th through the 14th were the dates of Austin's first training trip to California, which the above dates/invoices/checks covered. A March 11, 2009, Altour invoice showed that Pro Tect paid for further changes in the flight itinerary, with a check being sent from Pro Tect to Altour on March 12, 2009.

The paper trail by itself was fairly damning. First and foremost, Marvin Austin – while still a college student – was taking a trip to California to visit and presumably train at the facility of a registered NFL agent. Furthermore, the flight was paid for via check from one of his former high school coaches. What transcends these events as going from "very bad" to "orchestrated improprieties" are details extracted from John Blake's phone records, and contacts that were made around the pertinent dates above – with all centering around agent Gary Wichard, former high school coach Todd Amis, and Austin. Records show that on the days leading up to Austin's initial March 7th trip to California, John Blake spoke multiple times with those three aforementioned individuals – and in many instances within minutes of one another. Similar patterns showed up numerous times during Austin's week-long stay on the west coast.

Austin's impermissible training trips – or the knowledge and involvement of UNC – did not end with that initial March flight to California, however. Another invoice from Altour International was obtained that showed a date of July 17, 2009. Again a check from Todd Amis was shown as the method of payment, dated July 22. Marvin Austin's second impermissible trip to California was from July 23 to August 1, 2009.

As before, the phone records of associate head coach John Blake gave further details. Once again calls to (or from) Wichard, Amis, and Austin showed up within close proximity to one another. This time several contacts were made with head coach Butch Davis as well. All of the phone data made it clear that at least one member of UNC's football staff – Blake – was aware of the whereabouts of one of his star players. Based on his contact with Blake during Austin's second training trip to California, it is well within reason that Butch Davis could have been aware, too.

* * *

UNC's football team had a very successful 2009 season when Marvin Austin was a junior, going 8-3 during the regular season before losing a closely-contested bowl game. The future looked bright for the program, but the downside was that the team had a number of rising seniors who were highly rated by draft analysts and were strongly considering leaving early for 2010's NFL draft. That list included defensive backs Kendric Burney and Deunta Williams, linebackers Quan Sturdivant and Bruce Carter, wide receiver Greg Little, and defensive tackle Marvin Austin.

To the surprise of many in the college football world, how-ever, those six rising seniors shunned the upcoming NFL draft and left millions of contract dollars on the table. Instead, they announced on January 4, 2010, that they would all be returning to school for their senior year. With this unexpected turn of events, UNC was vaulted to the top of the projected standings for the 2010 Atlantic Coast Conference football season, and the team was immediately inserted into early discussions about the National Championship.

Following that announcement to remain at UNC, and while still unknown to the NCAA and the public at the actual days and times they were occurring, more questionable activities were going on by Marvin Austin behind the scenes. All of those events would eventually come to light, and in reality should have been noticed much earlier (by either the school or the NCAA). They showed a similar pattern and lifestyle as later displayed in his infamous Twitter message from the night-club in Miami, with red flags abounding.

Based on numerous Twitter pictures posted by Austin, he

was in Washington, DC, on April 23 and 24, 2010. He tweeted the following on the 23rd: "Jus got to DC an (sic) I'm feeln (sic) a shopn (sic) spree . . . nobody gon (sic) be fresh as ME!!!", as well as posting pictures showing himself and University of South Carolina player Wesyle Saunders in a DC hotel. Aside from boasting about going on a shopping spree and posting pictures of an expensive hotel, the bigger implications came once again from John Blake's phone records. Some interesting contacts took place not only on the actual days Austin was in DC, but also on the days immediately before and after the trip. Austin and Blake spoke once on the 20th, once on the 21st, and twice on the 22nd. The above tweet was on April 23rd. Austin and Blake then spoke nine times on the 24th, and then once on each day, the 25th, 26th, 27th, and 28th of April – the days following the trip. The connections did not stop there, however. At 10:27 PM on April 23 (the night of the tweet), Blake spoke with NFL agent Gary Wichard. And then on the 24th (when Blake had spoken to Austin nine times), Blake also spoke with Wichard seven times. And to top things off, the third party from the previous California trips – Todd Amis – made his appearance in the records as well. On April 24th, only 23 minutes after getting off the phone with Austin, Blake spoke with Amis for 20 minutes. Less than an hour before those calls – and then a little over an hour after them – Blake spoke with Wichard.

Approximately two weeks later Marvin Austin was back in the nation's capital for another visit, and more incriminating pictures and tweets would follow. On May 7th Austin tweeted a picture of a Gucci gift certificate card, and followed that up the next day by tweeting the message, "Tables, bottles, beautiful (sic) people!!!!! LIVE…" On May 10th Austin ate dinner at a Cheesecake Factory restaurant, and then posted the picture of his $143 bill on Twitter. He also included a picture of a dozen doughnuts, price tag $40.

As with the first DC trip, more information from John Blake's phone records give insight as to the days leading up to the trip, during the visit, and then immediately following. On the 5th of May (two days before the Gucci tweet) Blake spoke to Austin six times. That same evening, he spoke with NFL agent Gary Wichard. On May 10th (the date of the Cheesecake Factory dinner) Blake spoke to Austin seven times, and with Wichard three times – all in close proximity to Austin's calls. Then on May 11th Blake spoke to Austin three times, Wichard twice, and then Todd Amis once – though it was only two minutes after getting off the phone with Austin, and the call with Amis lasted 14 minutes.

There would be two other incidents of note on May 11th. The first was a Twitter message from Ed Shields to Marvin Austin: "Marvin I will bring the wallets to u today." It was established earlier that Todd Amis was Austin's top high school assistant coach, and had worked under head coach Moe Ware. Ware resigned after Austin's graduation, and the new head coach at Ballou was Ed Shields. The next occurrence was a phone call that took place on John Blake's phone, immediately between calls with Todd Amis and Austin. Blake spoke with sports agent Melvin Bratton, as opposed to the usual suspicious contact with Gary Wichard. Bratton was a former collegiate player with the Miami Hurricanes in the mid 1980's, and helped lead his team to the 1987 National Championship. He went on to spend two seasons in the NFL before injuries ended his career. An interesting note is that Bratton's years at the University of Miami coincided with Butch Davis' first stint at the school as an assistant coach. This would seemingly only further complicate matters regarding UNC and the contact that some of their players (and coaches) were having with agents – especially those who had close prior relationships with some of the coaches.

All told, John Blake had contact with Bratton a minimum of 13 times during 2009, and a minimum of 30 times during 2010. When the NCAA's sanctions against UNC were finally levied a year later, agent Gary Wichard of Pro Tect Management was discussed and represented. No mention of Bratton was ever made. Whether that was due to his complete innocence in the scandal is unknown. Another scenario could simply be that the NCAA may not have known about his past connection to Butch Davis, not to mention his current connection to John Blake – including the aptly timed calls surrounding Blake's contact with key figures such as Marvin Austin and Todd Amis.

* * *

The next major chronological event to happen in the spring of 2010 was the one that first tipped off the NCAA and media to possible infractions – the Miami club tweet that was mentioned at the onset of this chapter. Quickly following his earlier excursions to California and DC, Austin was off on another trip to southern Florida. Aside from the tweet that was sent out at 3:07 AM from the night club, other evidence of questionable activities also emerged from that jaunt, including a photograph of Austin and fellow rising senior Greg Little that appears to have been taken at poolside during an agent's party. Timestamps and records would show that Austin and Little were in the Miami area from May 29th through the 31st.

The eventual email from Chance Miller of the NCAA to UNC would be sent on June 21st, and a full investigation would soon be underway. Those first interviews were conducted with players in Chapel Hill on July 12th and 13th. Once again, the phone records of John Blake would turn up some interesting trends.

Calls placed on the night of July 11 would show that Blake called numerous players very late that evening, which was just prior to the first round of NCAA interviews. While seemingly harmless on the surface, it should be noted that the NCAA forced Georgia Tech to vacate their 2009 football championship game victory in part due to members of their coaching staff forewarning players that they would be interviewed by the NCAA. The Association's first email to UNC was on June 21, and according to an interview with Athletics Director Dick Baddour on July 15, "One of the things that they instructed us in very clearly is that we are to maintain the confidence of their visit and their review. They've requested that we not discuss it publicly. Obviously, we're going to fully cooperate with the NCAA in every way that we can by making things available to them and in particular by following their instructions on discussing it publicly."

Despite this warning, it appears as if John Blake may have committed one of the same offenses that caused trouble for Georgia Tech. On the night of July 11, the day immediately preceding the first player interviews, Blake made a number of late-night calls to team members who would eventually be interviewed and/or investigated, as well as two members of the program's staff who, once more information was uncovered, seemingly had a very close relationship and confidence with Blake.

At 10:21 PM on July 11th Blake called player Robert Quinn. At 10:26 he called then player-development assistant Norris

McCleary, whose name will become more prominent later. At 10:28 Blake called player Quinton Coples. At 10:29 he called player Marvin Austin. At 10:32 he called player Robert Quinn. At 10:33 he called then video/media assistant Johnny Vines, who like McCleary would become more prominent later. And at 10:37 Blake called player Michael McAdoo. The very next morning the NCAA interviews would commence. Was Blake calling to warn them? To set up a meeting where possible tactics could be discussed? Those details may never be known because the timing of the calls was never addressed by the NCAA when the official allegations (and later the sanctions) were eventually released.

* * *

To further augment the university's rapidly increasing problems, on July 21st the North Carolina Secretary of State began its own investigation into laws that were potentially broken by sports agencies tied to the school and its players. As the summer would wear on, this would be a harbinger of things to come as more and more issues would continue to arise. The most serious – academic misconduct tied to the school's basketball program – was still over a full year away.

* * *

The essential (and unanswered) questions:

-- Was there more to Marvin Austin's sudden recruiting affinity towards UNC than simply meeting head coach Butch Davis at a Washington, DC, function?

-- Did members of UNC's staff other than John Blake have connections with sports agents?

-- Why were the (public) social media accounts of UNC players not being adequately monitored by the school?

-- Why were John Blake's school-issued phone records not being adequately monitored by the school?

-- Did Blake forewarn members of the football team regarding the impending NCAA interviews?

CHAPTER TWO

JOHN BLAKE RESIGNS; FOOTBALL PLAYERS SUSPENDED

O n August 26, 2010, just over a month after the NC Secretary of State had opened its investigation into possible agent infractions, the NCAA announced that it may have discovered potential academic fraud at UNC. The details were first divulged in an August 26, 2010, email from Joni Worthington, the Vice President for Communications at UNC, to Erskine Bowles, who at the time was President of the University of North Carolina System. The email exchange would eventually be made public, along with a follow-up message he sent to the UNC System Board of Governors later that evening. Bowles is a 1967 graduate of UNC.

The initial email from Worthington to Bowles contained

information from a variety of media stories that would soon be dispersed to the public, all based on a news conference that was held at UNC on the evening of the 26th. In the emails were numerous quotes from UNC officials as they had become aware of the academic issues. With the news that the NCAA had expanded its investigations into academics, Chancellor Holden Thorp was quoted as saying, "We are treating this with the seriousness you would expect from this university. We will figure this out... We hope the scope of this is limited." Athletics Director Dick Baddour indicated that while the current focus was on football, that the school would look at it as an opportunity to look into the tutoring program within other athletic programs. A quote within Worthington's email from head football coach Butch Davis read, "Nothing is more important than the character... and integrity of this football program."

Other vitally important information regarding Butch Davis was included in the forthcoming news stories that were documented in Worthington's email to Bowles. A former UNC tutor was at the center of the NCAA's current investigation, and Davis revealed that the tutor in question "is someone that has previously been employed by our family." The woman in question, Jennifer Wiley, was let go from her job by UNC as a tutor – but was then, according to Davis, hired by his family "to be an academic coach and academic advisor. This is someone who worked with our son, and to be honest with you, we're a little bit surprised and possibly disappointed."

The follow-up email that Bowles sent to the other members of the Board of Governors stated in part that, "We do not know the extent of these problems at this time. But we are investigating this matter fully and as expeditiously as possible, and we will get to the bottom of it. And when we do we will deal with it appropriately as you would expect the university to do." The "University," of course, being the school from where he graduated. And to further punctuate that theme, a total of eleven Board members received their undergraduate degrees at UNC, far out-pacing the other universities in the system. The next highly-represented school had only four undergraduate members on the Board of Governors. When the parameters were widened to include graduate degrees, UNC checked in with well over twenty representatives on the Board of Governors.

* * *

Player suspensions would begin to follow soon thereafter, though only one was mandated by the school. Despite being at the center of the controversy for several months, Marvin Austin had been allowed to continue representing the university and the football team. On September 1st, however, it was announced that coach Butch Davis had suspended him indefinitely for "violating unspecified team rules," according to various news agencies, including a story that appeared on ESPN's website. Even still, UNC tried to distance itself from the negative stigma of an NCAA investigation – something that would be a common tactic in the years to come. Instead of referring to the NCAA's presence as an investigation, whenever a UNC official spoke of the issues it was simply referred to as a "review." This was seemingly an attempt to lessen the seriousness of the charges in the eyes and ears of the general public.

With regards to Austin, Butch Davis had this to say: "This decision is not a result of the ongoing NCAA review. Marvin has violated team rules and has neglected his responsibilities to the team." This suspension was issued just three days prior to the team's season-opening game against Louisiana State University, and early indications from unnamed sources said that the team might be without other players for that contest as well. That same ESPN article reported that the school was exploring the possibility of "rolling suspensions" that would allow them to spread the absence of players over multiple games, in effect lessening the impact on the team as a whole. In what would appear to be an attempted gag order, the school cancelled all scheduled media availability with players prior to the LSU game.

It was also reported that the school was working with the NCAA in order to determine who would and would not be allowed to make the trip, and which players should be held out for precautionary reasons. That is, which players' names might surface in the near future in relation to NCAA violations. Through past examples of other schools' transgressions, it was well known that if a player is later determined to have played while ineligible, then the school would have to retroactively vacate any and all team wins in which that player participated. This common understanding would be a major point in the years and events yet to come in the scandal, especially once UNC's basketball team (and its numerous national titles) entered the fray.

* * *

On September 3rd, one day before the LSU football game, six UNC starters were initially declared ineligible for "violating school and/or NCAA rules," the university announced. Those starters included Marvin Austin, which was somewhat expected, as well as Charles Brown, Robert Quinn, Michael McAdoo, Kendric Burney, and Greg Little. Six non-starters were withheld from the game based on the current and ongoing NCAA investigation. Those players were Shaun Draughn, Linwan Euwell, Brian Gupton, Ryan Houston, Da'Norris Searcy, and Jonathan Smith. Furthermore, safety Deunta Williams was declared ineligible late Friday (the night before the game), while two other players – linebackers Quan Sturdivant and Bruce Carter – were cleared to play.

Many of the facts were still unknown at this point, especially in terms of the actual violations. As noted by the various news reports that were referenced at the beginning of the chapter via Joni Worthington's email to Erskine Bowles, the NCAA was investigating not only possible improper contact with agents, but also looking into allegations of academic misconduct by some of the players. UNC Athletics Director Dick Baddour said in a statement, "We are still working with the NCAA staff to resolve these eligibility issues. The NCAA is focusing on each of their situations on a case-by-case basis. Together we are working to determine their status in as thorough and fair a process as is possible." It was also revealed on that same Friday that investigators from the NC Secretary of State's office had subpoenaed Marvin Austin in relation to sports-agent laws. UNC would go on to lose that opening game against LSU, 30-24.

* * *

On September 5th, the day after the LSU loss, another domino in the scandal would fall. John Blake, who had been near the center of the ignominy and its blossoming controversies, resigned his coaching position with the football team. He gave a fairly detailed statement:

"While I have enjoyed my tenure at the University of North Carolina, it has become apparent to me over the course of the past few weeks that my presence has become a distraction to my family and to this great University, too. Consequently, I have determined that it is in the best interests of my family, the University community at large, and the Football Program for me to step down from my position as associate head football coach effective today, September 5, 2010.

"I thank the Lord for the opportunity I have had to work with Butch Davis while at the University of North Carolina. I have grown to love and respect the school, my fellow coaches, and the young men who have worked so diligently to improve both as students and as football players. That love and respect has led me to the conclusion that the best decision for all involved is for me to step aside at this time. I wish the players, the coaches, and the University all the best.

"I thank the Tar Heel Nation for the overwhelming support I have received. The memories I have made here will last a lifetime. May God bless you all."

Furthermore, statements were also given by head coach Butch Davis and also Athletics Director Dick Baddour. The words from Davis especially stood out, as once again they reiterated the close working relationship that the two men had shared over the years:

"Knowing John as I have over the years, it is clear that this was a difficult decision for him to make. I know how much John loves the players, coaching and the game of football. I am grateful for all of his hard work and effort in helping build this program. As difficult as this situation is, I have accepted his resignation. Throughout his career, I know he has worked hard to help young men become better people and football players. He and his family have made positive contributions to our football program.

"The Tar Heel family has tremendous passion for the University and everything it represents. It's one of the things that made me want to be a Tar Heel four years ago. All of us who are part of the football program have been both disappointed and embarrassed by recent events. Our student athletes, coaches and I are committed to working every day, both on and off the field, to build a better football program, one that everyone associated with the University of North Carolina can and will be proud of."

In a somewhat puzzling move, the university chose to pay Blake a prorated amount of his annual $240,000 salary equaling $74,500, which was equivalent to the amount he would have received had he completed the football season through the month of December. This decision was made despite the mounting evidence that seemed to indicate that Blake had broken numerous NCAA rules, as well as put the school in jeopardy for further sanctions.

* * *

Following the resignation of John Blake, it was announced that linebackers' coach Art Kaufman along with Norris McCleary, a member of the team's support staff in player development and a former NFL lineman, would take over some of the defensive line coaching duties that Blake had left vacant. Butch Davis also indicated that he would become more involved with some of the day-to-day coaching and meetings than in the past, according to an online *USA Today* article published on September 7th.

McCleary's name was one that showed up in great detail within John Blake's university phone records, and during some troubling stretches of times. His prior background was one that was heavily entrenched in athletics. He played football at East Carolina University, and then had a multi-year stint in the NFL as a defensive lineman. Though he was only officially promoted to an on-field "coaching" position once John Blake resigned, the phone records seemed to indicate that he had a very close relationship with Blake, regardless.

On the afternoon and evening of the NCAA's first on-campus interviews with UNC players, John Blake spoke with McCleary four different times. These calls were within close proximity with contacts Blake made with Todd Amis, NFL agent Gary Wichard, and several players who were under scrutiny by the NCAA. All told, Blake and McCleary had over 350 phone contacts between April and September of 2010, some of the prime months of the blossoming agent portion of the scandal. These were often closely intermixed with calls Blake had to (or from) players such as Marvin Austin, Robert Quinn, and Quinton Coples, and also with NFL agent Wichard.

McCleary's departure from the school was unceremonious and apparently without fanfare, as few news stories on him are to be found. According to his LinkedIn page, his employment with UNC ended in December of 2012. As of late 2013 he was listed under several job capacities. He was working as a coach with the West Charlotte football team, he was a broker in the Charlotte area, and was also CEO of Mack's Player Development. Regarding the latter position, he indicates on that same LinkedIn page that he "train develop current college an NFL players. I've train 1st round picks and college free agents." One area that catches the eye is that from early 2008 until March of 2010 – his date of hire at UNC – he was self-described as being involved in "Pro Athlete Investment." As evidenced by his own stated past work parameters, he was involved with the training and apparent integration of professional athletes both immediately before and immediately after his coaching tenure at UNC. Whether coincidentally or not, the many phone contacts he had with John Blake show a timely connection with NFL agents – again, while he was on staff at UNC.

Another member of the football team's assistance staff who (on paper) held a relatively minor role was Johnny Vines. Like McCleary, however, he appeared to play a much larger role based on his contacts with John Blake. Vines was a simple video coordinator for the football team at the time, but phone records show a pattern very similar to that of McCleary's. The contacts Blake had with Vines were often surrounded by names such as Marvin Austin, Gary Wichard, and others who were entangled in impermissible benefits. And along with McCleary, Johnny Vines was the only non-player whom John Blake contacted during that late night flurry of calls on July 11th, just prior to the first NCAA interviews.

* * *

According to a *USA Today* article published during the second week of September, 2010, several of the university's decision-making organizations had finally begun to take notice of the scandal. Bob Winston, the chairman of the school's Board of Trustees, indicated that the issues would likely be discussed during their next meeting. Furthermore, the university's 92-member faculty council was scheduled to get a briefing in the following few days from Chancellor Holden Thorp. Regarding that upcoming meeting, faculty chair McKay Coble said, "I think it will be respectful. And I think there will be some pointed questions."

All of the negative attention was something that many who

were associated with the university were unaccustomed to. At the time, only seven programs in what were considered college athletics' "marquee" conferences had gone as long as the past 26 years without a major NCAA infractions case. UNC was one of those, which undoubtedly contributed to the "Carolina Way" mantra that had been repeated by its supporters over the years. According to Chancellor Thorp, "We're concerned and devastated to be in this situation. We've had 50 years here without having to go through this sort of thing. The way we respond is really important."

Board of Trustees Chairman Bob Winston displayed a similar sentiment, saying "Everybody has the same idea... that we've got to get to the bottom of this, whatever it is it is, and deal with it and, if there are changes to be made, make the changes. But this isn't the way we're going to do business." Winston went on to reiterate, "We will look ourselves in the mirror at the end, and make sure the answer is it's incidental." That line of thought was often repeated at the beginning of the scandal by those who represented the school, either athletically, administratively, academically, or via the alumni – that the university would do whatever it took to get to the bottom of the issues. As documentation would later show, that tone would change a number of months later – once football was no longer the sole athletic program that had exhibited questionable practices.

* * *

After a couple of weeks of relative silence, more bad news surfaced on September 22nd with an official suspension (via the NCAA) of defensive players Kendric Burney and Deunta Williams. The offense was receiving improper benefits, and the NCAA stipulated for Burney to miss a total of six games and Williams four. As covered in Chapter One, Burney and Williams were among six underclassmen who chose to return to UNC for their senior seasons instead of entering the NFL draft, along with fellow suspended players Marvin Austin and Greg Little. The final two players, Quan Sturdivant and Bruce Carter, had recently been cleared by the school. Any potential NCAA penalties against them were still up in the air at that point in time.

The impermissible benefits given to Burney and Williams were associated with trips to California, Atlanta, and Las Vegas for Burney, and two trips to California for Williams. Based on comments made by head coach Butch Davis on his radio show, the players would apparently only face penalties from the NCAA. "If and when they come back," said Davis, "they'll certainly be welcome additions." Dick Baddour described the length of the suspensions as being "unduly harsh."

Sources familiar with the situation at the time told the Associated Press that the "agent" in Burney's case was Chris Hawkins, a former football player initially at UNC (from 2001-03) before getting kicked off the team. He would eventually continue his career with Marshall University. A week prior, in response to questions regarding Hawkins, Athletics Director Baddour said that Hawkins had been around the players and program "periodically" over the years. According to a source that spoke with espn.com for a September 2010 article, UNC players told investigators that Hawkins had contacted several sports agents about their interest in representing UNC players in the NFL draft. Hawkins was designated as an agent by the NCAA in part due to his connection with University of Georgia receiver A.J. Green. Hawkins purchased a jersey from Green for $1,000, which would land Green with a multiple-game suspension.

A UNC official stated (in the same ESPN article) that Hawkins had frequently visited the North Carolina football facility during the previous few years, including a visit during the summer of 2010 in which he worked out with former UNC (and Pittsburgh Steeler) player Willie Parker in UNC's weight room. According to the school official, Hawkins had often described himself as Parker's manager. At the time of Burney's suspension announcement Hawkins had pending felony charges of trafficking cocaine, as well as misdemeanor charges of possession of marijuana. The legal troubles would later continue for Hawkins. In May of 2012 he was arrested by the Kinston (NC) Department of Public Safety and charged with discharging a weapon into an occupied dwelling.

* * *

Despite having already resigned from UNC's staff, a huge blow was dealt to the reputation of former associate head coach John Blake with the release of a Yahoo! Sports article on September 29th. The investigative article (penned by Charles Robinson) detailed just how closely Blake was associated with NFL agent Gary Wichard, and supplied even deeper details into their professional relationship. The four-month investigation by Yahoo! Sports showed that Blake and Wichard had engaged in multiple financial transactions over the prior three-plus years. Hotel receipts from one of Marvin Austin's California training trips were obtained, and they listed Austin's name along with Pro Tect Management, which was Gary Wichard's agency.

A myriad of facts were presented, which included evidence of at least six wire transfers from Wichard's private bank to

Blake, a $45,000 personal loan to Blake from that same bank, and a credit card in the name of Wichard's NFL agency – Pro Tect Management – issued in Blake's name. As previously established, Todd Amis wrote checks to cover Marvin Austin's flights to California, and Blake was often in contact with Amis – a minimum of 80 times in 2009, and a minimum of 69 times in 2010.

Shortly after the release of Charles Robinson's article, UNC head football coach Butch Davis issued a bold statement: "Let me tell you, here's how I feel: I am very sorry that all of this stuff has tainted the football program. But I'm going to tell you what I'm more sorry about, I'm sorry that I trusted John Blake. I can promise and tell you, that if we would've ever known that if any of these allegations were absolutely true, Coach Blake would have been dismissed. I would have fired him." This was in reference to a man whom Davis had taught in high school, whom he had coached with on the same NFL defensive staff, and whom he had hired away from Nebraska to be his associate head coach and recruiting coordinator. A man whom, by all indications, Davis was very familiar with – and for a very long time. And a man whom the university chose to pay nearly $75,000, despite the fact that Blake resigned by his own accord, and could have soon been fired for just cause regardless.

* * *

More bad news would surface less than two weeks later when, on October 11, 2010, football players Gregg Little and Robert Quinn would be declared permanently ineligible by the NCAA. According to an espn.com article, Little and Quinn received travel accommodations and jewelry, and then lied about it to investigators in three separate interviews. In a twist of irony, it was not fully revealed until late 2013 that Little was never completely honest even then, and that the NCAA was unable to uncover the true amounts of illegal benefits. It was only during the series of Secretary of State indictments (covered in a later chapter) that those full details would emerge.

At the time, Athletics Director Dick Baddour said that head coach Butch Davis continues to have "my complete support." He went on to say, "I feel very strong about our compliance staff, about our compliance program. I feel very strong about this football program, as I do the other programs that we have. I think we're in good stead. I'm going to fight the institutional control issues because of what we had in place and because of the way we're handling it." Baddour went on to acknowledge that the football program should have done more to monitor its high-profile players. "We should've been doing something else. We should've acknowledged the level that these guys are and that there were going to be people coming at them... I wish we had done more. I'd like to relive that part." Regarding Greg Little's illegal benefits, Baddour was quick to point out that none of those impermissible extras were received during Little's 10-game stint as a reserve on the university's prized basketball team during its Final Four run in 2008.

* * *

A disturbing story of potential bias surfaced on November 14, 2010, via the Raleigh *News and Observer*. It reported that Cynthia Reynolds, formerly the UNC football team's academic coordinator, had filed an age discrimination grievance against the school with the Equal Employment Opportunity Commission. According to documents that were filed a month earlier, Reynolds claims she was moved out of her position because head coach Butch Davis wanted a younger "face" for the academic support program for recruiting purposes. Reynolds, 56 years old at the time, had been hired by the university in 2002 as an associate director of the Academic Support Program for Student Athletes. She had primarily worked with the football program until she was reassigned to Olympic sports in August of 2009, and she was eventually not renewed in August of 2010.

Reynolds' replacement was 29-year-old Beth Bridger, whom Reynolds described as an "excellent learning specialist" who also was in charge of hiring and training the mentors and tutors. Coincidentally, Jennifer Wiley – one of the primary suppliers of impermissible benefits during the football scandal – was a tutor with the school. Her significant role will be further expanded upon later. Reynolds originally filed a grievance with the university, reported the *News and Observer*, but that was denied by the panel of the EPA Non-Faculty Grievance Committee. She was notified of that decision via a letter she received from Chancellor Holden Thorp. Reynolds stated, "I think it's important to make the point that even though I was an 'at-will' employee, you can't get rid of somebody (because) you want someone younger in the position. There are policies, and you have to follow them."

* * *

In late 2010 the university released a list of names of individuals known to have provided impermissible benefits to football players. One was the previously-mentioned former tutor and student with the school, Jennifer Wiley. Amongst the remaining names was a Florida-based jeweler, three individuals tied to professional sports agencies, a former Maryland football player, and three former UNC football players – Hakeem Nicks,

Omar Brown, and Mahlon Carey.

In a November 18th meeting of the school's Board of Trustees, Chancellor Holden Thorp spoke (along with Athletics Director Dick Baddour and head football coach Butch Davis) in order to update the Board members on the scandal. Thorp concluded his comments that day by saying, "I hope you can see how diligently and sincere the three of us have worked on this. This is a challenge and a difficult thing that the University has gone through, but the difficult decisions that we had to make are ones that everybody agreed were in the best interest of the University. As a leader, what you look for is when you have a group of people responsible for doing difficult things, if everybody feels like they had a chance to speak their mind (and) if everybody agrees at the end to do what's best for the University. That's what makes me feel good about Butch Davis being our football coach, about Dick Baddour being our athletics director and about the football program at the University of North Carolina."

Head football coach Butch Davis made platitudes of his own, stating, "There is no one single player and there is no one single game and there is no one single season worth the character and integrity of this institution and this University. That's my commitment and my pledge to you as we move forward into the future of this program." Despite the mounting negative stories surrounding the school, many of which threatened its long-standing solid reputation, some affiliated with the school's Board appeared more interested in how athletics were faring. When it came time for follow-up questions from the members, an unidentified trustee could be heard on the live video feed of the meeting asking Butch Davis how the ongoing review was "affecting recruiting."

* * *

The essential (and unanswered) questions:

-- Did the heavy representation of UNC graduates on the Board of Governors play a role (at any time) during the scandal?

-- Why did the university choose to pay John Blake nearly $75,000 in pay that he had, by all indications, not earned?

-- What larger role (if any) did people like Norris McCleary and Johnny Vines play with regards to the football issues?

-- Why did the team allow a former player – who had been kicked out of the program years prior – to have on-facility access to their current players?

-- Why did head coach Butch Davis personally hire a former UNC tutor – even after it was known that the tutor had essentially been fired by the university?

CHAPTER THREE

PARKING TICKETS; TUTOR JENNIFER WILEY

Evidence of more wrongdoings had continued to surface in the late summer of 2010, and as a result local North Carolina media entities approached UNC with numerous public records requests. Instead of being forthright and releasing much of the information, however, the school chose to stonewall behind a team of lawyers and delay the release of key records and documents – a practice that actually continues to stretch into 2014. One set of records was finally released in June of 2011 after the State Court of Appeals denied the school's request to delay the release pending an appeal. According to a June 16, 2011, article from the Raleigh *News and Observer*, this was brought about following a lawsuit by a consortium of media outlets that had requested – and been denied by UNC – those numerous public records.

A key release dealt with on-campus parking tickets received by fewer than twelve football players. The players had been specifically named/requested by the media consortium due to the fact that they were some of the key pieces involved in the ongoing NCAA investigation. According to that same *News and Observer* article, those players tallied 395 parking violations from early 2007 through August 2010. The latter month and year was when several of the news entities had made their documents request, meaning the school had fought their release for almost a full year. This was a stark contrast to the comments made in the previous chapter by people such as Dick Baddour, Erskine Bowles, and Bob Winston who pledged to do whatever it took to get to the bottom of the school's scandalous issues.

The 395 tickets led to fines totaling $13,125. Some of the specific details behind those various numbers revealed much more, however, and would eventually lead to the discovery of deeper problems. According to the *News and Observer*, Greg Little, a former wide receiver who was ruled permanently ineligible the previous season due to NCAA agent violations, was responsible for 93 of the tickets. Even more shocking was the fact that Little was ticketed in five different vehicles, and that those vehicles had nine different license plates on them, apparently in part from the use of dealer tags. According to a wralsportsfan.com article, by law dealers cannot issue temporary tags to the same vehicle for consecutive months. However, the parking records showed that one of Little's vehicles bore temporary tags for the months of March and April of 2008. Both of those 30-day tags traced back to a company in Durham named 919 Imports. That auto dealer had closed by the time the parking records were finally released, and the business owner, Shawn E. Brown, was serving a federal sentence for money laundering. Interestingly, a somewhat related series of events would unfold two years later during the summer of 2013 when UNC star basketball player PJ Hairston would be connected to vehicles supplied by another convicted felon from Durham. Those events will be covered in full detail in a later chapter.

* * *

It would eventually be revealed that Jennifer Wiley, the UNC tutor noted in the previous chapter, paid $1,789 in August 2010 for some of Greg Little's aforementioned parking tickets. As more information about Wiley was uncovered, her role – and that of the academic support system at UNC – would become more prominent. According to a timeline provided by espn.go.com, Wiley began her employment with UNC's academic support center in August of 2007 during her junior year as a student at the university. During the subsequent three years she provided a number of impermissible educational benefits to athletes, mainly in the manner of making substantive changes to papers, and also composing entire sections in some cases. There was also the payment of Little's parking tickets, and at the time that summarized the basic extent of her impermissible assistance. Despite these impermissible transgressions that were still unknown at the time, Wiley was seen fit to receive an institutional award for tutoring excellence by the university upon her graduation in May of 2009. The fall of 2013 would shed much more light on her true role, however, and would later paint many of the comments made by those who had defended her in a very hypocritical light.

* * *

Beginning in October of 2013, the NC Secretary of State would begin issuing indictments based on its investigation into sports agents. Jennifer Wiley (now with the married last name of Thompson) was the first to be indicted, and the information that was revealed showed that much of her illegal involvement was never uncovered during the initial NCAA investigation of the scandal. Secretary of State documents showed that she received thousands of dollars in cash (through the mail) from sports agents, and would then pass that money on to football (and one-time basketball) player Greg Little. Again, the documents associated with the indictment would counter many of the supporting claims made by her defenders several years earlier. Those indictments will be covered in greater detail in a later chapter.

In March of 2012, Joseph B. Cheshire V, a Raleigh lawyer who was representing Wiley at the time, gave an interview with the Raleigh *News and Observer* in support of his client. In the coinciding news article Cheshire indicated that Wiley's father had sought his counsel shortly after her role in the scandal became public back in 2010. Cheshire, a well-known defense lawyer, said he agreed to advise Wiley at no charge because he believed in her and was sickened by "the extent people would go to destroy her life for their own sakes." As a predictable side note, Cheshire is a graduate of the University of North Carolina.

Up to that point in time Wiley had never talked with NCAA investigators, and it was later revealed that she stonewalled those from the Secretary of State as well. Cheshire stated that she was a "deeply religious" and "big-hearted" young woman, but conceded that the academic assistance that she had given UNC's players was "sometimes out of bounds without even knowing she was, but yes, occasionally just out of bounds." He went on to say that she broke "convoluted and arcane" NCAA rules, apparently referring to assistance on papers, but her efforts to help were no different from what "thousands of friends, family, fraternity members, suite mates, girl or boyfriend students" routinely do for students not affiliated with an athletics program. Cheshire said Wiley's motivation was simple: She wanted to help people who needed help.

The obvious question that is raised regarding Wiley (Thompson), especially with the fall 2013 Secretary of State indictments, deals with the illegal acts of accepting cash payments via the US Postal Service across state lines, and then funneling that money to collegiate athletes. Greg Little has since admitted to receiving more than $20,000 during his time at UNC. None of that was mentioned by her lawyer in the March 2012 article; he simply decried her as a victim who only wished to help athletes with their school work. So it begs the question: did Cheshire know that Wiley had accepted cash payments and was giving it to players? If so, did he deliberately omit that information when verbally defending his client? Or did Wiley simply lie to her lawyer, in essence continuing the lack of clarity and communication that she had shown the NCAA – and would later show the Secretary of State?

Other troubling facets of the Wiley situation were connected to her post-UNC employment. According to the same *News and Observer* article that is quoted in the previous paragraphs, rumors circulated in the summer of 2009 that she had become "too friendly" with student athletes, and her employment contract was not renewed as a result. According to an ESPN timeline, this decision was reached in August 2009 by the director of the Academic Support Center and the Assistant AD for Certification. However, she was soon thereafter hired directly by head football coach Butch Davis to help tutor his son, a high school student at the time. Wiley would continue to provide impermissible academic assistance to UNC players even after she was no longer employed by the university, and despite being sent a letter by the university that it was not okay to continue providing tutoring services to student athletes. She also continued to provide impermissible monetary gifts to players – again, during a timeframe that seemingly overlapped with her personal employment with head football coach Butch Davis.

Wiley, an Education major while at UNC, went on to teach for a short time in elementary schools in both Durham and Raleigh. Her employment stints were brief, however, due in part to her reputation and past involvement in the scandal. According to her lawyer, in September 2011 she resigned from Jeffreys Grove Elementary School in Raleigh after a little more than a month on the job. Cheshire said she quit because parents complained she was "the UNC tutor."

* * *

The essential (and unanswered) questions:

-- Why did the university fight and delay the release of so many public records (a practice that continues well into 2014), despite the continued insistence by its leaders that they want to fix the problems within their athletic programs?

-- What did Jennifer Wiley's lawyer know (in 2012) regarding her illegal funneling of money to UNC players?

-- Why would a head coach hire a former university tutor – a tutor whose prior university employment had been discontinued by the school due to her becoming "too close" to players (on his very own team)?

-- Were/are there deeper connections between UNC athletes and Durham felons regarding the use of vehicles?

CHAPTER FOUR

MCADOO'S PLAGIARISM; BUTCH DAVIS FIRED

n late May of 2011, with the release of its Notice of Allegations from the NCAA only weeks away, UNC players continued to put themselves in the negative spotlight of the news. According to an article by *The Daily Tar Heel*, the NCAA was back on the school's campus on May 18 to interview football player Quinton Coples. He had been seen in pictures of a post-NFL draft party he attended in Washington, DC, and the NCAA had questions about trip-related expenses. Coples had previously shown up throughout Associate Head Coach John Blake's phone records, and often in close proximity to calls to or from individuals involved in activities that were under scrutiny by the NCAA. Whether the collegiate association was ever made aware of that phone information, however, is unknown. Most of that revealing data had been previously exposed via the PackPride.com website.

According to *The Daily Tar Heel* article, the school had
instituted an internal policy in 2010 that dictated UNC football players to sign out before they left campus to go on trips.
Kevin Best, spokesman of the football program at the time,
declined to comment on the specifics of whether or not Coples
signed out when he attended the post-NFL draft party in April.
Washington, DC, was also the location of two of Marvin Austin's trips that drew the scrutiny of the NCAA. Coples would
ultimately avoid any NCAA penalties. He would go on to be
a first round draft pick in 2012, going 16th overall to the New
York Jets. He signed a four-year contract worth $8.8 million on
May 17, 2012.

* * *

On June 21, 2011, UNC received their Notice of Allegations (NOA) from the NCAA. This was essentially the list of
transgressions that the NCAA was saying the university had
committed, and the school then had 90 days to respond to those
claims before penalties were handed down. Within the NOA
was outlined numerous "potential major violations," according
to articles released by ESPN and the Associated Press. Those
included unethical conduct by a former assistant coach (John
Blake) as well as failure to adequately monitor the conduct of
former and current players.

The NOA discussed the various players who had received
improper benefits, and also attached dollar values to those benefits. As mentioned in earlier chapters, the eventual 2013 revelations about Greg Little and Jennifer Wiley (Thompson) proved
that the NCAA only had a fraction of those figures correct. Wiley was also cited in the NOA for refusing to cooperate with the
investigation. Another notable aspect was that the school was

also penalized for failing to monitor "social media activity" of the football team in 2010. Despite these clear explanations of the school's shortcomings, the lack of social media monitoring would ultimately continue for the university, and would eventually spread to the basketball program in the years to follow.

Chancellor Holden Thorp said in a statement, "I deeply regret that Carolina is in this position. We made mistakes, and we have to face that. … We will emerge with a stronger athletic program, and we will restore confidence in Carolina football." During the timespan that marked the beginning of the scandal and the release of the NOA, one of the supplementary figures – NFL agent Gary Wichard – died in March 2011 from complications due to diabetes and pancreatic cancer.

* * *

During the first week of July 2011, football player Michael McAdoo filed a lawsuit seeking an injunction to lift his permanent NCAA ban which had been handed down the previous year. According to a sportsillustrated.cnn.com article, the association's judicial system found him guilty of infractions serious enough to warrant a permanent ban, but McAdoo and his lawyers disagreed. The lawsuit claimed that McAdoo was "improperly and unjustly declared ineligible to play intercollegiate athletics by Defendant NCAA." His attorney was Noah Huffstetler, who received his undergraduate degree from UNC in 1973 and his law degree from the institution in 1976.

The previous year's NCAA investigation had found McAdoo guilty of accepting $110 in improper benefits, and that he also committed three instances of academic fraud related to parts of a paper actually being written by tutor Jennifer Wiley. Evidence of the academic fraud – which reportedly consisted

of Wiley adding citations and composing a works cited page
– were not uncovered by the NCAA, but rather by the university. The school's Honor Court, however, determined there was
not enough evidence to charge McAdoo with one of the three
counts and found him not guilty of another, according to the
same sportsillustrated.cnn.com article. According to the lawsuit, none of this was taken into account by the NCAA prior to
their ruling.

According to the university's website, "The Undergraduate
Honor Court is comprised of Undergraduate students from all
backgrounds and majors. Court members represent the values
and diversity that makes Carolina special. The Court is charged
with reviewing allegations of misconduct to determine if the
Honor Code was violated. If the Court determines a violation
has occurred, it will impose a disciplinary sanction consistent
with community values and University guidelines." At the
time, many in the sports media realm felt McAdoo had a fairly
strong case for reinstatement. However, new evidence would
surface just days later that would change all of that – and ultimately alter the landscape of UNC's ongoing scandal as well.

* * *

When Michael McAdoo's attorney filed the suit, one important addition was part of the proceedings: the research paper
in question was included as evidence. The Raleigh *News and
Observer* posted the various attached exhibits on its website,
and members of the N.C. State website PackPride.com started
to look through them. This wasn't the website's first foray into
their rival's scandal; as mentioned in the chapter's opening
paragraph, members of its message board had earlier meticulously dissected the phone records of John Blake, uncovering a

number of trends and violations that would later be recognized by sports writers as well as presumably the NCAA. This time, members descended upon the research paper and quickly made a startling discovery: the vast majority of it was plagiarized, and often lifted word-for-word from various internet sources. One section in particular came from a book originally published in 1911, and included terms and expressions that had been obsolete (when describing the paper's topic) for years.

McAdoo's suit instantly became more of a challenge, since according to a sportsillustrated.cnn.com article posted on July 8, 2011, the NCAA would likely view a plagiarized paper much more seriously that simply having a tutor reformat the citations. Other problems on the university's side were also exposed. Namely, why didn't the paper's original professor discover the plagiarism, considering that it only took some rival fans using Google a few minutes to unearth it? Furthermore, why was the school's Honor Court unable to detect it? And finally, Athletics Director Dick Baddour had also publicly supported McAdoo a few days earlier, saying the paper was the student's own work. This was obviously just an assumption by Baddour, or else it was something he was told by other factions within the university and he accepted as fact.

* * *

A distinction that an organization never wants is having the full attention of a newspaper's investigative reporter, especially a capable and talented one. With the discovery of the McAdoo plagiarism, that is exactly what would begin to happen in Chapel Hill. The Raleigh *News and Observer*'s Dan Kane began to focus his efforts on the story – not just on McAdoo, but on the academic and athletic issues within the university as a whole.

A graduate of St. John Fisher College in Rochester, New York, Kane had joined the *N&O* staff in 1997, and became a part of its prestigious investigative team in April 2009. His journalistic efforts had been recognized with several awards in the past.

In a July 17, 2011, article, Kane reiterated that the professor and the Honor Court missed the plagiarism, as did the involved factions of UNC's athletics department (academic support personnel, and even Dick Baddour). Kane also pointed out another party that apparently missed it prior to McAdoo's case going to trial: the NCAA. He went on to list another piece of information about the blossoming case that at the time seemed like a simple footnote, but would eventually lead to issues of monumental proportions. The professor who assigned the paper to McAdoo was Julius Nyang'oro, who was also the chairman of UNC's Department of African and Afro-American Studies (AFAM). He was out of the country at the time of Kane's article and could not be reached for comment. His name and actions, however, would surface many more times in the future.

UNC history professor Jay Smith, who will be covered in more detail in a later chapter, said at the time that he was not surprised the school's Honor Court missed McAdoo's plagiarism. He had been arguing for two years that the Honor Court system failed to get at the heart of the misconduct. Smith said he became a critic when he turned in a student for plagiarizing a paper in 2009. He said the Honor Court's prosecutor did not provide the correct evidence at the hearing, overlooking key information that Smith had clearly provided. The experience convinced Smith that students do not have the time or experience to handle complex misconduct cases.

The comment Professor Smith made regarding students

being unprepared for that type of authority may be understandable. But how does that explain the professor missing McA-
doo's offenses? And the athletics department, and the athletics
director? Smith went on to say in the *News and Observer* article that when an athletics department relies on the Honor Court
to determine facts crucial to a key football player's eligibility,
that puts the university's academic integrity at great risk. Student athletes on UNC's basketball and football teams help the
university collect millions of dollars in television rights, ticket
sales, and licensing fees, creating pressure to keep athletes
eligible. The athletics department puts "UNC's credibility on
the line without apparently doing the due diligence on the basic facts of the case," he said, "and I think that's a very serious
problem."

To further highlight the point, Smith indicated that earlier in
2011 he had surveyed members of the faculty about the Honor
Court. One surprising find was that many faculty said they do
not use the system, and reasons varied. Many felt that the court
was being too lenient on cheaters, and several key responses
suggested preferential treatment for student athletes by UNC
officials or the Honor Court. One of the faculty responders
wrote, "The evidence of cheating could not have been more obvious, and the excuse given was completely implausible. Also,
this case dealt with a student athlete, and I found the interven-
tions from the athletics department asking that the case not be
brought before the honor court unethical."

A related effect of the McAdoo case was the attention given
to the PackPride.com site, and a somewhat begrudged acceptance by the media of the effectiveness of some of the site's
members. The site had made other discoveries in the past, but
not until the McAdoo plagiarism incident were those findings

prominently featured in the mainstream media. The poster at
the heart of the McAdoo case would actually be featured in an
article on the respected Poynter website. He was quoted under
a username, as his real name was withheld in the article by request. One of the main points of the feature was that important
news was initially broken on a fan internet site, and then only
afterwards did expanding media coverage of the event follow.
Unfortunately for UNC, this trend would repeat itself several
times in the future – with each successive story having a bigger
and bigger impact.

Michael McAdoo's case would eventually be dismissed, and
he remained ineligible to play collegiate sports. Many sports
journalists felt those ultimate decisions were in part due to the
discovery of the plagiarism. Paul Sun, the attorney who represented the NCAA in the suit, said that the association "correctly
and fairly" applied its rules in the case. McAdoo would eventually be signed by the NFL's Baltimore Ravens as an undrafted
free agent in August 2011. He tore his Achilles tendon during
the summer of 2012, which forced him to miss the entire NFL
season that year. He was released by the Ravens a year later,
and signed with Winnipeg of the Canadian Football League
in late 2013. McAdoo gave an interview with the New York
Times that was published in 2013, and which will be covered
in more detail in a later chapter. Part of the topic dealt with
academic cheating and irregularities, and also the educational
restrictions that schools sometimes placed on athletes. McAdoo
was quoted as saying, "I would still like to get a college degree
someday, but not at the University of North Carolina. They just
wasted my time."

* * *

On July 27, 2011, less than three weeks after the discovery of McAdoo's plagiarism, the university fired head football coach Butch Davis. According to articles released at the time by espn.com, Davis had apparently survived the most dangerous days of the NCAA's investigation, as he had lead the previous year's suspension-decimated team to eight wins and a bowl victory. However, the school's administration would eventually alter its opinion, saying that the turmoil caused by the investigation was doing too much damage to the university's reputation. In a direct quote from Chancellor Holden Thorp, he said he had "lost confidence in (the school's) ability to come through this without harming the way people think of this institution." He continued by saying that "our academic integrity is paramount, and we must work diligently to protect it. The only way to move forward and put this behind us is to make a change."

With football's late-summer training camp just over a week away, the team now found itself without a clear figurehead. After his firing, Davis said "I can honestly say I leave with the full confidence that I have done nothing wrong. I was the head coach and I realize the responsibility that comes with that role. But I was not personally involved in, nor aware of, any actions that prompted the NCAA investigation."

Holden Thorp and Dick Baddour both spoke at a news conference held on the following day. Several questions were raised by reporters with regards to the payout that Davis would receive. Chancellor Thorp indicated that it would cost $2.7 million, at which time a reporter pointed out that if it was determined Davis was fired "with cause" it would potentially cost the school nothing, according to the contract that Davis signed. Thorp replied, "I've reached the conclusion that even though this is a terrible time, that the athletics program will need to pay whatever it is that we need to pay to make the separation happen." In a quick follow-up question regarding the wording of the contract, Thorp made clear that the school would not be dismissing Davis "for cause."

Roughly ten minutes later and after a number of other questions and topics were posed, attention was once again turned to the topic of Davis's contract. A third reporter revived the line of questioning with Thorp: "Chancellor, you were talking about the reputation of the university. And given the budget crisis of the university… you're saying that you're not going to fire (Davis) for cause. I have his contract right in front of me. It says, 'serious disrespect for the integrity and ethics of the university'. Given the crisis financially that you're in, what would motivate you to pay him to go away?" To which Thorp responded, "As I said earlier, that is what has made this a difficult decision. Any money that is paid to Coach Davis will be from the athletics department, not general support funds for the university. As I said, that is the conclusion that we have come to with extensive consultation. With lots of folks." Later dissection by the media of the contract's wording would indicate that the university could, in fact, have fired Davis "with cause." Why they did not is unclear.

An interesting subplot to the timing of Davis's firing was that Thorp's decision came the day that a new university Board of Trustees chairman was elected. According to a sportsillustrated.cnn.com article published on July 28, 2011, former Chairman Bob Winston had long been known as a Davis supporter. He had served as chairman since 2009, and Winston and UNC administrators had shown their support of Davis numerous times during that time span. On the day that Wade Hargrove replaced Winston as chairman, however, the tone of the discussions regarding Davis obviously changed while the trustees were meeting in a closed session. The culminating result was the ultimate firing of Davis.

An ongoing matter that had been discussed in the media for weeks leading up to the firing had been the personal cell phone records of Davis. Despite being issued a university-supplied cell phone, Davis had made virtually zero calls on it during his years with the school, instead opting to use his personal cell phone. After the phone records of John Blake showed a number of NCAA-related violations, the media had long been after the records of Davis, as well. Even though the phone records in question were for his personal cell, the fact that Davis used it for university business seemingly made them public record. The matter had been contended by Davis, and was at the time of his firing still in limbo. At the news conference a reporter asked Thorp how the firing of Davis would affect the pending release of his personal cell phone records which had tentatively been scheduled to happen in the coming weeks. The question to Thorp was, "Are you still planning on releasing the private cell phone records of Butch Davis? I know he was in the process of redacting them." To which Thorp replied, "That's up to Coach Davis". As it would turn out, once Davis was fired from the university then UNC absolved itself from the equation. The records would go on to be entangled in legal proceedings for more than a year.

At the same news conference discussing the firing of Butch Davis, another big announcement was made. It was revealed that Athletics Director Dick Baddour would be stepping down as soon as a replacement could be found. Baddour had been part of the Tar Heel "family" for 45 years, and had held the position of athletics director for the past 14. Prior to that, he had been the senior associate of UNC's former athletics director, John Swofford. When Swofford left to become Commissioner of the ACC (a title he still held during UNC's scandal) in 1997, Baddour took over as athletics director. With the firing of Butch Davis and the announced retirement/resignation of Dick Baddour, and adding to the previous resignation of John Blake, the number of jobs directly affected by the scandal – which included firings, resignations, retirements, and transfers within the university – now stood at three. That number would continue to rise.

* * *

Reactions to the firing of Davis were mixed. Numerous former players took to the social media airways in support of Davis, while select other individuals who were in some way professionally or financially connected to the school supported Thorp and his decision. According to an article on wralsportsfan.com, Hannah Gage, a member of the Board of Governors and a UNC graduate, said, "It wasn't an easy decision, but I believe it's the right decision for the university. The Chancellor made it clear today that he's not willing to compromise the university's academic integrity or its reputation."

University President Tom Ross, a graduate of UNC's School of Law, supported Thorp's decision. He said, "This has been a difficult decision for the Chancellor, but I am pleased that he made the decision only after receiving and studying all of the facts so that he would both be fair to the individuals involved and look out for the best interests of the University. He believes deeply in academic integrity and understands that academic integrity and a successful athletics program are both achievable simultaneously. For this to happen, he has now concluded that a change in the football program is necessary." The comments by both Gage and Ross speak to high academic standards and an uncompromising attitude by the school. Those comments would be viewed under a different and more hypocritical light in the near future, however, as much more serious academic issues would arise – and UNC would ultimately not act with such an uncompromising and fact-seeking attitude when basketball was involved in the allegations.

* * *

Several weeks following the termination of Butch Davis, one final troubling story related to him (other than the eventual release of his phone records) would see the light of day. In an online article by local ABC affiliate WTVD on August 17, 2011, it was revealed that a UNC police officer had responded to an on-campus crash involving several of the school's football players. On May 29, 2011, Sergeant Shawn Smith was the investigating officer of the accident in question. Smith had also been the assigned personal officer to coach Butch Davis during home and away football games, according to the news station.

The article said that football player Herman Davidson crashed a vehicle that also included players Carl Gaskins, Jr., Dion Guy, and Ebele Okakpu as passengers. The police report indicated that Davidson had alcohol on his breath, but was not impaired. The initial report said the car was traveling the speed limit at the time of the crash. Nearly 16 hours later, however, the report was changed to say the car was going 45 mph in a 25 mph zone. Davidson only received a citation for not having a driver's license. He was not issued a speeding ticket, and none of the players were taken into custody. The crash caused $18,000 in damage to the car Davidson was driving, which belonged to Okakpu's father.

UNC said that Smith resigned on July 15, 2011, six weeks after the crash. The school did not indicate to WTVD if the crash led to his resignation. Smith denied a cover-up, but when asked about his resignation he told the station's I-Team it was a "self-inflicted wound" and a "hard lesson learned." The former officer claimed on his Twitter page (@Tar_Heel_Smitty) to be "the BIGGEST Tar Heel fan in existence!" He said, "I let my love for UNC interfere with real life and I paid the price." The athletics department told the station that it was aware of the crash, and that the players had been disciplined by then football coach Davis.

* * *

The essential (and unanswered) questions:

-- How did Michael McAdoo's professor miss the plagiarism? How did the Honor Court and the school's athletics director miss it? Was it a case (amongst one or more of those entities) of simply choosing to not notice/acknowledge it?

-- Based on faculty survey responses, how long had UNC athletes possibly been receiving preferential treatment in the school's Honor Court system?

-- Why would the school choose to pay fired head coach Butch Davis $2.7 million when apparently they had the legal right to withhold that money? What would be the advantage to "pay him to go away?" And was this decision in any way related to the impending release of his personal cell phone records?

CHAPTER FIVE

MARVIN AUSTIN'S TRANSCRIPT; JULIUS NYANG'ORO; CARL CAREY

The academic scandal at UNC might eventually be reflected upon as phases that unfolded little by little. The plagiarism exhibited by Michael McAdoo was essentially phase one, as it showed the lack of institutional oversight with regards to the work being submitted by student athletes. It also introduced Julius Nyang'oro, the chairman of the Department of African and Afro-American Students (AFAM), where he also served as a professor. It was Nyang'oro who assigned (and presumably graded) McAdoo's paper.

Phase two began to unravel on August 21, 2011. It was on that date that the Raleigh ran a front-page story about an academic transcript it had obtained for former UNC star Marvin

Austin, who had been near the center of the school's agent-related NCAA violations. The details showed anomalies beginning with Austin's very first classes at the university, and were dissected by noted investigative reporter Dan Kane.

In a summer 2007 session at UNC, just prior to his first full semester as a freshman, Austin took a 400-level class in AFAM. This was during the same time span when daily football workouts were being held, yet Austin managed to receive a B-plus in the course. The instructor was Julius Nyang'oro. To further muddy the situation, Austin had been allowed to enroll in the course (and apparently excel in it) despite having a score on the written portion of the SAT that was deemed low enough that he needed to take a remedial writing class. Austin did not take that writing class, however, until the immediately subsequent fall semester – after he had received the B-plus in a 400-level course.

According to Kane's article, Julia Nichols, the student services manager for UNC's Academic Advising Program, said it is unusual for a freshman to begin his or her college education with a 400 level course. There were exceptions, though, but they were reserved for incoming students who had "demonstrated an aptitude, either through advanced placement classes or other experience," and who petition the professor to be allowed to take the course. Based on Austin's reported SAT scores, the quoted levels of aptitude certainly did not appear to match up well with his personal academic parameters. Nichols concluded by saying, "As a general, blanketed rule, freshmen are not normally allowed to take 400 or 500 level classes."

Another UNC spokesman, Mike McFarland, said the course Austin took did not require a prerequisite and was therefore open to all students. But he confirmed that students could not just sign up for the course via open registration. They had to first get permission from the African Studies department, which was led by Nyang'oro at the time. McFarland also said that a 400 level course also often suggested it had a level of sophistication that would pose a challenge to a newly arrived freshman. UNC officials could not produce a syllabus outlining the course requirements for the 2007 class. A description of the class, "Bioethics in Afro-American Studies," was provided on the unaffiliated website CourseRank.com. It described it as a course that would "examine the process involved in resolving moral dilemmas pertaining to people of the African Diaspora." Yet Austin, a sub-standard student based on SAT scores, not only was placed in a course normally reserved for upperclassmen, but also received a grade of a B-plus.

Jon Ericson, a retired Drake University provost who started an organization called The Drake Group that advocates reforming college sports, was also quoted in the *News and Observer* article. "You don't start at the senior level seminar and then work your way down to remedial writing," Ericson said. He said that Austin's transcript suggested that Austin was assigned to a class that was intended to provide him a good grade to maintain his eligibility on the football field. Ericson said he advocates releasing the grades for athletes in high-dollar programs, but not their names. The grades would help show which departments and classes were serving to protect student athletes' eligibility, and, hopefully, he said, prompt faculty to speak out against the erosion of academic standards. That last point would be especially pertinent to UNC's situation, as throughout the scandal the vast majority of its faculty chose to remain mute on the subject – even while more and more evidence of orchestrated cheating was strongly suggested through data and records.

A 2.0 grade point average (GPA), or a C average, was required at the time to remain in good academic standing at UNC, according to its handbook. In total, Austin was carrying a 2.21 GPA after more than three semesters and three summer classes. The transcript showed that Austin received grades of C-minus or lower in seven of 17 classes and labs, including one F and three D's. None of those four "lowest" grades were in the AFAM department. It was just the opposite; Austin had taken three classes within the African Studies department by the end of his second year, earning the grades of the aforementioned B-plus along with two B-minuses – grades that mathematically helped to balance the lower grades he received in numerous non-AFAM courses.

More revealing data was included in Kane's article regarding the AFAM department and Nyang'oro in particular. MyEdu.com was a website that received grading data from UNC. It reported that a majority of students taking the "Bioethics" class over the previous five years scored an A-minus or better. It also showed that no students had received less than a B-minus during that same timeframe. A month earlier Chancellor Holden Thorp had commented on the AFAM department, marking it as an important one for the university. He also went on to refer to Julius Nyang'oro as "a great colleague." Prior to being named chancellor of the university, Thorp had held the position of Dean of the College of Arts and Science – a position that coincidentally oversaw both the AFAM department and its head, Julius Nyang'oro.

Information held within Nyang'oro's curriculum vitae indicated that he first worked at the University of North Carolina in 1984 as a visiting assistant professor in the Department of African and Afro-American Studies. He was a Post-Doctoral Fellow in the department from 1985-1987, and in the fall of 1989 was an instructor/coordinator for UNITAS, a multi-cultural living and academic program at UNC. In 1989 and 1990 he was the executive director of UNC's Institute for the Comparative Study of African and Afro-America, which was later renamed the Institute for African American Research. From 1990 to 1992 he was an assistant professor in AFAM, and then from 1992 to 1995 was an associate professor. In 1995 he was given the title of "present professor" in the AFAM department, as well as adjunct professor in the Department of Political Science. He was named the chairperson of the AFAM department in 1992, a position he would hold until shortly after the release of not only Austin's transcript, but also other suspiciously correlating information that soon followed.

* * *

Less than a week later another article by Dan Kane and the *News and Observer* would appear revealing details that would further damage the image of Nyang'oro, his department, and his university superiors. The August 27, 2011, article showed that during the same time the school's football program was still dealing with issues that had been uncovered regarding sports agents with connections to both coaches and players, Nyang'oro had hired another agent to actually teach a summer class on the school's campus.

The agent was Carl Carey, Jr., whose top client was former UNC football and basketball star Julius Peppers. Furthermore, at the time of the summer class Carey was representing two other UNC football players who had been selected in the NFL draft held only months earlier. Even more damning was the fact that while he was teaching the class, he was also trying to retain one of those players – Robert Quinn – whose business manager was questioning Carey's ability to represent Quinn. Quinn and his business manager (his girlfriend) were both living in Chapel Hill at the time. Carey had also previously signed yet another UNC player, Quan Sturdivant, but Sturdivant had later switched to a different agent.

Julius Nyang'oro hired Carey to teach a course during the first summer session called Foundations of Black Education. Carey had formerly been an adjunct professor and academic adviser to football players at UNC before eventually leaving the university in 2002 and starting an advising business for athletes. He would go on to become a sports agent in 2005, with his biggest client being the aforementioned former UNC star Julius Peppers. Much more on the massive impact that Peppers had on the overall UNC scandal will be revealed in Chapter Nine.

Karen Gil, UNC's Dean of the College of Arts and Sciences who oversaw Nyang'oro, approved the hire of Carey – but said she did not know he was a sports agent. "In hindsight," she said in an email to the *News and Observer*, "it would have been better to know." She did not make herself available for an interview, nor did she respond to further questions the newspaper had about the hire. Other UNC officials indicated that Carey was allowed to teach the class because he had the credentials and experience. He held a PhD in Educational Psychology, and he had also taught the exact same class 11 years prior in the same department under Nyang'oro.

* * *

Carl Carey told the *News and Observer* that he knew little about Nyang'oro – despite the fact that he had previously taught under the department chairman in the early 2000's. He also claims he told Nyang'oro that he was a sports agent. Carey said, "I was there because of my love for teaching students. I was not there for any other purpose but to teach the class." The fact that he had entered into a monetary arrangement with Robert Quinn, however, would raise suspicions to those claims. At the time of the article's release, Carey was suing Quinn, a first-round pick of the NFL's St. Louis Rams, in an attempt to recover nearly $300,000. Carey indicated that the money was comprised of loans and advances he gave Quinn in advance of an expected professional contract. As mentioned earlier, Quinn was also living in Chapel Hill at the time. Regarding the depth of the past relationship between Julius Nyang'oro and Carl Carey, Nyang'oro was unable to confirm or refute Carey's statements, as the head of the AFAM department did not respond to numerous requests for interviews – for this current story, for any of the past ones, or any that would arise in the future.

Carole Browne, a Wake Forest University biology professor who also had recently served as a co-chairman for the Coalition on Intercollegiate Athletics, was also interviewed for the article. The Coalition had previously proposed reforms for college athletics, and Browne said that hiring a sports agent to teach a class was "absolutely an atrocious thing to do." She continued by saying, "It's giving the agent the opportunity to run into students even incidentally, which could generate problems." As future information regarding UNC's athletes and the AFAM department would surface, enrollment data would show that possible contact within the hallways of that department with the school's premier athletes would be anything but incidental.

The hiring of Carey would be the third direct questionable activity to which Nyang'oro was tied. Previously he had missed obvious plagiarism in a paper by football player Michael McAdoo. Next, the transcript of Marvin Austin showed he was allowed to take an upper-level class as an incoming freshman, despite the doubtful signs of Austin's preparedness for collegiate work. Unfortunately for Nyang'oro, the AFAM department, and the university as a whole, more was yet to come.

* * *

On September 1, 2011, less than two weeks after the partial transcript of Marvin Austin showed questionable academic practices, and only a few days following the disclosure that a sports agent was hired to teach at the school, Julius Nyang'oro resigned from his position as chairman of the Department of African and Afro-American Studies. Chancellor Holden Thorp announced in a statement that the university would also be looking at "possible irregularities with courses that included undergraduate students." Despite a bold proclamation in the statement by Thorp that said, "Because academic integrity is paramount, we have every obligation to get to the bottom of these issues," future deliberate stonewalling measures taken by the school would bring those words into question.

Even though Nyang'oro would be ceding his position as chairman, the statement indicated that he would continue to teach, according to the September 1st article by the *News and Observer*. As a result of leaving the chairman's post, Nyang'oro would lose $12,000 in salary. He had previously been making $171,000 a year, overseeing a staff of 22. Once again, Nyang'oro declined to comment on all matters. When reached at his office, he referred the reporter to the university administration.

In a column posted in *The Daily Tar Heel* several days later, author Will Doran opined that when Nyang'oro resigned his chairman position the previous week, "it was several years too late." In a hard-hitting centerpiece from the university's campus-centric newspaper, Doran pointed out many of the "elephants in the room"; topics that had previously only been skirted around by the mainstream media. The author noted that Nyang'oro missed the plagiarism by Michael McAdoo – or perhaps ignored it. He cited Marvin Austin's suspiciously high grade, and the hiring of Carl Carey. Also referenced was UNC's "much-touted academic integrity," with ironic emphasis given towards those words throughout the remainder of the article.

According to the column, university registrar data on the class rating website unc.blinkness.com showed that between 2003 and 2009, Nyang'oro gave out 74 percent A's, 25 percent B's, and only 1 percent C's to a total of 1,126 students. In the words of the author, those numbers "might not seem out of place in an elementary school classroom, but they should have been scoffed at in the rigorous academic atmosphere" that UNC "claims to value." Instead, he noted, many of the former chairman's department colleagues followed his grading lead, with statistics supplied. "The consensus from anonymous reviewers on Blinkness was that participation and attendance would be enough to get an A," the article stated. "Several others also said a bit of reading might not hurt."

The article concluded by touching on Chancellor Thorp's edict that the university would be looking into areas of the department. "Let's not stop with this department," the article suggested. "Administrators should investigate all the departments that inflate grades so far that the University's integrity pops... We're paying for a stellar education, not a stellar transcript. Anyone who truly believes in the lofty ideal of academic integrity must desire it at all steps, not just on the football field." There was at least one part of the reviewer-comments on Blinkness that would later appear to be off the mark to a degree. Regarding some AFAM classes and the notion that attendance would be needed in order to get a good grade, data would soon emerge to show that even being present in a classroom wasn't always necessary for achievement at UNC.

* * *

The essential (and unanswered) questions:

-- Who was ultimately responsible for enrolling/allowing Austin to take (and receive a high grade in) a 400-level class?

-- Why wasn't there more institutional oversight regarding the extremely questionable hiring of a professional sports agent to teach an on-campus class?

-- How close was Carl Carey's relationship with Julius Nyang'oro – not only when he was hired in the summer of 2011, but also back when Carey taught in the department in the early 2000's?

CHAPTER SIX

FOOTBALL PENALTIES

The final few months of 2011 were relatively quiet in terms of new information on the scandal. Julius Nyang'oro had resigned his chairman post in the AFAM department and would eventually retire from the university. The school had made its appearance before the NCAA regarding the infractions charged in the Notice of Allegations – a meeting attended not only by Chancellor Holden Thorp and Director of Athletics Dick Baddour, but also by John Swofford – who was not only the commissioner of the ACC, but conveniently also a former UNC athletics director, athlete, and a graduate of the school. Happening behind the scenes, though, was the on-campus look into possible irregularities within the Department of African and Afro-American Studies (AFAM). Those findings would be revealed at a later date. The next major news, however, would be the formal sanctions handed down by the NCAA against the school's football program.

* * *

An article dated March 12, 2012, from the Raleigh *News and Observer* hit the highlights of the NCAA's sanctions. Many of them had previously been covered in the original Notice of Allegations, with the difference now being that penalties were attached. The wording of some of the infractions, though, would be especially important regarding future activities by the university and some of its players. Essentially, the school would later commit similar infractions – but would not be held to the same standards and penalties by the NCAA. The main difference would seemingly be the sports that were affected. As has been noted before, the school's level of defense of its football issues versus basketball issues would eventually be great indeed.

The football program was cited for allowing some of its players to receive impermissible benefits in the forms of money, travel, and other expenses – often provided by tutor Jennifer Wiley, who at one time had worked personally for head coach Butch Davis's family. It would later be shown through a series of Secretary of State indictments that not only did agents also supply players with money, but that the dollar amounts the NCAA stated in its 2012 sanctions were substantially below the actual transaction levels.

Another major violation – and one that would appear to drive all of the university's stonewalling attempts in the future regarding uncovering the truth of its academic improprieties – dealt with the impermissible participation of athletes. The formal sanctions stated that during the 2008-09 academic year and the summer of 2009, three student athletes engaged in academic fraud. As a result, one of those athletes competed while ineligible during the 2008 football season, another competed while ineligible during the 2009 and 2010 football seasons, and the third competed while ineligible during the 2008 and 2009 football seasons. The culminating result was that the football program was forced to vacate 16 victories during that timeframe – as games where ineligible players participated were retroactively forfeited. This is a well-known mantra of both the NCAA and college sports in general. And it is also presumably what would eventually lead the school to fight tooth and nail over improprieties involving its basketball program. Much more on that matter will be discussed in the upcoming chapters, but the implication is clear: If a basketball player were ever deemed to have cheated academically, then the team would have to forfeit any games/seasons in which that player participated – even one involving the winning of a National Championship.

* * *

Back to the March 2012 football sanctions: The program lost a handful of scholarships spread out over the forthcoming three seasons, and was also banned from postseason competition in 2012, which included any potential conference championship game or bowl game. In a decision by the school considered hypocritical by many, however, it chose to award its players with "Division Champion" rings after the 2012 season, despite not being eligible for the championship game due to its past violations. This decision was apparently justified by the university because the team finished in a three-way tie for first in the Coastal Division. The school also proclaimed itself "Coast Division Champions" in a variety of advertising mediums, including a prominent billboard in Charlotte. All of this in spite of the fact that Georgia Tech officially won the division and played in the ACC championship game.

Another penalty from the NCAA dealt with compliance. The notes said that "the school must also educate athletes, coaches and relevant school personnel on NCAA rules and regulations." This edict would fall on at least a few deaf ears in the future, however, as the summer of 2013 would find even more UNC athletes receiving benefits that were clearly impermissible based on multiple NCAA regulations. One final notation dealt with how the school would be monitored and treated moving forward in terms of any potential new violations that might occur. The sanctions stated that the institution is on probation for three years. This would seem to infer that if other infractions were to occur during the three years to follow – in any sport – that stricter penalties would be levied. Whether that ultimately ends up being the case (stricter penalties being levied) remains to be seen, as other infractions have undoubtedly been committed by the school and its players in the aftermath of those announced March 2012 sanctions.

Following the announcement of the official violations and penalties, a number of individuals associated with UNC (both past and present) commented on the matter. Regarding a potential appeal, Chancellor Holden Thorp said, "We decided it wouldn't make sense to appeal, given how long the appeal would take, given the (lack of) success other schools have had with appeals." Former head coach Butch Davis maintained his innocence in the matter by saying through a released statement, "As was stated by the Chancellor this summer, and has been noted in this report, I was not named in any of these allegations." Former UNC Athletics Director Dick Baddour took a more grandiose approach with his comments, eliciting the very term that has been brought into question through the university's actions and events over the past two decades: "Well there's still a Carolina Way," Baddour said. "The way we did this investigation, it was my strong belief that it was the Carolina Way. We set out four guiding principles when we started. Number four was that we would be better as a result of this."

In a *News and Observer* editorial released on that same date of March 12, 2012, staff writer Caulton Tudor commented that the school was given a tough punishment, but that it could have been worse. He noted that more scholarships could have potentially been lost, and that ultimately only a one-year bowl ban wasn't too bad. An important observation he also made was that, "Sixteen wins have been vacated, but that sort of reprimand doesn't carry much weight." That is likely true, given that the football team had never competed for a national championship during the affected timeframe. But once again, the issue of vacated victories would eventually become the centerpiece of the university's fierce struggle to keep public information hidden from the media. Because if the school was ever forced to vacate victories in basketball via the spreading academic scandal, then past national championships definitely would be in jeopardy. Tudor ended his piece by stating, "Perhaps the most important retribution of all is the damage to UNC's image and reputation."

An editorial by *News and Observer* staff columnist Tom Sorensen appeared the following day, and like Tudor's closing remark it also made comments regarding the university's reputation. The article began by taking the stance that UNC's football program – and head coach Davis – deserved the sanctions it received. Sorenson insinuated that there was little discipline within Davis's former program, as he reiterated the multiple offenses that were by then well known: ineligible players competing, the acceptance of illegal benefits, a tutor enabling players to engage in academic fraud, and more. As has been the case throughout the school's three-plus year ordeal, however, items were pointed out by an observer in an article that would later be contradictory to how things ultimately have unfolded. Sorensen said the school "got one thing right. The Tar Heels acknowledged their misdeeds." He went on to ask, "How many times has an athlete, celebrity, politician or official been caught cheating and compounded his or her mistake by lying about it?" The ultimate irony would be that the ongoing investigation into the school's Department of African and Afro-American Studies would uncover misdeeds, and it would uncover cheating – yet when faced with a different set of potential prospects and penalties, the school would do exactly as Sorensen described: compound the mistake through various forms of obfuscation.

Sorensen took a final jab at the university's historical sense of entitlement by saying, "The NCAA did omit one penalty: The Tar Heels forfeit the right to condescend. While (other schools) were caught cheating, the Tar Heels avoided serious scandal. As a result, their fans were free to take shots at violators. And they did. The lesser among those fans will continue to. But they have no credibility."

* * *

The essential (and unanswered) questions:

-- Why would the school choose to publicly flaunt a division championship, and also purchase championship rings for the players on its football team, all while being banned from post-season play – which included the ACC Championship Game?

-- Even after being informed to do so by the NCAA, why would the school not take the (apparently adequate) steps to "educate its athletes, coaches, and relevant school personnel on NCAA rules and regulations?"

-- Considering that the "institution" was placed on three-year's probation, would the future violations that would be uncovered in 2012 and 2013 lead to stricter NCAA penalties on the school – due to UNC still being within its probationary period?

CHAPTER SEVEN

ACADEMIC FRAUD; AFAM GRADE CHANGES; DEBORAH CROWDER

In May of 2012 UNC released the report from a faculty-led internal investigation into the school's Department of African and Afro-American Studies (AFAM). According to a May 4, 2012, article by investigative reporter Dan Kane of the Raleigh *News and Observer*, evidence had been found of academic fraud involving more than 50 classes that ranged from no-show professors to unauthorized grade changes. The report would give many details, but also seemingly leave just as many important questions unanswered.

According to Kane's article, one of the no-show classes was a Swahili course taken by former football player Michael McAdoo. That same course had earlier been at the center of the NCAA claims that McAdoo had received impermissible tutoring, which then led to the discovery of a paper being heavily plagiarized. The vast majority of the suspect AFAM classes were found to have been taught by former department chairman Julius Nyang'oro. Along with the release of the report, the university also said that Nyang'oro would be retiring effective July 1. According to Nancy Davis, the Associate Vice Chancellor for University Relations, "Professor Nyang'oro offered to retire, and we agreed that was in the best interest of the department, the college and the university."

The report attempted to make it clear that there was no evidence that student athletes received more favorable treatment (via the suspect courses) than students who were not athletes. In fact, this would become a common sentiment to be proclaimed by UNC leadership in the months and years to come, and was the school's main argument that its athletic teams should not be punished due to the academic fraud: because non-athletes were part of the classes as well. Possible insight into why non-athletes were in those classes would eventually be revealed, but not for over a year after the release of the May 2012 report. As such, that information will be discussed in a later chapter.

A direct line from Kane's article stated, "The findings were so serious that the university consulted with the district attorney and the SBI about investigating forgery allegations, as some professors said their signatures were forged in documents certifying that they had taught some of the classes in question. Professors also said they had not authorized grade changes for students that the department submitted to the registrar's office."

An immediate set of questions would arise from the

lines in the above paragraph. The most obvious dealt with the grade changes. For whom were they changed, and what were the new/old grades? And what effects, if any, did it have on those students' overall grade point averages? If they were athletes, did the changes allow them to keep their eligibility in a particular sport? More than a year and a half later, the school has still not revealed that information.

* * *

According to the report, law enforcement officials declined to investigate because they did not think the forgeries rose to the level of criminal activity. What was apparently not considered, however, was the fact that some of the forgeries dealt with classes that were "on record" with the school, and where students received grades. They were part of the monetary framework of the university's financial and bookkeeping structure. Yet no one taught them – since the professors' said signatures were forged. Did anyone receive the pay for having taught those classes, even though no "teaching" took place?

Jonathan Hartlyn and William L. Andrews were the two senior faculty administrators who conducted the investigation. In a joint statement they said, "We are deeply disturbed by what we have learned in the course of our review. Our review has exposed numerous violations of professional trust, affecting the relationship of faculty and students and the relationships among faculty colleagues in this department. These violations have undermined the educational experience of a number of students, have the potential to generate unfounded doubt and mistrust toward the department and faculty, and could harm the academic reputation of the university."

Information that would become extremely important in the

future was that the timeframe covered in the report only went
back as far as the summer of 2007, and ended with the summer
of 2011. A reason for this was given in a later interview by
Chancellor Holden Thorp, who said the course review did not
go back before summer 2007 because the university wanted to
obtain the most accurate records and recollections available.
Another possible explanation, though obviously never stated by
the university, was that the summer of 2007 coincided with the
first time the recruits of former football coach Butch Davis were
on campus. Furthermore, Davis was fired in late July of 2011,
showing that his tenure at the school essentially mirrored the
time period UNC chose to focus its AFAM report. Many in the
social media world would suggest, perhaps rightfully so, that
the school was attempting to pin all of its academic troubles on
the now-ended Davis regime and his football players

* * *

Much more valuable insight was provided via the report
and the aforementioned article by Dan Kane. It showed that
the AFAM department's long-time administrator, Deborah
Crowder, would have overseen much of the course scheduling and grade recording. She retired in September 2009 and
declined to be interviewed for the internal investigation. The
newspaper reported that she made $36,130 a year before re-
tiring, but she could also not be reached for further comment
by the newspaper. Like the pattern that followed the initial
mentioning of Nyang'oro's name a year earlier, Crowder would
also soon become a much more central figure in the academic
scandal.

One of the classes that was deemed a "no-show" course
was the 400-level class where Marvin Austin received a B-plus

during his first summer on campus. Kane's article noted that Nyang'oro had been unable to produce a syllabus for that class, "Bioethics in Afro-American Studies," or the Swahili class that Michael McAdoo had taken. That was another red flag, according to the school's report, because documents provided by other professors teaching similar courses focused on reading and writing in Swahili, not writing papers about Swahili culture in English, as McAdoo had submitted.

More problems arose when Nyang'oro told the university investigators that he did not teach the aforementioned Swahili class, yet the plagiarized paper McAdoo submitted listed Nyang'oro's name as the course professor. The investigation found it was one of nine classes in which there was no evidence that any professor "actually supervised the course and graded the work, although grade rolls were signed and submitted." And as stated earlier, other professors who were listed on grade rolls for those classes said their names were forged on course documents. McAdoo was one of 59 students taking those classes. Yet again, an obvious question was left unasked and thus unanswered: who were the other students? Were they athletes whose eligibility was somehow affected by the fake grades?

The report also found a "strikingly high" percentage of cases in Nyang'oro's classes in which temporary grades were converted to permanent ones. Several other faculty members said they had not authorized grade changes for students. It was not detailed in the report whether the newer, "permanent" grades were higher than the "temporary" ones, despite this being a seemingly obvious set of data to seek in order to uncover motive. And once again, the issue of athletic eligibility was completely ignored by the report – despite the clear evidence of Marvin Austin and Michael McAdoo benefitting from taking the classes, McAdoo's plagiarism withstanding. As detailed when discussing Austin's transcript in Chapter Five, a 2.0 grade point average was required to be in good academic standing at the school. If temporary grades were later changed to permanent ones, and the ensuing result was that an athlete's GPA was bumped above the 2.0 threshold, then clear intent would be established. Again, none of that was addressed in the report. Whether the investigators looked into the matter and then chose to not include it, based on what they possibly discovered, is unknown.

Indeed, the report did not cast any blame on the athletics department. However, information obtained by the *News and Observer* showed the AFAM's independent study courses were popular with athletes, and that Nyang'oro was often teaching them. Such courses had drawn suspicion in the past due to the sometimes lax attendance and work policies, and athletic programs at other universities had gotten into trouble based on some independent study courses, according to the *N&O*.

In all, nine courses from the summer 2007 through summer 2011 timeframe were found to be aberrant, meaning there was evidence that students completed written work, submitted it to the department and received grades, but there was no evidence that the faculty member listed as instructor of record or any other faculty member actually supervised the course and graded the work. Those nine courses had a collective total of 59 registered students, according to the report. Furthermore, an additional 43 courses with a collective total of 599 registered students were either aberrant or were taught irregularly. The latter meant that the instructor provided an assignment and evidently graded the resultant paper, but engaged in limited or no classroom or other instructional contact with students.

* * *

The AFAM's long-time administrator, Deborah Crowder, was earlier mentioned as being the person who would have overseen much of the course scheduling and grade recording within the department. Crowder began working at the university in 1979, and retired in 2009. Details would emerge that showed a very close relationship between Crowder and the men's basketball program. She had been in a long-standing relationship with former basketball player Warren Martin, who played on the 1982 National Championship team. At the time the various fraudulent classes were being revealed, Crowder also had a Facebook social media page. When the report was publicly revealed her Facebook page was still open to public view, and her "friends" list contained a staggering collection of former UNC men's basketball players – many of whom had played on past National Championship teams.

Included were:

- Wayne Ellington (played from 2006-09, and was a member of the 2009 National Championship team)

- Bobby Frasor (2006-09, and a member of the 2009 National Championship team)

- Tyler Hansbrough (2005-09, and a member of the 2009 National Championship team)

- Quentin Thomas (2004-08, and a member of the 2005 National Championship team)

- Wes Miller (2004-07, and a member of the 2005 National Championship team)

- Byron Sanders (2003-06, and a member of the 2005 National Championship team)

- David Noel (2002-06, and a member of the 2005 National Championship team)

- Rashad McCants (2002-05, and a member of the 2005 National Championship team)

- (The wife of) Jawad Williams (2001-05, and a member of the 2005 National Championship team)

- (The wife of) Jackie Manuel (2001-05, and a member of the 2005 National Championship team)

- Will Johnson (1999-03)

- Terrence Newby (1997-00)

- Ademola Okulaja (1995-99)

- Donald Williams (1992-95, and a member of the 1993 National Championship team)

- Derrick Phelps (1990-94, and a member of the 1993 National Championship team)

- Kevin Salvadori (1990-94, and a member of the 1993 National Championship team)

- J.R. Reid (1986-89)

- David Popson (1984-87)

One other name of note stood out amongst Crowder's "friends" list: Kay Thomas. Thomas was a long-time secretary of the UNC men's basketball team. According to a 2012 interview with the website keepingitheel.com, Thomas worked for the basketball program under Coach Dean Smith until he retired.

Also of significant interest was the emerging revelation that Crowder was very close to Burgess McSwain, a long-time academic adviser to UNC's men's basketball team. A story that originally appeared in the Chapel Hill News in February of 2004 detailed many of McSwain's accomplishments involving academics and the school's basketball team. There was even a quote given by Julius Nyang'oro in the article. It followed a lead-in that proclaimed that McSwain's efforts and skills as a teacher had won the respect of numerous UNC faculty members who regularly teach student athletes. Nyang'oro's remarks immediately followed, part of which stated, "Burgess has a clear sense of what a teacher needs to do to convey the key concepts that need to be understood. She is another transmission belt in the teaching process." In fact, that specific topic, "faculty members who regularly teach student athletes," was immediately changed following Nyang'oro's quotes, leaving him as the only faculty member featured in the section. Later in the article McSwain was quoted as saying, "I tell people who ask me that it's not a sham at Carolina. I can't say what happens at other schools, but at Carolina, while we may spoon-feed them a little bit, they go in and take their own exams and write their own papers. We don't do their work for them." Whether she was aware of the fraudulent activities within the AFAM department that benefitted basketball players is unknown. McSwain died on July 9, 2004, after a long illness.

According to information that would surface later in 2012 via an article from the Charlotte *Observer*, Crowder had received $100,000 and some Hummel figurines in 2008 from the estate of Burgess McSwain's father. The payment was said to have arisen from a "close" friendship Crowder had with Ms. McSwain. The money and items were reported to be in exchange for taking care of the father's dogs.

* * *

More notable information from the AFAM investigative report surfaced just a few days later via another *News and Observer* article penned by Dan Kane, which made heavy use of statistics gleaned from the documents. It revealed that football and basketball players accounted for nearly four of every ten students enrolled in fifty-four classes at the heart of the academic fraud investigation. The actual number of athletically-associated enrollments might have even been higher, as trainers, volunteers, and other "support" members of the teams were not identified – only those who were official sports participants. While perhaps shocking to the general public, there were signs beforehand that should have hinted at the news, what with Austin and McAdoo's earlier transgressions, and then Crowder's close ties with the basketball program.

Crowder's presence brought up another huge red flag once the percentage of basketball enrollees was revealed, and led to a topic that few in the media (and none at UNC or even the NCAA) seemed to want to tackle: As previously mentioned, there were unauthorized grade changes. For whom were they changed? Were they for football and/or basketball players? And if so, how did it affect the GPA's and eventual eligibility of those players? Someone at the university – and likely the AFAM department – changed those grades. A fair line of reasoning to follow up on would be to look at people who had connections and/or a vested interest in the athletic programs.

Deborah Crowder unequivocally fit those parameters, especially with the basketball program. Yet the grades of past basketball players were never looked into by the university – or if they were, it was never publicly acknowledged by the university. As explained in an earlier chapter, if players were found to have participated while ineligible, then victories would have to be forfeited. The UNC men's basketball team won national titles in the very recent years of 2009 and 2005. It also won a title in 1993, which just happened to be the year after Julius Nyang'oro took over as the chairman of the AFAM department. And it won a title in 1982, a team on which Deborah Crowder's boyfriend, Warren Martin, played. Yet no questions were asked regarding this massive set of coinciding and suggestive information.

According to the *News and Observer*'s article, university officials say they found no evidence that the suspect classes were part of a plan between Nyang'oro and the athletics department for eligibility-maintaining purposes. And once again the same reasoning was given that Hartlyn and Andrews had used in their report: Student athletes were treated no differently in the classes than students who were not athletes. It should be noted that in the summer of 2011 the university hired a Raleigh public relations firm to help with their handling of the ongoing scandal. As time would go on, more and more people associated with UNC would repeat some of the same phrases over and over again, emphasizing points that would appear to convey less wrongdoing on the university's part, and thus hopefully keep the NCAA from returning to the school – such as the "student athletes vs. non-student athletes" technicality.

* * *

Former State Supreme Court Justice Bob Orr, at the time an attorney, was quoted as saying, "These kids are putting in enormous amounts of time, and in at least some of the sports that are very physically demanding, they are missing a number of classes because of conflicts, and then if they are a marginal student to begin with, you've got to send them to Professor Nyang'oro's class. I think the academic counselors realized that and the tutors realized it and frankly the folks up the food chain for the most part recognized it. But nobody wants to rock the boat because it's big money."

Kane's article went on to further break down the reported enrollments in the suspect classes. Of the 686 students, 246 of the enrollments, or 36 percent, were football players, and 23 enrollments, or three percent, were basketball players, according to UNC. Kane went on to point out that football and basketball players accounted for less than one percent of the total undergraduate enrollment – about 120 of the more than 18,500 undergraduate students on campus – yet they accounted for nearly 40 percent of the enrollments in fraudulent classes.

Some in the social media realm tried to immediately downplay basketball's involvement, pointing to the relatively low "three percent" statistic (23 enrollments). That argument was statistically flawed, however. The short timeframe of the school's investigative report into AFAM classes was from 2007 to 2011. During that same time period, there were 26 total scholarship players who participated on the four men's basketball teams that covered the same timeframe. There are several counterarguments that could shed a different light on that data: If each of those 23 basketball AFAM enrollees only took one fraudulent class apiece, then all but three men's basketball members from 2007 to 2011 would retroactively lose their eligibility (assuming the academic fraud was appropriately acted upon by the NCAA, or even the university itself). If a group of players took two classes apiece, that would still mean that at least 11 players would retroactively lose their eligibility – 42 percent of the players from 2007 to 2011. In either scenario, the team would be forced to vacate all of its victories during that timeframe – including the 2009 National Championship. So once again, it became increasingly apparent why the university was unwilling to dig any deeper into the AFAM fraud. The basketball team and its past accomplishments were coming close to being placed at the center of the microscope, and those glories were as much a part UNC's image as any academic reputation had ever been.

* * *

As more dissecting of the university's investigative report continued, even more questions appeared to be left unanswered. According to the May 7, 2012, article in the *News and Observer*, university officials could not say why no one brought the suspect classes to their attention before the previous summer. Jonathan Hartlyn and William Andrews, the two UNC academic officials who conducted the probe, did not interview students for the report – despite the fact that they must have known all of the students' names who were in the classes, as they reportedly had open access to all past records. However, Nancy Davis, a university spokeswoman, said the university's counsel, Leslie Strohm, and its former faculty athletics representative, Jack Evans, did talk to students. Inexplicably, those interviews were not reflected in the report. As noted before, other information that was not reflected in the report was for whom specific grades were altered. While the Family Educational Rights and Privacy Act (FERPA) would prevent the report from naming specific students, it could have very easily indicated whether the grades of athletes were changed – and what effect it had on those athletes' overall GPA. But once again, that was not pursued by the report's investigators or by the university as a whole.

Tom Ross, the UNC system president and a graduate of UNC's School of Law, stated a theme that would be oft-repeated in the coming months by those closely associated with the university: It was time to look forward, and not backwards. He said in a statement that he saw no need to look further into the academic improprieties. "I believe that this was an isolated situation," Ross said, "and that the campus has taken appropriate steps to correct problems and put additional safeguards in place." On what information he was basing his assumption that it was an isolated situation, however, was certainly unclear. Hannah Gage, chairman of the UNC System's Board of Governors and another UNC graduate, said she would not know if the board would be seeking more information until she had talked to others. As pointed out in Chapter Two, UNC graduates held a significantly higher percentage of the BOG seats than any other university in the 16-institution system.

* * *

The essential (and unanswered) questions:

-- Who changed the grades for the students?

-- Who forged the professors' signatures?

-- Who was ultimately paid for the various classes where the teacher was "unknown?"

-- How many athletes took part in the fraudulent classes, and for which sports?

-- Did those grades affect their GPA's, and if deemed impermissible, then retroactively their eligibility?

-- Had the matter been pursued, would team wins need to vacated, even if it meant national championships?

-- Even though Deborah Crowder retired in 2009, the fraudulent AFAM anomalies continued for at least two more years. Was Nyang'oro solely responsible? If not, who else played a role in the improprieties now that Crowder was gone?

-- Why did the university and its on-staff investigators refuse to ask the above questions and seek answers in a manner that would appear to uphold the honorable and high standards it had long claimed to hold for the institution?

CHAPTER EIGHT

NO-SHOW CLASSES; INTERNAL REPORT REVEALS MORE ACADEMIC FRAUD

Following the release of the university's AFAM report in early May that dealt with academic fraud, the opinions, comments, and fallout would commence from various entities who were in some way connected to the university. Some expressed outrage, while others seemed to offer veiled excuses. All the while the media (and especially the investigative team at the Raleigh *News and Observer*) seemingly recognized the blatant fraud and cheating for what it clearly appeared to be – a method to keep athletes eligible via easy and/or nonexistent classes – and continued to report on various aspects of the story.

A May 11, 2012, article by the Raleigh *News and Observer*

indicated that UNC was considering taking monetary action against former African and Afro-American Studies chairman Julius Nyang'oro. It stated that he had taught a course the previous summer with 19 students enrolled. However, following an inquiry the newspaper made about summer school payments to Nyang'oro, university officials said they might seek action against the professor for not teaching a class as they had anticipated. According to Nancy Davis, a UNC spokeswoman, "Through our review, we learned that Professor Nyang'oro provided instruction for a course in independent study format that had been approved to be taught in lecture format. Had the summer school been aware that he was treating it as independent study, he would not have been paid for the course. We are reviewing appropriate next steps."

Nyang'oro was the instructor of record for 45 similar classes, and university officials said they followed the same pattern: A course typically intended for classroom instruction was converted into an independent study format, which meant no classes and an expectation that a paper or other project would be produced at the end. This would appear to be the format that was followed in the class that former football player Michael McAdoo took, and in which he turned in a paper that was heavily plagiarized. That paper would eventually lead to the NCAA ruling him permanently ineligible. The university refused to investigate how many other athletes may have followed the same impermissible blueprint as McAdoo, and to date the NCAA has not investigated the matter, either.

With growing regularity certain words would be spoken by university individuals in positions of influence that supported the "let's look forward, not into the past" plan of action in an attempt to protect the university's reputation. Wade Hargrove, chairman of UNC's Board of Trustees, said, "All of (the academic issues are) deeply troubling. My concern at this point is making sure that measures are in place to prevent these things from ever happening again at this university."

Nyang'oro received money for teaching courses during the summer sessions, as well as $8,400 for being a summer school administrator, according to university records. The particular class in question, AFAM 280, reopened questions as to whether additional investigation was needed, according to the *News and Observer*. Orange County District Attorney Jim Woodall said the evidence regarding the prior forgery allegations did not appear to be enough to launch a criminal investigation. "But," he said, "if there were some payments for a teacher teaching classes that were not taught, well, that would be a different issue." The potential payment information that Woodall referred to was not included anywhere in the university's investigative report on the AFAM department.

* * *

Art Chansky, a graduate of UNC and the author of several UNC-related books, had been a long-time employee of Tar Heel Sports Properties, a company that owned and managed the multimedia rights for the university. Chansky had worked for the company for 18 years, most recently serving as Associate General Manager and Account Executive, according to a story by WTVD-TV. Depending on which account of the events was true, he either resigned or was fired from that company almost two years earlier in December of 2010. The break came just days after an email sent by Chansky to Chancellor Holden Thorp was made public. The email was dated October 6, 2010, which was several months after the initial football issues arose, and the subject line was "Private and Confidential." In the letter Chansky offered the names and numbers of people who could assist Thorp with a potential search for a new football coach, should Thorp choose to fire Butch Davis. Once the email became public, Chansky's tenure at Tar Heel Sports Properties quickly came to an end. (Davis would not be fired by the university for another eight months.)

After leaving Tar Heel Sports Properties, Chansky would move on to work with various other business entities, and also penned occasional articles for the Chapelboro.com website. An article posted on May 21, 2012, touched on the topic of the AFAM investigative report, and specifically on former chairman Julius Nyang'oro. In the article Chansky began by pointing out the timeframe of the investigation into the department, and how it coincided with Butch Davis's time on campus. This may have been due to Chansky's possible dislike towards Davis (based on his email sent to Thorp that had become public), or it could simply be that Chansky repeated the party line that many associated with the university had hoped to suggest at the time: this started and ended with Butch. He even threw in a quote in an apparent attempt to absolve basketball, when he noted that a week prior coach Roy Williams had said of his players, "They went to class and did the work that was assigned them." To which Chansky followed up with: maybe all the basketball players did, but apparently not all the athletes; again insinuating the issue was a football one. His article concluded with a seeming call for justice. "Let's hope"… any criminal fraud is detected… "quickly and the right people are held accountable." Of course, similar words of "wanting to get to the bottom of things" had been heard before from others in positions of administrative and/or media influence. The sincerity of those claims would soon be put to test, however.

* * *

Members of the university's Board of Trustees finally began to weigh in on the subject after being briefed on Thursday, May 24, 2012. An article that appeared the following day in the Raleigh *News and Observer* indicated that the trustees had asked "pointed questions" about accountability in the university's academic operations. Chairman Wade Hargrove described the findings of the internal AFAM investigation as "major indiscretions that raise serious questions of unprofessional and unethical conduct." He went on to say that he read the report with a mixture of "disappointment and dismay and outrage," and that "academic freedom is not to be confused with academic irresponsibility or academic fraud. We all know the difference." According to information the trustees were given, new rules would now govern independent study courses, and a review of teaching assignments would be conducted annually – apparently a practice that had not taken place beforehand. Chancellor Holden Thorp was quoted as saying, "I know that you're all as deeply troubled as I am, as disturbed as I am and as angry as I am that these things could have happened. They are completely at odds with what we stand for as an institution."

Trustee Peter Grauer asked how courses with little or no supervision from professors could have gone unnoticed for years. Karen Gil, Dean of the College of Arts and Sciences answered him, saying, "That's a good question, and I understand the concern. There are checks and balances all over the system, but in this case they did not detect the problems. There were no student complaints about these courses." The obvious follow-up questions were not asked by the trustees, nor were they offered by the university officials: Why were there no complaints? What would have been the possible reasons that students –

many of them student athletes on the basketball and football teams – would continue to take classes that were in essence fake, and never say anything? More than just "taking" the classes, though, they were actually signed up for those classes by their sports programs' academic advisors. But again, those deeper issues were never sought out by the adult leadership of the university.

* * *

William Andrews, a senior associate dean who was one of the investigators, indicated that the AFAM review took nine months and was difficult to piece together. He said that lax oversight in the department was part of the problem in reconstructing what happened. When asked by one trustee why the review covered only four years, Andrews said it was clear that many of the problems ended with the 2009 retirement of the department's longtime administrator, Deborah Crowder. Furthermore, four years of data revealed issues linked only to Nyang'oro and Crowder, he said, and there was no evidence to indicate others would have been involved even if the probe had covered a longer period. This statement – and reasoning – appeared to be grossly flawed, however. While Nyang'oro was the teacher of record of the majority of classes, he was not the only one. He had been the department head since 1992, yet the school chose to only look back to 2007? And Crowder had worked for the school since 1979, yet the school chose to only look back to 2007? Essentially the statements by Andrews were assumptions, and not based on the available data at his disposal. As would be proven less than two months later, in fact, Andrews was indeed incorrect in his statements regarding the beginning point of the fraudulent classes.

Bobbi Owen, a senior associate dean for undergraduate education, said it was hard to know why students ended up in any particular course. "Word of mouth is potent," she said. "Students drift to places where they understand they will be accommodated." What she did not mention, however, was that scholarship athletes of major programs (such as basketball and football) have team academic advisors who were largely responsible for enrolling his/her team's athletes in classes. The basketball team had such as person. A much closer look at that individual will be given later. The football team also had such a person. According to a New York *Times* article that was published in April of 2012, former UNC player Deunta Williams said that athletes could only take the classes the athletics department wanted them to take. It was always better that the classes not be too difficult, he said – otherwise, there might be eligibility problems. He went on to indicate that freshmen football players took Swahili as their language requirement, because the athletics department tutors were strong in that language. Swahili was one of the main courses taught by Julius Nyang'oro.

The May 25, 2012, *News and Observer* article that covered the Board of Trustees meeting ended with a quote from Holden Thorp: "I'm chancellor at this university, but I've been a student and a faculty member, and I'm still a faculty member," he said. "These findings are a kick in the gut to those of us who take great pride in what we do here." He said he hoped the investigation would send a strong message that the university took its academic reputation seriously. Unfortunately for the school, the stronger message that was eventually sent dealt with the information that the report purposely ignored.

* * *

On June 7, 2012, Chancellor Thorp offered a letter to the university's Board of Trustees giving an update on the ongoing scandal. In it, Thorp said that the school had sent a letter informing Professor Julius Nyang'oro that it would be taking back $12,000 that Nyang'oro had accepted as payment for a summer school 2011 course. The letter went on to explain that Nyang'oro's teaching of the course did not meet the university's instructional expectations, and they did not believe that he should have been paid. What was not mentioned in Thorp's update to the Board of Trustees was whether restitution would be sought for the over 50 other courses that apparently did not meet the university's instructional expectations, either. A key point that showed up near the very beginning of Thorp's letter was the reasoning/rationale that had already begun to spread amongst UNC leaders and administrators. The chancellor made sure to include that "most of the irregularly taught and aberrant classes detailed in the review of courses in the department included both student athletes and students who weren't athletes." As touched on various times before, this would be key in the university's eventual insistence that the academic fraud should not be an NCAA issue.

Thorp said in the letter to the trustees that the school was trying to determine how the summer school 2011 class was created, and how students were registered for it. This uncertainty seemed odd in the current era, where virtually every on-campus scheduling transaction happened via computer. Furthermore, as pointed out earlier, most major-sport athletes got preferential (and early) treatment in terms of signing up for courses in order to accommodate their practice and game schedules, which was often performed via the team's academic adviser. Thorp even went so far as to confirm that staff in the Academic Support Program for Student Athletes helped the students (who were all athletes) register. As would become a pattern over the months (and years) to follow, the university either neglected to check the emails of its various staff members for clues as to possible motives – or else the university checked but never revealed those findings.

Thorp also stated his official reason/stance on why the covered period of the AFAM report was only from the summer of 2007 through summer 2011, instead of spanning further into the past. The letter said, "The review focused on the last five consecutive summers and four academic years because we wanted to obtain the most accurate recollections and records available. We also wanted to cover the summers of 2007 and 2009, when the first irregularities known to us had occurred. The further back we go, the less reliable and available the data become since faculty are required to keep course records for only one year. People's memories also become less clear and less reliable going back in time." Many in the social media world were expecting there to be a punch line after this line of "reasoning," but it truly was the actual explanation given to the university's Board of Trustees – despite the fact that computer records at major universities are kept intact for decades, and that any individual student can return to campus and request his or her past transcript, which would show the classes taken and the grades received – no matter the year of graduation. Yet according to Thorp, going back any further than 2007 would have yielded data that was "less reliable and available."

As noted above, Chancellor Thorp indicated that older records of grades given in a particular class would be difficult to locate. Even if that were the case, a transcript for each individual student (who took that particular class) would be available for perusal. According to the UNC's "Office of the University

Registrar" webpage, "Transcripts can be ordered online by current students and alumni of the university. Online transcript ordering is convenient, can be done from any location 24/7, and provides emails to inform students/alumni on the status of their request." Nowhere on the site does it give a limitation of how far back (in terms of a student's graduation year) it can provide a transcript. The frequently-asked-questions page of the site notes that a request can take up to two weeks to fulfill due to the large volume of transcript requests it receives, which in reality is a very reasonable turnaround time. But Chancellor Thorp and other administrative leaders would have the school's Board of Trustees, as well as members of the media, believe that it was virtually impossible to get accurate data on AFAM classes prior to 2007 – despite all of that pertinent information being available in the registrar's office if anyone had taken the time and effort to do the research. The initial university-sanctioned report on AFAM's courses would prove to not be the last time that the school avoided obvious methods of data-collection. Specific methods would have most certainly led to clarity into the academic and athletic fraud that had taken place over several decades, yet they would continue to be overlooked in the future. As a result, a pattern of seemingly deliberate laxity in uncovering the truth would be repeated time and again.

* * *

The Raleigh *News and Observer* continued its strong coverage of the scandal, releasing an article on June 8, 2012 – a day after Thorp's letter to the Board of Trustees. The article focused on the summer 2011 class that was filled entirely with athletes (which was also created just days before the summer session began), and also noted that the academic advisers had known that there would be no instruction. The academic support staff reported to the university's College of Arts and Sciences, the article said, but was actually housed in the athletics department's student support center within Kenan Stadium.

Thorp could not be reached by the newspaper for comment, but new Athletics Director Bubba Cunningham said he was concerned. "I just think this has uncovered some information that quite frankly, the university, we're not proud of." He would then repeat a line similar to one that was earlier spoken by Board of Trustees chairman Wade Hargrove, and which was the same sentiment that would be repeated later by others in positions of leadership within the school: "But we'll continue to work to ensure that it doesn't happen going forward." Future prevention was clearly in the university's plans. Past detection and accountability were apparently not. Members of the Board of Trustees either declined comment for the article or could not be reached.

Email correspondence that had been recently released showed that Professor Nyang'oro went to another professor in the AFAM department, Tim McMillan, on June 14, 2011, to add the summer course in question (AFAM 280) to the summer calendar. McMillan was reportedly the one who normally taught the class. "Sure," McMillan replied via email. "How many students will I have?" To which Nyang'oro responded, "No more than 5. I will be the instructor of record and relieve you of responsibility and bother. A big relief for you?????" Nyang'oro then talked to a journalism professor, Jan Yopp, who also was serving as the dean for summer school that year. On June 16, 2011, the day the summer semester began, Yopp sent word to Nyang'oro that the class was open for registration. Four days later, Nyang'oro revealed in an email to Yopp that 18 students had enrolled in the class, though there was no mention that all of them were athletes. "I am totally taken by surprise!" Nyang'oro expressed in his correspondence.

Nancy Davis, a spokeswoman for the university, and Jonathan Hartlyn, a senior associate dean who oversaw the African Studies department and was one of the staff members who conducted the internal review, were contacted for the *News and Observer*'s article. Echoing almost word for word what Chancellor Holden Thorp said in the previous day's letter to the UNC Board of Trustees, both Davis and Hartlyn continued to stress than non-athletes also took the suspect classes and received the same treatment grade-wise.

As pointed out earlier, the university had hired a public relations firm the previous year (which was still employed by the school at the time – and troubling data would eventually emerge regarding just how much money the university had spent for PR assistance). Ben Silverman is a businessman totally unrelated to the UNC scandal. His past professional experience, however, helps to put UNC's use of a public relations firm into perspective. For over six years Silverman was an author for PR Fuel, an award-winning consultancy that was launched in 2001 and has won numerous awards. According to Silverman's LinkedIn page, his work for PR Fuel was "Author of weekly, best practices newsletter for the public relations industry."

In one of Silverman's past articles, "Note to PR Pros: Keep Your Key Messages Consistent," he wrote the following: "Consistency in public relations is important. Public relations consultants and corporate executives are often told to 'stay on message' and not to stray from a script. Companies and organizations put an enormous amount of time and energy into hammering home a consistent key message, be it through public statements, advertising, or simple branding. Consistency gives comfort to people, and public relations professionals are charged with providing a comforting view of a company or client. When a public relations strategy is inconsistent, trouble usually follows." That sense of consistency was exactly what began to emerge through the comments of various UNC officials. They stressed that they would be looking towards the future to make sure that the issues never happened again (with a veiled inference being that they did not want to look back). They also stressed that both athletes and non-athletes were enrolled in the classes (with the inference being that as a result, the NCAA should not view it as an athletic scandal). These patterns fit standard PR operating procedures; multiple people were repeating the same message, in an effort to provide "a comforting view of a company or client."

Several final and important pieces of information were included in the *N&O*'s June 8, 2012, article. It was now being reported that 58 percent of the enrollees in the fraudulent classes were athletes, as opposed to the originally-reported 39 percent. More insight into the information-gathering process for the report was also given. Once again the point was stated that it was unclear how the students – athletes and non-athletes – ended up in the classes. Jonathan Hartlyn interviewed students for the probe, according to the article, along with Jack Evans, a professor who had been a liaison to the athletics department, as well as university counsel Leslie Strohm. Hartlyn, however, declined to say what those interviewed students said. As before, information that could have given insight into motive was either ignored or was purposely withheld.

* * *

Details would continue to emerge and questions would continue to be asked by those not associated with UNC. The university itself, though, would carry on with its obstinate nature and would deflect direct questions that otherwise might clarify aspects of the ongoing scandal. On July 8, 2012, the Raleigh *News and Observer* reported that athletes did in fact account for the majority of the enrollees in the fraudulent courses in the Department of African and Afro-American Studies. Furthermore, data had emerged that suggested the irregularities within the department and university might go back as far as 1999.

The first parts of the article penned by tenacious investigative reporter Dan Kane indicated that past students who possibly wanted to enroll in summer courses taught by Julius Nyang'oro would have been met with obstacles. This was due to the fact that of the 38 courses the university said he was responsible for over the five summers covered in the AFAM report, 26 of them listed a maximum capacity of just one student. Despite that restrictive parameter, however, university records show more than one student was enrolled in most of those courses. Furthermore, a substantial number of those students were often athletes. Registration records showed that many of the courses had no classroom or class time.

To augment the confusion of the situation – as well as to hint at the possibility of a third, influential party being in the equation – was the fact that Julius Nyang'oro was not officially paid by the university for 29 of those suspect summer classes. Professors were typically paid per class because the summer work was considered beyond their normal nine-month work year. According to summer school Dean Jan Yopp, faculty were generally only allowed to be paid for two courses each summer, which might explain why Nyang'oro did not receive payment for some of the 29 courses. It does not, however, explain why Nyang'oro would so readily agree to take on the workload to teach (or at least grade papers in) more than two dozen courses for no apparent and traceable compensation. Overall, 75 courses were linked to Nyang'oro over a four-year period, according to the *News and Observer*. University officials said that was an extraordinary number for a professor, let alone a department chairman, to have responsibility for. No one apparently noticed the exorbitant number until the AFAM fraud investigation began.

While very few members of UNC's faculty had spoken out publicly up to that time about the academic fraud, Professor Jay Smith had made his opposing opinions known. He and Willis Brooks, a fellow UNC history professor like Smith, told the *News and Observer* they were concerned about the case's impact on the university's academic integrity. They said the enrollment and pay data suggested Nyang'oro had set up a system for athletes to get into classes they could pass. "The only logic I can conjure is (Nyang'oro) was protecting seats," said Brooks, a professor emeritus who served on the faculty athletic committee in the early 1990's. "And since the preponderance of people who took the seats are athletes, there is circumstantial evidence," he said.

The Raleigh newspaper reviewed a number of archived internet pages that showed that as far back as 1999, some of the same AFAM class offerings were listed with a maximum of one student. When questioned about the more than decade-old pattern, the university said it would be difficult at the current date to determine how many of the students in those classes were athletes. However, as detailed in an earlier section of this chapter, the information was readily available to the school via a review of past athletes' transcripts. It would, however, require that the school display not only the effort to determine whether athletes had taken part in those much older courses, but also the desire.

* * *

At the end of the *News and Observer*'s June 8th article a month earlier, the percentage of athletes in the fraudulent cours-es had risen from the school's initial reporting of 39 percent up to 58 percent. In a newer July 8, 2012, article, the percentage had risen yet again. The university said that athletes and former athletes made up 64 percent of the enrollments. While it may have been frustrating to the media that the initial numbers had been incorrect and continued to change, what was more trou-bling was the fact that, according to the *News and Observer*, UNC officials had released little information beyond the enroll-ment figures to back up their claims that athletes didn't receive special treatment.

The university had not released any of the information about its interviews with students regarding how they got into the classes. Furthermore, it revealed very little from its interview with Nyang'oro, an individual who seemingly would have been able to give some very insightful details into the courses and the reasons for their fraudulent nature – especially considering that he had chaired the department for twenty years. At a recent UNC Board of Governors meeting, the *News and Observer* at-tempted to ask Chancellor Holden Thorp about what Nyang'oro said in his interview. University spokeswoman Nancy Davis quickly interjected, preventing Thorp from answering. "You need to talk to (Nyang'oro) about that," she said. "That's not for us to answer." It was well known at the time that Nyang'oro had given no comment to virtually every question and interview request by the media – something that Nancy Davis, given her important position as university spokeswoman, was likely very aware of.

That blocking of information was a far cry from Holden Thorp's claims from the summer of 2010. When the football program was first being scrutinized for impermissible benefits and academic irregularities, Thorp and many other influential figures surrounding the university boldly proclaimed that they would do whatever it took to get to the bottom of the issues. Former Athletics Director Dick Baddour felt that the school had handled the football investigation in "The Carolina Way," and had used certain guiding principles during the process – one of which dealt with integrity. Now, however, lawyers were being hired, PR firms had their fingerprints on quotes and statements, and information was being withheld from the media.

Another person whom UNC officials could have interviewed had they truly desired to discover the nature and intent of the fraudulent athletic courses was Deborah Crowder, the AFAM department's former manager. The school had claimed that she and Nyang'oro were the only two in the department suspected of improper behavior, and that Crowder had responsibility for scheduling classes. Once again, the extensive degree of Crowder's longstanding (and easily uncovered) ties to the school's basketball program should have been all the school needed to ask pointed questions on the matter. Whether they ever spoke to Crowder, however, is unknown.

The PackPride.com message boards once again helped with portions of a news story, as the July 8, 2012, article in the *News and Observer* noted that a fan on that website posted other information regarding some archived registration records. The data showed that 44 of the suspect AFAM classes listed the maximum seating at one student. Other university records show that 31 of those one-seat-maximum classes had athletes as the majority of the enrollees. University spokeswoman Nancy Davis and others said there were several possible legitimate reasons why a class might be listed as having only one seat available. One example given was that a teacher might be trying to protect seats for students who needed the classes to complete their majors. This was, unfortunately, yet more speculation and hypothetical excuses on a matter that could have been definitively verified through a simple review of past records and data. Those suspect class rosters could have been pulled, and the students' majors reviewed. If there were situations that did not fit the legitimate reasons Davis offered, then there would obviously be another explanation. Were the students who did not fit those legitimate parameters athletes? Did they benefit by taking the courses by way of receiving a high grade that boosted their grade point average? Simple questions and simple methods of getting the answers, yet the university chose to ignore that logical and morally-correct path.

* * *

Following the report and data regarding the AFAM program and the 54 fraudulent courses from 2007 to 2011, UNC had a special faculty committee look into the academic fraud scandal at the university. The 13-page report was released in late July, and its authors were Steven Bachenheimer, a professor of microbiology and immunology; Michael Gerhardt, a law professor; and Laurie F. Maffly-Kipp, a professor of religious studies. The Raleigh *News and Observer* ran an article on July 26, 2012, to cover the findings of the report.

According to Dan Kane's article, the committee found "an athletics program divorced from the faculty, academic counselors for athletes improperly helping them enroll in classes and poor oversight of faculty administrators who have wide latitude in running their departments." Bachenheimer, Gerhardt, and Maffly-Kipp called for an independent commission of outside experts in higher education to review athletics and academics at the school. The report was almost entirely focused on what it called an atmosphere of distrust on a "campus with two cultures," one academic and one athletic.

The report said an unidentified "departmental staff manager" within African Studies may have directed athletes to enroll in the no-show classes, and that "it seems likely" someone in the department was calling counselors for athletes to tell them "certain courses" were available. Deborah Crowder was clearly the referenced staff manager, as that was the position she had long held up until her retirement in 2009. No mention in the report, however, was made regarding her extremely close ties with the basketball program. Neither her email nor phone records were checked in order to verify the suspicions, either. The report went on to say, "We were told that athletes claimed they had been sent to Julius Nyang'oro by the (Academic Support Program for Student Athletes)."

The report in many ways described an athletics program that had too much control, noting that the admissions office under its then-current director had never rejected a student athlete with a subpar academic record that had received a recommendation from a special advisory committee. The report's authors went on reveal a troubling side note: the academic support program for athletes was supposed to be run by the College of Arts and Sciences, but its funding came from the athletics department. And its director, Robert Mercer, also reported to John Blanchard, a senior athletics director. "This reporting system is ambiguous, lacks clarity, and is likely not very productive," the report said.

The report went on to suggest that the university should examine athletes' course selections over a period of roughly 10 years to see if they were clustering in certain classes and departments with the intent of protecting their eligibility in sports. According to Chancellor Holden Thorp's earlier words, however, that would be a very formidable task – and was the main reason why the initial AFAM investigation did not go back any further than 2007. Yet there were three respected university professors, who presumably were well versed in the data-collection methods currently at the university's disposal regarding past records and results, who were suggesting a larger view of the past be taken.

In a section of the report with the heading "Need for Institutional Transparency Regarding Athletics," the following bold statement was made: "Generally, (the faculty) call for an external review of athletic advising, independent of the athletics department, as well as more forthright statements from the administration about the compromises made to host Division I athletics at UNC." Ironically, it would later be shown that prior to its release the three-member report had been altered and partially censored by people within leadership positions at UNC in yet another attempt to shield the school's top athletic programs from future penalties. Those details would not emerge for another year; another, different startling discovery would be made less than two weeks later, however.

* * *

The essential (and unanswered) questions:

-- Why weren't papers from athletes in other AFAM classes ever checked for the same types of plagiarism that showed up in Michael McAdoo's assignment?

-- How had the university managed for years to overlook dozens of unsupervised courses?

-- Who was ultimately responsible for the decision to only go as far back as 2007 in the initial AFAM report?

-- Why did the school seek restitution for only one of Nyang'oro's improperly-taught classes?

-- Why didn't the university simply look at past students' transcripts if they wanted information on older AFAM courses and grades?

-- Why were the information and data gathered from the student interviews (conducted during the AFAM report) never released?

-- Why did Professor Nyang'oro agree to teach (or at least have his name connected to) so many classes filled primarily with athletes, yet apparently do so without compensation?

-- Why did the university refuse to state what its interviews with Nyang'oro had revealed regarding the originations and motives behind the fraudulent, athlete-filled classes?

-- Why did Chancellor Thorp and others in positions of leadership offer full transparency and cooperation in 2010 during the football portion of the scandal, but then in 2012 block the release of so much pertinent information?

-- Why was Deborah Crowder never contacted and interviewed

by the school? Or if she was, why was the resulting information withheld from the public?

-- Why had the school purposely avoided mentioning Deborah Crowder's personal ties to the basketball program?

-- Did the athletes who eventually enrolled in the "one-seat-maximum" courses benefit, in terms of athletic eligibility, from the fraudulent classes and final grades they received?

-- Why did the athletics department fund an academic support program that was supposed to be run by the College of Arts and Sciences?

CHAPTER NINE

THE JULIUS PEPPERS TRANSCRIPT

T‌**he previous chapter** in part covered the limited scope of the university's look into the AFAM infractions of the past, as it chose to only go back as far as the year 2007. The school's poor reasoning was that past records might be unreliable. It was clearly detailed, though, how information could be accumulated from former players' transcripts in order to piece together evidence of earlier potential fraudulent classes – if the school had so chosen. Ironically, the topic of transcripts would be at the center of the next major turning point of the school's worsening academic scandal.

On August 10, 2012, the Raleigh *News and Observer* printed an article titled "UNC reluctant to dig deeper on scandal." It laid out in clear words the stalling and lack of cooperation UNC had shown ever since data had surfaced suggesting its storied men's basketball program might have been complicit in the academic fraud. Writer Dan Kane noted that in the previous month Chancellor Holden Thorp had promised full cooperation with a special UNC Board of Governors' panel that would be reviewing the academic fraud, as well as cooperation with others who were trying to learn what went wrong at the university. "We welcome the involvement of the Board of Governors' panel, our trustees, our faculty, and others who care about the university," Thorp said. However, the reporter noted that Thorp and the school had shown little interest in digging into two separate and very specific matters that had been brought to their attention by the *News and Observer*. Those details, Kane said, could have potentially proven that the scandal involving no-show classes went back several years beyond what the university had confirmed.

In late July of 2012, approximately two weeks before Kane's August 12 article, the newspaper had given the university the name of a former UNC student who had been in a fall 2005 AFAM class taught by Julius Nyang'oro. According to the student, the class had never met – and the newspaper offered emails from that person backing up his claim. Nancy Davis, the university spokeswoman who had handled much of the media-relations dialogue during the summer of 2012, repeatedly said that officials would not investigate unless the former student came to them directly. Just prior to the newspaper's article being published, however, she slightly revised the university's position in an email that said: "The former student's experience was consistent with the patterns we identified in our review." She declined, however, to provide further explanation. And the school's review, of course, had only gone back as far as the summer sessions of 2007; the course the student spoke of had occurred a full two years earlier.

A second matter the newspaper shared with the university was also met with indifference, and that dealt with a "test transcript" that an *N&O* reporter found on UNC's website. In June of 2012 the reporter showed the university officials the "test transcript," as it was characterized on the school's website, which was purportedly developed to help students and advisers use a computer program that told them what courses a student still needed to graduate. The test transcript, which dated back to 2001, had several distinguishing characteristics that were consistent with the issues raised in the recent AFAM academic scandal. UNC officials said it was a fictitious transcript, but they declined to look at records to verify and be certain that it was not lifted from a real student's records, either in whole or in part.

As had already been suspected by many in the social media realm, the *News and Observer*'s article verbalized an observation that was becoming clearer by the day: "The lack of investigation into these and other matters raises questions about whether the university is seeking information beyond what it has already reported." Jay Smith, a history professor at the school, agreed that the university should have been digging into both of the new matters because they could have shed light on how long the academic fraud took place, as well as who was intended to benefit from it. "My sense of it, and it's only a sense," Smith said, "is that they really want to keep this episode to the Butch Davis era, and conveniently also confined to the football team." As documented earlier, head football coach Butch Davis was fired after a prolonged NCAA investigation largely revealed impermissible agent benefits, but also minimal instances of academic improprieties. That particular NCAA investigation did not, however, uncover the mass academic fraud within the AFAM department.

* * *

One vital distinction about the fall 2005 class was that it showed that questionable courses were being offered well over a year before Butch Davis would ever arrive on UNC's campus. The student (who wished for his name to be withheld) provided emails to the *News and Observer* that showed he enrolled in the class primarily because it was originally listed in the registration records with a Friday afternoon time, which fit his schedule. The student later discovered, however, that no class time or classroom was given. He emailed the teacher of record, Julius Nyang'oro, who replied via email, "You need to come see me." The former student said that when he met with Nyang'oro he was told there would be no class, and Nyang'oro instead assigned him a research paper. The student said he worked hard on a 20-page paper and received an A-minus. The *News and Observer* noted that as of the article's press time, UNC officials had still not contacted the student regarding the class.

As briefly covered earlier, the second item the newspaper brought to light dealt with the "test transcript," and especially the various peculiar traits it displayed. The 2001 transcript was for a fictitious student, according to the university, and listed grades and a Scholastic Aptitude Test (SAT) score. The SAT score was 870, well below the 1230 average SAT score for UNC students during the late-1990s/early-2000's timeframe. The student was also entering his/her senior year of college with a grade point average just over 2.0. Seemingly even more coincidental was the fact that the student was listed as an African and Afro-American Studies major, the department which was currently at the center of the school's academic scandal. The student had completed 12 classes in that department, according to the transcript, with a 2.6 GPA for those courses. The document also showed that the student was exempt from taking a physical fitness class, a practice that was typically granted to scholarship athletes.

There were a number of courses on the 2001 test transcript that matched up with those shown to be "no-show" classes in the university's recent 2012 review of AFAM. The student received grades of B or better in all of them. For example, the transcript showed an A for a course known as AFAM seminar, and according to the *News and Observer* that class had turned up four times as a no-show class in UNC's review. The fictional student also took three independent study courses, receiving B's or better in all of them, and notations indicated he/she was registered for a fourth. One of the school's internal reviews in 2012 had cast doubt on the department's handling of its independent studies, and since the emergence of the scandal a stricter limit had been placed on who could take them. One final distinguishing factor of the test transcript was that the student only took a full "five course" load in one fall semester. The remaining spring and fall semesters only had four classes each, with classes being taken in summer in order for him or her to stay on track. That is also a scheduling pattern often employed by athletes participating in major collegiate sports.

* * *

UNC Professor Jay Smith told the *News and Observer* that even if the transcript was proven to be a mock-up, it was surprising that someone would draw up one that casted the African Studies department in such a poor light. He also mentioned the uncanny resemblance to the current academic scandal. "It's either a real transcript, or it is a startling Freudian slip that reveals the reality of the system," Smith said. The most recent university data had shown that athletes made up nearly two-thirds of the enrollments in the 54 no-show classes identified by the school. In two of those classes, the sole enrollee was a men's basketball player.

Despite all of the forewarning given to UNC, and despite Chancellor Holden Thorp's quote about welcoming the involvement of others, the newspaper's tips on those two matters (the fall 2005 class and the test transcript) went largely ignored by the university. Neither the current 2012 UNC registrar Chris Derickson nor the registrar at the time of the transcript's making, David Lanier, thought it reflected the transcript of an actual student. Lanier even questioned why a transcript representing an athlete would be drawn up, since they had special academic counselors assigned to them. Derickson, who became registrar in 2010, said there were many test transcripts pulled together over the years as the university developed the computer program that tracked progress toward a college degree.

At least one official appeared to show interest in the newly-discovered fraudulent class and the test transcript. Peter Hans had recently been elected chairman of the UNC Board of Governors. "I would like to share this with the members of the review panel and ask them to look at it," he said. "Maybe there's a good explanation, but we need to ask those questions." As it turned out, the answers would be revealed in the very near future, but not from any proactive fact-seeking steps taken by UNC.

* * *

The *News and Observer* article that introduced the test transcript topic to the public was published on Friday, August 10, 2012. It would only take approximately 48 hours for many of the unanswered pieces to begin falling into place. In the late afternoon hours of Sunday, August 12, a noted messageboard user on the PackPride.com site indicated that he believed he had connected the "test transcript" on UNC's website to a real, former student, and that he would be posting definitive news on the site as soon as a final few details could be verified. From looking at various archived discussion-board threads from that evening of August 12th, the PackPride site began to immediately buzz with anticipation. Often internet messageboards and chat rooms are filled with wild and inaccurate claims, and much of it can be easily dismissed. This particular poster, however, was well known by the users of the site. According to older threads, he had been largely responsible for the meticulous dissection of John Blake's phone records that had resulted in the uncovering of several questionable trends and connections, and had also posted data and information regarding the AFAM department and its independent study courses, which lead to further questions about the longevity of the academic scandal. In short, he appeared to be a trusted source, and thus the fans on the site reacted with great anticipation to the upcoming news.

Within an hour of that initial premonition, a new thread was started on the PackPride.com site with the title stating the owner of the "test transcript" had indeed been identified. The narrative of the post gave elaborate pieces of data and information, citing years, test scores, dates, and also a bevy of quotes from past news articles – some of which were almost a decade old. The data all culminated in the announcement of the test transcript being the actual, real transcript of Julius Peppers, a former star athlete for UNC who had played for both the football team and the men's basketball team.

The depth of the researched connections in that messageboard post was extremely convincing. The final blow of confirmation would seemingly come approximately an hour later on that Sunday evening. According to the archived thread, users on the site began to revisit the UNC webpage where the transcript was housed. One noticed that the root directory for the transcript could be accessed by simply removing some of the extensions from his internet browser's address bar. Once that was done one was taken to the root directory where a number of files were listed. After clicking on several of those files a discovery was made: the authentic transcript of Peppers, with his full name printed at the top, was there for anyone to see. The school had apparently housed his transcript in one of the server's public directories, made a copy of it on another page, and replaced his name with "test transcript." They had not, however, taken the time to remove his real transcript from the server. As a result, it had essentially been accessible to the public for over 10 years. News about the PackPride.com connections and discovery began to spread throughout the social media world, and by the next morning it was one of the top sports topics being covered on a multitude of reputable media sites.

* * *

Reporter Dan Kane of the *News and Observer* submitted a blog post to the newspaper's website in the early morning hours of Monday, August 13, 2012, with a full article to later follow. He restated many of the findings from the previous evening's PackPride.com thread, along with reiterating important information from some of his earlier articles. The reporter began by saying a 2001 academic transcript published by the newspaper on Friday that UNC officials had insisted was fake could actually be the real thing, and it could also belong to one of the most popular athletes in the university's history – Julius Peppers.

Specific dates were given with regards to Peppers' collegiate career, in that he was a star football player from 1999 to 2001, and was a member of the basketball team for two seasons – including one that included an appearance in a Final Four.

If proven authentic, Kane said, the university could be in far deeper trouble with regard to an ongoing academic scandal that was still coming into view. At issue, he reminded his readers, was whether individuals in the university set up a series of bogus, no-show classes that were predominantly taken by athletes with the possible intent of helping them maintain their eligibility to play sports. The Peppers' revelation would also suggest that fraudulent classes for athletes may have been going on much longer than university officials had been willing to look into and confirm.

According to Kane, a review of the website-linked transcript featuring Peppers' name at the top alongside the "test transcript" on the site showed a perfect match for 34 of 36 listed classes. The two that were not exact showed the same class and semester, but differed on the grade. The Peppers transcript showed an incomplete for one of the classes, "Black Nationalism," while the test transcript showed the student received a B-plus. For the second and final anomaly, the Peppers transcript showed he was registered to take an "African American Seminar" class, while the test transcript showed an A grade. As a reminder of the school's earlier investigation into the AFAM department, a number of unauthorized grade changes had been made to students' marks from the year 2007 to 2011. This could have easily been the case with the two minor grade anomalies on Peppers' transcript, as well.

Kane would continue to seemingly point out the obvious,

but his persistence in explanation was certainly understandable given the obtuse lack of cooperation and concern that his newspaper and other media outlets had recently received from UNC officials. If the information about the transcript proved true, he wrote, the discovery could cause huge problems for the school. For one, the newspaper had reported the test transcript because it shared several characteristics with the ongoing major academic fraud scandal at the school – a scandal that UNC officials had been reluctant to determine just how far back it went.

As a first specific example that the scandal may have had much earlier roots, Kane showed that the "African-American Seminar" class that was shown on the website transcript was known as AFAM 070 in 2001, but as AFAM 396 during the present day. It had appeared four times as a no-show class in the internal review that had found 54 such classes from 2007 to 2011, leading to serious questions as to whether it was a no-show class in 2001 as well. As further evidence, the transcript showed grades of B or better on two other classes that had surfaced as suspect classes, and three independent studies in which grades of B or better were given. The independent studies were also suspect because university officials could not verify that anyone taught or supervised the students who took them. The upshot of the multitude of questionable classes and the high grades those classes provided Peppers was that without them he likely would not have been eligible to play – either football or basketball.

The Sunday night messageboard post on PackPride.com had also highlighted another confirming detail which Kane made reference to in his later blog entry: a 2003 ESPN feature story on Peppers in which his agent, Carl Carey, was described as having saved Peppers from receiving a failing grade during

Peppers' first semester. According to the article, Carey convinced a professor to give Peppers a re-test on the final exam in an "Elements of Drama" class in order to receive an overall passing grade. The transcripts (both "test" and real) showed a D for that class. The very first lines from that 2003 ESPN article by Tom Friend, in fact, were: "Behind every great college athlete is… a tutor. And behind every great two-sport college athlete is… a miracle worker." It discussed various aspects of Peppers' time while a student athlete at UNC, including him being thrown out of UNC's summer orientation program for repeatedly missing curfew and for ordering a pair of Air Jordan shoes with his university stipend money, which was impermissible. It also mentioned the fact that in the same summer Carl Carey had accepted a job as a UNC academic advisor, he had essentially been assigned to Peppers in order to "straighten him out." Next was the episode of the discussion with the drama teacher. Then an anecdote of how Peppers didn't want to do his school work, and would sometimes be 12 hours late for study sessions with Carey. Yet, as the article pointed out, "he'd always stay eligible."

If the tutor's name (Carl Carey) sounds familiar, that is because not only was he currently (in 2012) Peppers' agent, but he was also previously mentioned in Chapter Five of this book. He was the sports agent who was hired by AFAM Chairman Julius Nyang'oro to teach a 2011 summer class on UNC's campus – during the ongoing NCAA investigation – and who also had taught in the AFAM department a decade earlier. Following his initial stint serving as an academic advisor with UNC and also teaching in the AFAM department, he would then leave to become a sports agent. He would sign Julius Peppers – the athlete whom he helped to get through college – as his premier client in 2002.

On the Monday morning following the Sunday-night Pack-Pride.com messageboard post, university officials could not be reached by the *News and Observer* for comment. Kane reminded readers once again that over the previous several weeks UNC officials had repeatedly said that the test transcript was just that, a mock-up put together to test a university computer program that helped students learn what other courses were needed to obtain a degree. However, those officials refused to check academic records to back up their claims, and as a result were left to deal with the embarrassing – and potentially damning – fallout.

* * *

On August 13, 2012, the *USA Today* website posted an article consisting of multiple pieces of information gathered from wire reports. According to the article, UNC had released a statement late on Monday saying it had removed the transcript link and that it couldn't discuss confidential student information covered by federal privacy laws. The school did not confirm the authenticity of the partial grade summary, despite having the full name "Julius Frazier Peppers" at the top. A released quote said, "Student academic records should never be accessible to the public, and the university is investigating reports of what appears to be a former student transcript on the university's website."

Other information from the *USA Today* article recounted some of the previous details from both PackPride.com and the *News and Observer*'s Dan Kane, while adding other bits of data, as well. It was pointed out that nine of the ten classes in which Peppers earned a B-plus, B, or B-minus – grades that helped to ensure his eligibility – came in the AFAM department where he was majoring. Once again it was made clear that Peppers had also played for UNC's basketball team, under former coaches Bill Guthridge – a long-time assistant to Hall of Fame coach Dean Smith, and then Matt Doherty – a former player of Smith's. In June, over a month prior to the discovery of the Peppers transcript, NCAA spokeswoman Stacey Osburn had referred questions to the school when asked whether investigators would return to Chapel Hill in the aftermath of the initial AFAM university review. Osburn did not immediately return an email for comment following the newest developments that spanned much further into the past, the article said.

* * *

In the days following the discovery of the apparent Peppers transcript, some interesting side stories would emerge. One dealt with *News and Observer* reporter Dan Kane, and the matter was discussed in a blog article posted on August 14, 2012, by one of the newspaper's editors, Steve Riley. In it he mentioned that Kane had attracted a lot of attention due to his numerous investigative articles on UNC's academic fraud scandal, with one resulting effect being a website that had shown up earlier in the year called dirtydankane.com. A sports site called The Big Lead had recently raised the question of whether Julius Peppers' agent had set up the site in order to vent his anger about Kane. "In a word, yes," *N&O* editor Steve Riley wrote. "But the site set up by Carl Carey Jr. goes back a few months, and it isn't related to Dan's work Monday and Tuesday about the UNC transcript bearing Peppers' name." As it would turn out, Carey was apparently upset when Kane had reported in August of 2011 that Carey had been hired by UNC to teach a summer course while the school was under investigation for, among other things, athletes receiving improper benefits from agents. "Sure, I picked a horrible time to go back and teach at UNC," Carey had written the *News and Observer* in an earlier email. "I was totally unaware of the depth of the issues going on there." After the August 2011 article, Carey felt that he had been somehow linked to the agent issues at UNC and resented it, at one point threatening to sue the *News and Observer*. That August 2011 article showed up when a person Googled him, Carey said, and he wanted something negative to show up when someone Googled Kane. Riley closed his article by saying, "I'm Dan's editor, and I can tell you that I've never seen a more dogged and determined reporter. But I've also not seen one any more dedicated to being fair and placing things in their proper context. He will keep reporting this story, regardless of the web site assembled in his honor."

The website sportsagentblog.com gave some further details on the matter in an article it posted on August 16, 2012. It stated that Jason McIntyre of "The Big Lead" surmised that Carey was the owner of the dirtydankane website based on a whois.com search which reveals who registered virtually any particular website. It is possible to make a website's registration anonymous, but that precaution was not taken, however. The whois.com search revealed that a Cary Carey of Houston, Texas, registered the dirtydankane website in question. This was information that the *News and Observer*'s Steve Riley had alluded to in his article. However, when sources from sportsagentblog.com reached out to Carey, he gave the response that "I am not the owner of a website designed to smear anyone." Apparently he was unaware of public internet documentation of website registrations, such as the whois.com site.

* * *

The Raleigh *News and Observer* entered the fray once again on August 17, 2012, exactly one week after its article about the "test transcript" that UNC officials had claimed was fictional, and which the school had refused to look into further. More research had been conducted by the newspaper, and as the article's title referenced, "Transcript shows low hurdles for UNC athletes to stay eligible." Details included the breakdowns of Peppers' grade point average for each semester, and possible scenarios for how he had managed to continue playing sports.

The article began by noting how numerous media members (and also people in the social media realm) had wondered how an athlete with such poor grades as shown on the transcript could have remained eligible to play both football and basketball at a presumably premier academic institution as UNC. The transcript showed that Peppers received D's or F's in eleven classes. He ended his first full semester at the school with a 1.08 GPA, it never went above a 1.95 during his entire collegiate-playing career, and yet he was never academically ineligible. The article's author, Andrew Carter, pointed out that Peppers often came close to ineligibility, though. Peppers ended his spring 2001 semester with a 1.82 GPA. According to the school's minimum standards for athletes at the time, he would have needed a GPA of at least a 1.9 to play football in the fall of 2001. His named transcript did not list any grades after the 2001 spring semester, but the one identified as a "test transcript" offered clues about how he kept his eligibility. The *N&O* would also remind its readers that the test transcript was an almost exact match for the one with Peppers' name.

According to the transcript, when he was in the most jeopardy to lose his eligibility Peppers received two very specific and notable grades. The first was a B-plus in the spring of 2001 in a course entitled "Black Nationalism." The second was in the summer of 2001 in an African and Afro-American Studies seminar, in which he received an A. Those two grades – both in the AFAM department that was embroiled in an academic scandal centered around fraudulent no-show classes and forged grade changes – were ultimately enough to improve his GPA as to be eligible to play sports in the fall of 2001, his final season before entering the NFL.

The *News and Observer* article interviewed one of the very few faculty members willing to speak out against the academic embarrassment, UNC history professor Jay Smith. He had studied Peppers' transcript with interest, and said, "Assuming it's a legitimate transcript – and I guess everything suggests that it is – I was struck by the very poor showing in the student's very first semester. And (by) the pattern that quickly developed of the student doing a kind of high-wire act – barely staying eligible, or even falling under the eligibility bar in the course of the academic year and then getting back over the bar with courses over the summer." And the courses that always allowed Peppers to retain his eligibility? They were classes in the fraudulent AFAM department.

Indeed, the data mined by the *N&O* showed that Peppers carried a 2.16 GPA in AFAM courses. Not a stellar academic performance by any means, but suitable enough to balance out his non-AFAM courses – in which he received a cumulative 1.41 GPA. Other stark contrasts were shown between his work in the more standard fall and spring semesters when compared to his work in summer classes. He produced a 1.65 GPA in his first six fall and spring semesters, but a 2.93 GPA in the four summer classes for which letter grades were listed on the transcript. At the time of the article, UNC officials were still not confirming that the transcript was Peppers'. They had said, however, that Peppers was academically eligible to compete during his career at the school.

The article reported that to ultimately remain eligible during Peppers' years at UNC the university required athletes to have at least a 1.5 GPA entering their third semester, a 1.75 entering their fifth semester, and a 1.9 entering their seventh semester. It wasn't until athletes entered their ninth semester – their fifth year of eligibility – that they would have needed a 2.0 GPA to be academically eligible. "In retrospect," Professor Jay Smith said, "it's kind of amazing that the floor was ever that low." Coincidentally or not, Peppers managed to stay just above the eligibility threshold entering each of those semester benchmarks, and it was always thanks to high grades received in AFAM courses. He left for the NFL prior to his ninth semester.

In the fall of 2006 UNC adopted stricter academic eligibility requirements. Jay Smith praised the school's improved standards but questioned what it really meant. "I guess that's one thing that has changed for the positive in the last few years," he said. "Although, I doubt that the stricter GPA guidelines have done much to change the nature of the overall game that is played. The game is still, it seems to me at most big-time sports universities, to find course schedules that will keep players eligible."

* * *

There was also a legal angle to consider regarding the possible inadvertent publishing of Peppers' transcript by the school. According to an article on wral.com, the simple fact that the document appeared online could have been a violation of a federal law. At the time of the article UNC had still not confirmed or denied that it was in fact authentic, but were reportedly looking into the validity of it and were seeking answers to how it may have ended up on the university's website. According to a U.S. Department of Education official, the Federal Educational Rights and Privacy Act "protects the education record of the student who is or has been in attendance at the school." The official told wral.com that it made no difference whether the student was current or former. "Under FERPA, a consent for disclosure of education records must be signed and dated and must specify the records that may be disclosed; state the purpose of the disclosure; and identify the party or class of parties to whom the disclosure may be made," the official said in a statement. "If a student contacts this office alleging that his or her rights under FERPA had been violated, we may open an investigation." In extreme cases, an institution that violated FERPA could even lose federal funding.

Professor Jay Smith spoke on a morning radio show two days after the transcript's discovery. "I have come to the conclusion the problem is a systemic one," he told hosts on 99.9 The Fan ESPN Radio. "It is a systemic problem across the (UNC) campus." Board of Trustees Chairman Wade Hargrove also spoke up on the matter, though he was noncommittal. "The university is continuing this investigation. (It) is not over, and when there is factual information to disclose it will be discussed." UNC did not answer any additional questions for wral.com, and multiple calls to Peppers and his agent had gone unanswered. A U.S. Department of Education official said that a student would have to complain about a potential FERPA violation before any potential action could be taken against an institution. Once Peppers finally spoke up, however, it quickly became apparent that restitution from the university would not be sought by its former star athlete.

* * *

On Saturday, August 18, 2012, numerous articles began to be published indicating that Julius Peppers had released a statement to the Chicago *Tribune*, the hometown paper of the NFL's Chicago Bears, for whom Peppers played at the time. He confirmed the transcript was his, and displayed disappointment that it had been inadvertently published. He did not, however, indicate that he would be taking any sort of legal action against UNC. Instead, the statement was largely void of negativity towards the university; he even thanked the school's academic and athletic staff for their help and guidance during his time at UNC. He said he was currently "thinking of ways that I can use my experiences and resources" to help support students early in their college career. The meaning behind that quote would become apparent two days later.

According to an August 20, 2012, article on ESPN.com, the school announced that Peppers had earlier that day donated $250,000 to UNC's "Light on the Hill Society" scholarship fund, which supported African-American students. Peppers had previously donated $100,000 to the scholarship fund in 2009. "This gift is indicative of the kind of man Julius Peppers has become," Richard Williams, chair of the Light on the Hill Society board, said in a prepared statement. "I am very proud that he credits his experiences at Chapel Hill for helping to shape him."

* * *

Once again questions would arise from the media regarding just how long the academic improprieties had been occurring at UNC. Chancellor Holden Thorp had repeatedly defended the school's decision to only look as far back as 2007 in its search for fraudulent classes. His reasoning had already been proven to be tenuous due to the abundance of available student data at the university's disposal. With the virtual assurance of past indiscretions dating back at least to 1999 (by way of the information held within Peppers' transcript), the poor choice of the school's limited 2007 timeframe was further exposed. Based on an article published by *The Daily Tar Heel* on August 21, 2012, Thorp also appeared to be showing some signs of agitation on the matter. When questioned about how long the academic deceit had been occurring at the university, Thorp replied, "We never said it just started in 2007," offering yet another deflection away from the inadequate in-house investigation the school had sanctioned earlier in 2012.

In late August UNC would finally reveal how Peppers' academic transcript ended up on the university website. Based on an article by triangle.news14.com, Thorp told a five-member UNC Board of Governors panel that two staffers had made a mistake more than a decade earlier that resulted in the transcript's display. "Neither staff member protected student confidential information to the degree that they should have," Thorp said. "The first staff member has been disciplined; the second no longer works at the university. These incidents happened a long time ago and the university has long since changed the protocol for how test student records are set up and maintained." Thorp indicated that the staff members had been updating the university's old student information system at the time.

In that same article it was revealed that beginning with the 2013 school year, the Department of African and Afro-American Studies would have a new name. It would be called the African, African American and Diaspora (AAAD). The change had been approved by the administrative board, and the department reportedly felt the new name better reflected what they taught. Chancellor Thorp said he felt that new safeguards could turn the university into a model for other schools struggling with similar issues. He also took the opportunity to repeat one of the school's key PR themes of "looking forward" when he said, "We will fix this and it will never happen again." The damage of the release of Peppers' transcript – and all its deep insinuations – had begun to spread, however. Multiple factions within the media were finally coming to the full realization that numerous basketball players of UNC's various national title teams had almost certainly profited from the dishonest academic system that was being exposed.

* * *

The essential (and unanswered) questions:

-- Why did the university refuse to look into a student's claim that he took a no-show course in AFAM in 2005, which was two years prior to the earliest search parameter of the school's internal review?

-- Why would the university not take the time to verify if the "test transcript" that had been brought to its attention actually belonged to a real student?

-- Why was a messageboard user able to research and connect the test transcript to Julius Peppers in a matter of hours, yet the school had been unable – or unwilling – to previously come to the same conclusion?

-- How many of the nearly twenty AFAM courses that Peppers took during his college career – courses that were responsible for allowing him to remain eligible to participate in athletics – were fraudulent?

-- Why was the NCAA remaining silent regarding obvious and blatant instances of academic fraud involving athletes?

-- Why was Professor Jay Smith the only UNC faculty member willing to speak out regarding the embarrassment that athletics continued to cause the university?

CHAPTER TEN

THE BASKETALL PROGRAM'S TIES TO AFAM; WAYNE WALDEN

Following the discovery of information contained within Julius Peppers' transcript, several realizations began to set in: the academic fraud had apparently been going on at UNC for an extended time, and the school's storied basketball program had likely been a main beneficiary of the impermissible transgressions. Several very candid and critical news articles along those lines were written in the days following the uncovering of the transcript. In addition, there were numerous older articles that when re-examined and viewed under this new umbrella of knowledge, showed some amazing coincidences that would provide further damage to UNC's academic/athletic past. By way of those older articles, even more connections between the AFAM department and people within the basketball program would be shown.

The first article to directly call out UNC basketball appeared on August 14, 2012, just two days after Peppers' transcript was revealed. The article, penned by national columnist Gregg Doyel, was featured on the CBSsports.com website. He raised many bold questions of the program, wondered how so many abnormalities could have been overlooked for so long by both UNC and the NCAA, and briefly compared the school to others that had committed academic fraud.

"It's astounding," Doyel wrote, "how this academic scandal could go on for so many years and help so many UNC athletes without being stopped. Where was North Carolina's leadership in all of this? Where was the UNC president, the athletics director, the coaches for football and – yes – basketball? Where was the NCAA?" He also asked where the media (himself included) had been for not noticing any potential problems earlier. He owned up to his own oversight: "(I was) in disbelief that what seemed to be happening at North Carolina actually was happening. This was an indictment of UNC academics, and that didn't jibe with me, maybe because I didn't want it to jibe. … I didn't want to believe this school… could be so shameful."

When mentioning that it was individuals from a rival school's fan site that discovered the transcript, he said it added humiliation to the episode, but not just for the sake of a rivalry. "(It is) humiliating also because it underscores just how ignorant North Carolina wanted to be. UNC officials didn't want to know what was happening, so they stuck their heads in the dirt – and it just got worse. How bad? Maybe the ugliest academic scandal in NCAA history. This one is worse than what happened in 2007 at Florida State. I mean, it's not even close. Florida State had some numbers that looked bad – 61 athletes from 10 different teams – but this UNC scandal dwarfs it. FSU had 61 tainted players, almost all from the same class. North Carolina has at least 54 classes." The figure Doyel used of 54 classes, of course, was only from the 2007-2011 review – and did not include others that were likely fraudulent beginning with the years of the Peppers transcript, and perhaps even earlier. Indeed, unbeknownst to him, the number of classes would exponentially grow in the future as more data would be revealed.

Doyel continued with that line of thinking: "How many athletes were given free grades from the Department of African and Afro-American Studies? We don't know. UNC never wanted to find out, but the school has no choice now. The school mustered a halfhearted search for the truth earlier this year when it found those 54 tainted classes, but its search went back only to 2007. Despite efforts from the Raleigh *News and Observer* that suggested otherwise, the school held firm that the academic fraud started in 2007."

Once the transcript from 2001 was uncovered, he said, everything changed. "We have evidence not only of grades being given to athletes for at least a decade – but also that UNC academic support staff steered athletes to those classes. This can't be dismissed as the rogue actions of a man named Julius Nyang'oro, the embattled former head of the Department of African and Afro-American Studies. If it was just him, well, that could be explained away to a certain extent. The school would be vulnerable to NCAA sanctions, but one man running amok? That's not horrible."

Doyel then laid out the alternative to a Nyang'oro-only

setup, one which was becoming increasingly more likely given all the data that was emerging from the UNC scandal. "So what actually happened at North Carolina? Academic advisers steering athletes to Nyang'oro's department. Athletes staying eligible by getting grades in some classes that didn't even exist. Athletes who played football and men's basketball. Did the coaches know? Well, ask yourself this: Are we to believe that academic advisers were steering famous athletes to bogus classes behind the backs of the millionaire coaches who recruited, coached and needed those athletes to remain eligible?"

Doyel went on to give more numerical figures, and spell out more likely conclusions. "Answers are coming, but we already know this: The scandal spanned the decade from 2001-11. Know what happened that decade? The UNC men's basketball team played in three Final Fours. It won national titles in 2005 and 2009. Did any players on those NCAA championship teams attend bogus classes? According to the *News and Observer*, almost 67 percent of the students in those 54 classes were athletes. Most played football, but the newspaper reported that UNC records showed 'basketball players had also enrolled. In two classes, the sole enrollee was a basketball player.'"

Doyel then returned to the topic of Florida State, a school which had recently been punished for academic improprieties. "See, this is so much worse than what happened at Florida State – and Florida State vacated two seasons of saintly Bobby Bowden's victories, suffered scholarship restrictions and received four years of probation. What happens to North Carolina? Well, that depends. First, the NCAA has to show it cares. Incredibly, to date, the NCAA has not. Trained NCAA investigators missed the very stuff that is seeping out now, including the transcript discovered by a single N.C. State fan. The NCAA poked around, found some stuff, but didn't find this. (They) didn't find 54 bogus classes from 2007-11, or the unknown number of classes dating to 2001, filled mostly by UNC athletes. The NCAA hasn't uttered a peep in recent days about these new allegations, either. Neither has the school. Not Roy Williams. Not anybody."

Doyel closed his article with what would appear to be the obvious next steps to be taken – assuming such steps were dictated by morals, ethics, and rules. The first would have been by the NCAA, and the next by the school: "It's time for the NCAA to start digging. In the meantime, North Carolina should get a head start on some of its own chores. For starters? There are some banners at the Smith Center that need to come down."

* * *

Another scathing yet insightful article appeared by national writer Pat Forde on August 17, 2012. Forde was a respected senior writer for Yahoo! Sports. He began his piece by referencing the recent sanctions that the NCAA had given to Penn State University, and voiced questions as to whether that governing body would continue to show a strong policy of judgment with regards to UNC.

"After the NCAA circumvented its own crime-and-punishment process and blew up Penn State last month," Forde wrote, "we all wondered how long it would take for a follow-up test case to measure the willingness of the 'new NCAA' to flex its precedent-setting muscles again. Was the Penn State case a sign of a new era in policing of athletic programs gone bad, or an isolated blip brought on by a school's unique abdication of morals and responsibilities? Lo and behold, we have the festering scandal at North Carolina to give us a quick answer".

"As the Raleigh News & Observer and North Carolina State message-board vigilantes continue to go where UNC's timorous administration wouldn't in plumbing the depths of the Tar Heels' academic mess," Forde continued, "the situation demands a signal from NCAA president Mark Emmert. Will he and the NCAA executive committee cowboy up again? Will they circumvent the rules manual and due process and go after Carolina on the basis of general principle, a la Penn State?"

Forde then highlighted some of Penn State's sanctions: a four-year bowl ban, $60 million fine, scholarship cuts, and more than 100 vacated victories. All, he noted, without the benefit of an NCAA investigation or infractions hearing. Penn State had, however, been very forthcoming with its sharing of information – inviting Louis Freeh and his law firm, Freeh Sporkin & Sullivan LLP, onto campus. Freeh was a former Director of the Federal Bureau of Investigation, a native of New Jersey, and did not have any connections to Penn State or its administration. He was given full access to all of the school's past documents, emails, and records. His eventual findings would prompt the NCAA – and its president Mark Emmert – to hand down the heavy sanctions against Penn State.

Included in Forde's August 17 article were some of Emmert's quotes following the penalization of Penn State several months earlier: "While there's been much speculation about whether this fits this specific bylaw or that specific bylaw," Emmert had said, "it certainly hits the fundamental values of what athletics are supposed to be doing in the context of higher education. One of the grave dangers stemming from our love of sports is the sports themselves can become too big to fail and too big to even challenge. The result can be an erosion of academic values that are replaced by hero worship and winning at all costs." Forde pointed out that it seemed pretty clear there was an erosion of academic values at North Carolina, as well as a situation that threatened the fundamental value of what athletics were supposed to be doing in the context of higher education – situations taking place that in fact mirrored Emmert's words exactly.

Forde wrote, "The more we learn, the more it seems UNC has made a mockery of its ballyhooed academic mission for a long time in order to gain competitive advantage in football and men's basketball. With the introduction of what apparently is former two-sport star Julius Peppers' transcript into the public forum, it seems reasonable to assume that Carolina has been skating athletes through the African and Afro-America Studies department in order to maintain eligibility for more than a decade."

Forde said the problem wasn't isolated to one coach, one sport, or one professor. Instead, it was an institutional issue, "and that conjures one of those NCAA catch phrases that translate to big trouble: lack of institutional control." However, despite the overwhelming abundance of evidence that had already surfaced in 2012 even prior to the Peppers revelation, NCAA enforcement had for some reason shown no interest in returning to Chapel Hill and reopening its investigation.

This was where one of UNC's main public-relations "message points" apparently came into play. According to Forde's article, UNC said the NCAA's reasoning for staying away had been that the academic problems uncovered in the initial AFAM review were an institutional issue and not strict athletic rules violations. As school officials had made sure to state numerous times in the media over the previous several months, both athletes and non-athletes had taken the fraudulent classes, and thus it was the school's opinion that the improprieties fell outside the NCAA's realm of jurisdiction. This, despite the fact that the majority of students in the classes were athletes, and that numerous players on the school's basketball and football teams had chosen AFAM as their major over the past two decades. Also, Forde pointed out another note of incomprehensible hypocrisy: "And as much as the NCAA is hands-on with transcripts and grades of athletes coming out of high school," he wrote, "it is notably (and nonsensically) hands-off with transcripts and grades of athletes in college."

Forde then returned his argument to the Penn State case. He said that there was nothing about what happened at that school that fit "neatly" into the NCAA rules enforcement, yet the association felt that Penn State had placed sports ahead of the university itself, so the governing body acted. Forde asked if Emmert and the NCAA executive committee would penalize another program gone wrong (UNC) without a cut-and-dried bylaw violation (though it had become abundantly clear that fraud had occurred which directly benefited athletes). Or, had the NCAA simply penalized Penn State as part of a P.R. move to "appease the outraged and show that the NCAA could hit a bloated target at point-blank range?"

Forde made it very plain that he did not consider the crimes at North Carolina to be the same as the human atrocities at Penn State, a point that was also stressed in this book's introduction. Having made that point clear, he would then go on to say, "In terms of what's objectionable to the NCAA – alleged systematic academic fraud over a decade or more – that (is what) strikes at the core of the entire athletic franchise. And now that a 'Damn the Rulebook, Do What's Right' precedent has been established, is North Carolina's sad academic scandal a logical second act for the Emmert Posse? If not, I'd say the NCAA has some explaining to do."

Forde closed his article by referencing Josephine Potuto, a former member and chairwoman on the NCAA Committee on Infractions who was at the time the NCAA faculty athletic representative at Nebraska. She had told Yahoo! Sports in July of 2012 that she was concerned about the precedent the Penn State ruling had set for the NCAA to jump outside its standard operating procedures. She said that the NCAA would have to explain itself every time it chose not to get involved in an athletic issue on campus that was not directly related to NCAA bylaws. At the very least, UNC had just provided such an issue. Furthermore, depending on whether Emmert and his group chose to dig further into the school's blatant academic transgressions, issues that were much more clearly-defined (in terms of NCAA bylaws) could await. As Gregg Doyel had said in his previous news piece, however, the NCAA first had to show that it cared.

* * *

USA Today printed an article on August 16, 2012, that in part recounted a radio appearance that UNC basketball coach Roy Williams had made earlier that day. Williams made some puzzling remarks about the past that perhaps unintentionally alluded to issues and offered clues to certain patterns within the men's basketball program. Williams graduated from UNC, had been a longtime assistant to Dean Smith before leaving to be the head coach at Kansas, and then returned to coach his alma mater in 2003. He had since gone on to win two national titles at the school, in 2005 and 2009. "You know," Williams said, "I'm bothered by a lot of stuff. I'm bothered by some sensationalism going on. I'm bothered by problems that we have. I'm bothered by mistakes that we have made. But you know, I think in my opinion it's best for me to keep my mouth shut and let our administrative people take care of it." Even while referencing possible "mistakes" that had been made, Williams still defended his teams' academic records at both Kansas and UNC. His further comments, however, would continue to refer to issues and problems. "I don't think you can put your head in the sand and say, 'oh we're all right – it's just people making things up.' I'm not saying that. There's been some mistakes made, and there's been some serious mistakes." A closer look at earlier stories could possibly point to the source of those references, references which may have even been a Freudian slip of sorts.

* * *

An article appeared on indystar.com, the website of *The Indianapolis Star* newspaper, on April 2, 2010, several years prior to the discovery of UNC's academic fraud. The title was "They got game, but do NCAA players graduate?" Its topic dealt with some of the top men's basketball programs and players – and how those players performed in the classroom. In retrospect, it would end up giving some startling insight into UNC and its AFAM department. It painted a much clearer picture as to the extent the department may have impermissibly benefitted athletes in the past.

According to the article, *The Indianapolis Star* newspaper had used public records requests and spent four months collecting data and analyzing graduation rates to look at how athletes who played in the men's basketball Final Four from 1991 to 2007 fared in the classroom. The newspaper had obtained results for 357 athletes who played at least one minute in a Final

Four semifinal or championship game for a taxpayer-funded public university. UNC fell under that university distinction, and had furthermore advanced to the Final Four nine different times during the years covered – winning the national title on three of those occasions. Coincidence or not, the start of that successful time period which included nine Final Four trips and three national titles coincided almost exactly with Julius Nyang'oro being appointed as the chairman of UNC's AFAM department in 1992.

The article mentioned the term "clustering," which referred to a high percentage of teammates receiving the same degree. The school it used as the most glaring example was UNC, pointing out that of its basketball graduates, Communications and African and Afro-American Studies (AFAM) stood out as the two majors of choice. In fact, from the UNC team that won the 2005 national title, there were seven Tar Heels who had the same major, which was AFAM. That list included stars Sean May, Jackie Manuel, David Noel, Jawad Williams, Melvin Scott, Reyshawn Terry, and Marvin Williams. Sean May, who was named the tournament's Most Outstanding Player in 2005 and would go on to play in the NBA, gave some insight into the attractiveness of an AFAM major. He told the paper that Afro-American and African Studies offered "more independent electives, independent study. I could take a lot of classes during the season. Communications, I had to be there in the actual classroom. We just made sure all the classes I had to take, I could take during the summer."

The article didn't stop with those amazing bits of information that correlated with – and in large part seemed to verify – some of the data of current 2012 academic scandal. It noted that a small handful of past star basketball players had left college early but had still managed to graduate. Of the half-dozen listed, four were from North Carolina: Jerry Stackhouse, Antawn Jamison, Vince Carter, and the aforementioned May. All four of the athletes graduated with a degree in AFAM. Furthermore, an academic anecdote involving Marvin Williams was recounted in the article. He was the second pick overall in the 2005 NBA draft after just one season at UNC. Yet according to a school spokesman, Williams was working toward a degree and was (at the time of that 2010 article) a junior academically. His major, like the other star UNC players, was AFAM.

Kadie Otto, the head of the Drake Group at the time, told the newspaper that her concern with clustering was that it raised questions about whether athletes were being directed to a path of least academic resistance. "I'm fascinated at the longevity of North Carolina's clustering," Otto said. "It's unbelievable." She noted that big schools had mostly escaped penalties tied to the NCAA's academic progress rate (APR). "It begs the question, 'How are they doing it?'" Otto said. "They just seem to find a way." The NCAA's home offices were in Indianapolis, the same town as the "*Star*" newspaper. That made it especially convenient for the paper to ask an NCAA official about UNC's clustering. That official declined to comment, however, saying the clustering was a campus issue.

Data throughout the years shows that multiple UNC men's basketball players had chosen AFAM, the department rife with academic scandal, as their major. Along with the aforementioned seven players from the 2005 national title team, plus Stackhouse, Jamison, and Carter, other former players included Quentin Thomas, Mike Copeland, George Lynch, and Ed Cota. Those were just some of the ones who had declared AFAM as their major; numerous other basketball players throughout the years were known to have taken courses in the department in order to fill the needs of certain elective categories.

John Blanchard, a senior associate athletics director at UNC, told the paper it was reasonable that people in a peer group might gravitate to the same major. He said clustering "just doesn't bother us here (at UNC)". He continued: "The question is whether they are getting a good education, and the answer to that is a resounding yes." Two years later, as evidence of fraudulent courses would be exposed, that indystar.com article – and all the information held within, Blanchard's quotes included – was bathed in a much different light. The article also should have served as a warning bell in 2010 to higher authorities such as the NCAA, but that was not the case. The university may have heeded the warning to an extent, however, as the number of basketball players claiming AFAM as a major would coincidentally drop sharply following the publication of the *Star* article.

* * *

When Roy Williams left Kansas to become the head basketball coach at UNC in 2003, he did not come alone. Wayne Walden had been the academic adviser for the men's basketball team at Kansas for 15 years prior to his departure in 2003 to follow Williams to UNC where he had accepted a similar position on Williams' support staff for the Tar Heels. In a July 3, 2003, article that appeared on the Lawrence (Kansas) Journal-World website, Wayne Walden said that "The University of Kansas has been great to me. It's really tough to leave here. The biggest thing I'll miss is the relationships with the students." Walden himself was a 1984 alumnus of the Kansas. His loyalty, though, was apparently to Williams, and not to the school from which he graduated.

One of Walden's duties while at UNC, aside from being the main academic adviser for the basketball team, was also to apparently oversee the scheduling of classes for all of its players. According to the school's "Office of the University Registrar" webpage, members of the school's Priority Registration Advisory Committee (PRAC) decided which university groups or organizations would receive priority registration in any given semester or year. Athletic teams were always some of those groups, as they needed to try and schedule their players' classes around practice and game times. Past PRAC documents listed on UNC's website showed the teams which have received priority clearance, and also the person responsible for submitting those eventual scheduling requests. The past PRAC schedule documents showed that during his time working as the main academic adviser for UNC's men's basketball team, Wayne Walden was the person responsible for submitting the players' class registration requests to the Priority Registration Advisory Committee. Over the years, those registration requests would have included a multitude of courses in the AFAM department – for the many players who claimed it as a major, as well as for players who were taking such courses as electives. That would seem to indicate that Walden not only had intimate knowledge of the basketball players' course selections, but possibly also a direct hand in explicitly guiding them to those academic destinations.

Walden remained alongside head coach Roy Williams and with the men's basketball team until the summer of 2009, just after the team won its second national title during his (and Williams') time in Chapel Hill. During the closing remarks of the team banquet in mid-May of 2009, Roy Williams said the following: "You guys have heard… a lot of guys…. Wayne, stand up a second. Everybody clap for Wayne. I told Wayne that I wasn't going to do this, but Wayne I've said this to my team and they've gotten over it so you've got to get over it too. I lied. I've been a head coach for 21 years. … Wayne Walden has been with me for 21 years. And Wayne Walden came to North Carolina just trusting me and Coach Holladay that things were gonna work out alright… Wayne Walden found a jewel, and he's going to get married this summer, and Wayne Walden at the end of the summer will be leaving us. And it's funny … our academic guy is the best you can possibly be. I'd rather lose every assistant coach, together… than lose Wayne Walden. You guys heard it a little bit here… each young man talking about Wayne helping them with their academic side and getting their degree. For 21 years I've trusted one person… Coach Holladay helps, there's no question about that. He's the person on staff that's the main contact with Wayne. But for 21 years I've trusted one guy, with everything academically for every player I've ever coached. … I'd ask him about Ty… he's never had to go back and check and say I'll get back to you, because it's been his life. … I just want you to know that I've been lucky. To be at Kansas, I've been lucky to be at the University of North Carolina… but I've been really lucky to have the academic advisor I've had for 21 years. Wayne, thank you."

* * *

In a further example of just how little the mainstream media and the general public had been aware of the academic indiscretions that had been going on at UNC, an article entitled "Basketball champions make grades academically, too" had appeared on a variety of news websites on April 23, 2009. It was written by AP Sports Writer Michael Marot. Part of the article covered the presumed longstanding academic accomplishments of the UNC program. Head coach Roy Williams had been unavailable to comment for the article, but it noted that in the past "Williams has credited Wayne Walden, the associate director of the academic support center, for making academics a top priority." Then-current UNC Athletics Director Dick Baddour had given a statement commending the six Tar Heel teams that had appeared on a recent NCAA Academic Progress Rate "honor roll" list of sorts: "That's a credit to our coaches for recruiting true student athletes, to the student athletes for staying committed to academic integrity, to our staff for its timeless support and to the University of North Carolina for providing the education and inspiration to achieve academically."

The media and general public had obviously not been the only groups who had bought into the pristine image of the academics of UNC's athletes. NCAA spokesman Erick Christianson had said in that AP article, "There is a myth out there some hold that you have to somehow sacrifice your studies to do well on the court and that just isn't true. This (APR list) reinforces that you can excel in competition and in the classroom. So those who hold onto the dumb-jock myth, it's time to let it go." Three years after Christianson's statement, the AFAM discoveries at UNC in the summer of 2012 suggested otherwise. Christianson's parent association – the NCAA – was still nowhere to be found in Chapel Hill, however.

* * *

The essential (and unanswered) questions:

-- Why had Florida State been forced by the NCAA to vacate numerous victories due to an academic scandal that was essentially much narrower in scope than UNC's – yet the NCAA had thus far skipped judgment on the Tar Heel program?

-- Was the NCAA's penalizing of Penn State a public relations move, or would they be consistent and treat other schools which blatantly placed athletics above academics the same way?

-- Based on Roy Williams' references of "past mistakes," how much had he truly known beforehand about his players' involvement in the over decade-long AFAM academic scandal?

-- Why had the NCAA not investigated the suspicious pattern of athlete "clustering" at UNC when it was reported in the mainstream media in April of 2010?

-- How many of the seven AFAM majors on UNC's 2005 basketball national title team had taken a fraudulent course at the university?

-- How many of those players' transcripts, if investigated and reviewed by the NCAA, would have shown strikingly similar class and grade patterns as the transcript of Julius Peppers?

-- As an investigative result of the above two questions, how many of those players would have then been retroactively ineligible to participate in sports while at the UNC, meaning any victories in which they had participated would need to be vacated?

-- To what extent was academic adviser Wayne Walden involved in the scheduling of basketball players in AFAM classes that were possibly known (within the UNC infrastructure) to be fraudulent?

-- How would UNC's yearly Academic Progress Rates (APR's) looked without the benefit of the potentially numerous fraudulent AFAM courses?

CHAPTER ELEVEN

MARTIN INVESTIGATION ANNOUNCED; ROBERT MERCER, HAROLD WOODARD, AND VINCE ILLE

Following the inadvertent release of Julius Peppers' transcript, the university's leaders seemed to quickly realize that they had a big problem on their hands. A decade's worth of grades were now overwhelmingly considered suspect in at least one department, with more questions mounting by the day. The Peppers transcript was uncovered on August 12, 2012. Just four days later on August 16, the school announced a new investigation that would look even further into the past than the limited "2007" review had done earlier in the year. On the surface the university touted the new investigation as one that would have no limitations and would aggressively root out any past problems. A closer inspection, however, would lead to serious doubts of those claims.

An article published in the Raleigh *News and Observer* on August 16, 2012, helped to announce the upcoming investigation. UNC Chancellor Holden Thorp had been under increasing pressure from both the media and the general public to dig deeper into the school's academic fraud scandal that had recently multiplied in severity and drawn national attention as a result. On that Thursday Thorp said he was bringing in former North Carolina governor Jim Martin, along with a national management consulting firm, to look for "any additional academic irregularities that may have occurred." The firm, formerly known as Virchow, Krause & Co. before going on to operate under the name of Baker Tilley, would help to conduct an audit to try and find out whether the no-show classes and poorly supervised independent studies found earlier that year in the AFAM department extended beyond the initial four-year period that had been examined. "Obviously a lot of people are concerned that our review didn't go back far enough," Thorp said, "and we've come to the conclusion that we're not going to satisfy people's interest in that if we don't have an objective firm and an objective individual." Just how objective the individual tabbed to head the investigation would be, however, was immediately a contested matter – and would continue to be so long after the results were finally released.

Jim Martin was 76 years old when tabbed to lead the investigation into UNC's academic scandal that widely involved major-sport athletes. He had spent a career in politics, and had no specific investigative experience. He had served North Carolina in the U.S. House of Representatives for six terms, and also two terms as North Carolina governor – giving him plenty of political connections in the state. He had also served a term on the UNC Board of Governors, an entity that had historically shown a very high percentage of UNC graduates and influence.

Martin at one time served on the Board of Directors of a group called the Carolina Business Coalition. According to its website, it was a strategic organization that carried out a number of objectives designed to benefit North Carolina businesses and the state's economy. Its Board of Directors consisted of ten members. Of the ten, only two did not have direct academic connections to the University of North Carolina. One of those two, David H. Murdock was the CEO of the Dole Food Company and was a high school dropout prior to being drafted into World War II. Former Governor Martin was the other, having graduated from nearby Davidson College. The remaining eight members of the close-knit board were all graduates in one form or another of UNC. One of the members who attended the UNC School of Law, Roger W. Knight, had also previously served as legal counsel to Jim Martin in 1985-86 while Martin was governor.

There were other past ties between Martin and the school. He had previously chaired an advisory panel to UNC's Nutrition Research Institute at the N.C. Research Campus in Kannapolis, NC. Furthermore, there had also been a Merit Scholarship established in his name at UNC in the fall of 1999. The "Gov. James G. and Dottie Martin Carolina Scholar Award" was established by Jim and Mary McNab. Jim McNab had received his MBA from UNC in 1968. The McNab's daughter had graduated from the university in 1999 and went on to start law school there that fall as well.

An even more direct potential conflict of interest was the

revelation that Martin was the chairman of the Board of Directors for the Institute for Defense and Business, a nonprofit that helped the military apply business principles and technology to do a better job. The UNC associations again dealt with fellow Board members, one of whom was none other than Holden Thorp – the then-current Chancellor at UNC who had just chosen Martin to lead the investigation into Thorp's school. Other members included Roger Perry, a former UNC trustee, as well as James Moeser, the former Chancellor of UNC from 2000-2008 – the primary years that spanned the school's ongoing academic scandal. The board for the Institute for Defense and Business was based in Chapel Hill, the home town of UNC.

While none of those many connections necessarily proved collusion, they did show a stark difference in the approach that UNC took to its festering scandal when compared to the issues of other schools in the recent past. Yahoo! Sports writer Pat Forde had recently mentioned the Penn State case when wondering what disciplinary actions the NCAA would take against UNC's academic infractions. Penn State had opened its doors and records to Louis Freeh, the former director of the FBI. Freeh was unaffiliated with Penn State and had a vast background in criminal investigation. UNC could have sent a similar message that they desired to know the full truth of their past. Instead, they chose a former politician with multiple close relationships to associates of the university, both past and present. From the very first stages of the investigation's announcement, those in the media and general public who had been critical of UNC's blatant lack of transparency and cooperation once again displayed doubt in the university's desire to root out the true depths of the improprieties. Those doubts would in part eventually be justified, as documents released many months later would show just how limited the "investigative" aspect of

Martin's on-campus tenure had truly been.

* * *

According to the same *News and Observer* article, Chancellor Thorp indicated that once the audit of prior classes was completed, the Baker Tilley firm would also review numerous reforms that had been put in place to make sure the academic fraud didn't happen again. Once more, the same recurring public relations message was subtly delivered: look onward to prevent future problems, as opposed to clearly identifying the reasons behind the improprieties of the past. Thorp also said that Hunter Rawlings, president of the Association of American Universities, would come to the campus to help assess the relationship between athletics and academics and find ways to improve it. There would also be a university restructuring of the academic support unit for student athletes, including removing a line of authority between the unit and the athletics department. The unit would instead now answer solely to the College of Arts & Sciences.

The same newspaper article quoted Thorp as saying, "I'm totally devoted to this place and feel like we have to do whatever it takes to get us past this, and I think that the things that we are announcing today will." Thorp had earlier been criticized by at least one member of the UNC Board of Governors, former State Supreme Court Justice Burley Mitchell, for failing to dig deeply into the scandal. A member of the school's campus, UNC history professor Jay Smith, had also been outspoken about the need for a deeper investigation in order to protect the university's academic integrity. The examples of Mitchell and Smith were few and far between, however, as had been the case throughout much of the scandal. Few associated with leadership entities such as the Board of Governors or the university's Board of Trustees had publicly shown passionate concern, and even fewer UNC faculty members appeared to care about the damage to the school's image. That would be a woeful display that would continue well into 2014.

* * *

An article released by the *News and Observer* two days later, on August 18, 2012, revealed some very telling facts regarding the amount of information that the university had been withholding from the media, as well as for how long. According to the article, UNC Chancellor Holden Thorp had said in an interview that the school had reviewed some transcripts as part of its investigation from earlier that year and found dozens of classes in the African Studies department in which students, a majority of them athletes, did not have to show up. Thorp would not be more specific about what kinds of transcripts were looked at and what was discovered. Furthermore, the university had also not produced any information for the public that indicated UNC had undertaken a comprehensive inquiry into the types of classes taken by athletes and the grades they received. This, despite the fact that transcripts of two prominent former athletes – Marvin Austin and Julius Peppers – had shown likely widespread academic fraud.

For two years, beginning in 2010, university officials had declined to provide the *News and Observer* with athlete transcripts. The newspaper had asked for the documents with the personal information removed, such as the names and any other identifying details of the students. Despite the fact that the university had access to all of those records, and they also knew of the academic fraud, they refused. According to the newspaper, transcript information, if provided, would have shown whether there were "clusters of classes, disparities in grades, favored professors, and other such details at a university where a faculty report issued last month described a 'campus with two cultures,' one academic, one athletic."

Jon Ericson, the former provost at Drake University, indicated that if there was more openness and transparency about classes, professors, and grades, it would help expose which departments and classes were serving to protect athletes' eligibility. "If the faculty and the administrators and the athletic directors knew that the grades and the courses would be public, there wouldn't be courses to be embarrassed about," he said. Ericson and Minnesota lawyer Matthew Salzwedel had argued that universities could release much more information than they currently did about athletes' performances in the classroom. But schools don't, they argue, because administrators incorrectly cite federal privacy law and did not want to address academic "corruption" in college athletics. "Without (full) disclosure," they wrote in the Dartmouth Law Review in 2010, "isolated disclosures of academic corruption in college athletics by whistleblowers are treated as anecdotes, easily dismissed and often ridiculed. After all, no one likes a spoilsport." While that was perhaps a partial excuse for the complete silence from almost everyone associated with the UNC faculty, it was in no way a moral justification of the muteness – especially from a school and faculty that claimed to pride itself on doing things "the right way."

* * *

As stated earlier, the *News and Observer* first sought transcript information – with personal identifiers deleted – in late

2010. In early 2011, the university denied that request, saying that classes taken by athletes, even with names and other
personal details deleted, might still be "easily traceable" back
to the athlete and violate their privacy. "Our student athletes
attend class with other students on campus," Regina Stabile,
UNC's director of institutional records and reporting compliance, had written in a memo at the time. "That means that
many students on campus know which student athletes were in
a particular section of a particular course. Knowing the specific courses taken and the order in which they were taken could
too easily provide all the clues needed to match a de-identified
transcript with a specific student-athlete." Of course, since that
statement was made prior to the unveiling of dozens of no-show
courses where attendance was not required and classes never
actually met, it would eventually be viewed in an extremely
ironic and humorous light.

Matthew Salzwedel, a former tennis player at Drake who
chose to publish his own academic transcript in a law review
article, said that the particular "protective" approach Regina
Stabile and UNC had employed was typical of universities that
sought to protect big-time athletics. "It simply isn't credible
for UNC to say that because other students (many of whom are
long gone from UNC) might be able to discern individual athlete's transcripts, the redacted transcripts cannot be produced to
you, a reporter," he told the Raleigh newspaper. "In addition,
there should be no federal privacy protections for classes because, even as UNC admits, any student can watch an athlete
walk into class."

Following the university's refusal to fill the newspaper's request in early 2011, a subsequent entreaty of the data was submitted in a different format altogether. That new request sought

classes taken and grades earned for teams, asking UNC to organize the information not in the form of each athlete's transcript but instead by showing it for each semester. Well over a year later, that request was still pending at the time of the August 18, 2012, article. On top of the long amount of time that had already passed, Chancellor Thorp additionally said he would not consider the request again until the special audit/investigation was completed.

As the first full week following the revelation of Julius Peppers' transcript came to a close, Chancellor Thorp had written a letter to trustees, faculty, and staff that said, "Our focus every day remains on fixing the problems and ensuring they never happen again." Once again, one of UNC's main "public relations" talking points was front and center – to make sure the future was safe, as opposed to finding out what exactly happened in the past, and (most importantly) why. According to the *News and Observer*, Thorp also announced the new inquiries in that same letter, including the audit that he said would review "any additional academic irregularities that may have occurred." It was not otherwise clear what the scope or depth of the new audit would be, and no specific time frame was given for when it would be complete.

* * *

On August 21, 2012, another article appeared in the ever-vigilant *News and Observer*, pointing out a key employee reassignment that had recently taken place at UNC. When Chancellor Holden Thorp had announced a reorganization of the Academic Support Program for Student Athletes the previous week, he said the school had installed an interim director and was searching for a new, permanent one. According to the article, what Thorp did not say was what happened to the man who had held that director job for nearly a decade, Robert Mercer.

Mercer had been moved to a new position, outside of athletic advising, as a "special assistant for operations" at a center for undergraduate excellence, according to *N&O* reporter Dan Kane. Mercer's former boss, Harold Woodard (who was the person serving as interim director at the time), said Mercer had done nothing wrong. Instead, Woodard indicated that the issues that had arisen and built from the academic fraud investigation required a search for a "national" leader to run the program. "It's not about Robert, it really isn't," said Woodard, who was also an associate dean in charge of the university's academic support program for undergraduate students. "It's really about this opportunity for Carolina to claim the mantle of operating a model program." Yet another important aspect that was not mentioned, however, was Robert Mercer's close association with the scheduling of certain athletes' classes. The previous chapter discussed the PRAC scheduling assignments, and how Wayne Walden had been responsible for the vast majority of the semesters for the men's basketball team. There was at least one occasion, however – the fall of 2008 – where Robert Mercer was listed on the PRAC schedule as being responsible for the men's basketball team. That semester also happened to fall within the university's initial investigative parameter of the AFAM program that had uncovered over 50 fraudulent courses.

A letter was sent from Woodard to Mercer earlier in the month of August 2012 notifying him of the change in employment status. It stated that Mercer had been reassigned to the Johnston Center for Undergraduate Excellence, which handled honors programs and undergraduate research. "You will be referred to as the special assistant for operations and will assist with the facility and its operation, programming and other duties, as assigned," the letter said. Mercer would continue to make the same annual salary as before the reassignment, which was $81,900. He had been Director of the Academic Support Program for Student Athletes since October 2002, and had worked in the program as an administrator since 1996. All of those years would eventually fall under suspect of academic fraud.

The school's Academic Support Program for Student Athletes had garnered some unwanted attention in the UNC faculty report that had been released earlier in 2012. As mentioned previously, that report had said an unidentified "departmental staff manager" within African Studies may have directed athletes to enroll in the no-show classes, and that "it seems likely" someone in the department was calling counselors for athletes to tell them "certain courses" were available. "We were told that athletes claimed they had been sent to Julius Nyang'oro (by the Academic Support Program for Student Athletes)," the report said. Harold Woodard, Mercer's boss and the interim director who sent the letter of reassignment to Mercer, told the newspaper that he knew nothing about past claims of steering athletes to certain AFAM courses. "I'm not aware of what was happening in that department, and that's probably a good thing because it allows me to focus on where we want to take the staff during the interim," Woodard had said. A curious side note, however, was that Woodard had been a lecturer in the Curriculum of African-American Studies at UNC in the early 1990's – the exact same time period when Julius Nyang'oro was rapidly ascending to the position of chairman of the department.

* * *

Several other employee alterations were covered in that August 21, 2012 article by the *News and Observer*, though the full gravity of some of the scenarios would not be fully realized until later. A month earlier, Athletics Director Bubba Cunningham had announced a new senior associate director, Vince Ille, who had previously worked at the University of Illinois. Chancellor Thorp later said that part of Ille's job would be as a liaison between academic advisers who helped athletes pick classes, and separate academic counselors who made sure athletes were doing their school work and progressing toward degrees, as the NCAA required. Ille also would supervise the department's NCAA compliance efforts.

Documents released over a year later would eventually disclose more information on Ille. During his time at his previous job with the University of Illinois he had worked as a compliance officer with an individual named Jackie Thurnes. Ille had personally hired Thurnes while at Illinois. Ille would eventually take a job at UNC to become the university's top compliance officer for NCAA matters. Jackie Thurnes, though, would eventually leave Illinois to become an enforcement official with the NCAA itself. Those later-released documents showed continued email contact between the two former co-workers – one now working for UNC, the other working for the NCAA.

* * *

The Raleigh *News and Observer* published an article on August 31, 2012, that was largely based on quotes and updates from various university officials regarding the ongoing scandal. As was now seemingly the norm any time UNC officials gave public statements, there was always plenty of mention of the future, while trying to avoid digging up too much of the past. According to the newspaper article written by reporter Jane Stancill, those UNC officials had met with a Board of Governors' review panel earlier in the week, and their goal was clear: "Deans, faculty members, department heads and Athletics Director Bubba Cunningham lined up to convince (the review panel) that they would do whatever it takes to recover from perhaps the campus' worst academic and athletic scandal." Those university officials pledged more faculty involvement in athletics, a revamped African Studies department, new oversight rules for academic administrators, changes to the tutoring program for athletes, and a strategic plan for the university's entire sports enterprise. Noticeably not pledged, however, was the uncovering of the specific reasons why the academic fraud had happened in the first place.

The panel associated with the Board of Governors was just one of several entities looking into the school's problems, the article stated. UNC Chancellor Holden Thorp gave a brief update on the newly-formed Martin Investigation, but his choice of words left a good deal of flexibility in terms of their ultimate meaning. Thorp said he had met with former Governor Martin about three days prior, and Thorp had told Martin he was free to examine any data and talk with faculty, staff, and students as he deemed necessary. A specific goal (of the examination of data) was never stated, nor were specific documents (such as past athlete transcripts) deemed "absolutely necessary" in terms of being a part of the search parameter. And history would later reveal, in fact, that Martin and his team ultimately didn't look into key and obvious pieces of data that would have provided answers to many of the lingering questions. Instead, they apparently searched only where they "deemed necessary." Those critical details of the failed investigation, however, would not be divulged to the media and the general public until mid-2013, well after its conclusion.

* * *

Bubba Cunningham, UNC's athletics director, said that at
the time of the August 31 article the university had 720 student
athletes in 28 sports. Among the upperclassmen, 34 different
academic majors were represented. Only two majored in African and Afro-American Studies. That was a far cry from just a
few years prior. According to *the Indianapolis Star* article that
was thoroughly covered in the previous chapter, a large percentage of UNC men's basketball players had majored in AFAM
during the 1990's and especially the 2000's – years when the
program won three national titles. When the *Star* article publicly drew attention to the "clustering" of the UNC basketball
players, the number of AFAM majors would oddly begin to take
a sharp and significant drop.

Even though AFAM was no longer apparently chosen by
athletes as a preferred major, that did not necessarily mean
fraud was no longer taking place, however. Students could still
sign up for multiple AFAM courses no matter their major. For
example, the General Education curriculum at UNC was known
as the "Making Connections" program. According to information on the university's official website, that program was
divided into four broad categories known as "Foundations,"
"Approaches," "Connections," and "Supplement Education."
The program was essentially the first year or two of a student's
college career. It required a student to take a number of "elective" courses that would be in addition to the classes the student
would take within his/her major, though some overlapping
would appear likely to occur. Of those extra courses, multiple
classes could have come from the AFAM department based on

the parameters of the four above-noted categories – no matter the student's stated major.

The article closed with more comments from Thorp, all containing the same well-crafted theme and message that university officials had been pushing for months. He reiterated his promise to clean up the situation once and for all. "I am determined that we will fix this and that it will never happen again," Thorp said. "Nothing is more important than restoring confidence in this university that we all love."

* * *

Another article appeared on August 31, 2012, but this one was carried by espn.go.com. As was the case with many of the ESPN articles that covered UNC during the multi-year scandal, it seemed to reflect a more positive bias on the unfolding events. Coincidentally or not, ESPN's president – John Skipper – graduated from UNC. That August 31 article was based on a statement that UNC had released earlier that day, and one that would hold a great amount of future scrutiny and importance. According to the school's statement, the NCAA had told UNC officials that the university apparently did not break NCAA rules surrounding the school's African and Afro-American Studies department. UNC, which (according to the school) first notified the NCAA that it had identified potential academic issues involving student athletes in AFAM courses in late 2011, updated the NCAA enforcement staff on August 23 about the situation. As pointed out several paragraphs above, Jackie Thurnes was an enforcement official with the NCAA, who had formerly worked with UNC's top compliance officer on NCAA matters, Vince Ille. The two had previously worked closely together at the University of Illinois. Whether Thurnes was one of the NCAA officials involved (either directly or indirectly) in the late August updates was unknown.

"The NCAA staff reaffirmed to university officials that no NCAA rules appeared to have been broken," the school said in its statement. As noted in an earlier chapter, an article by Pat Forde of Yahoo! Sports stated that no specific rules or by-laws were broken by Penn State, either, yet the NCAA chose to heavily penalize them because the case had a direct effect on the university's athletic superstructure. He alluded that the same was unequivocally true at UNC. Academic fraud had occurred that directly affected athletes, and the NCAA had plenty of precedence to issue a punishment. At the very least, there was overwhelming data to justify a new NCAA investigation into everything that had been discovered in 2012.

The ESPN article said that according to UNC's released statement, an NCAA enforcement staff member made "several" trips to Chapel Hill in the fall of 2011 and found "no violations of current NCAA rules or student athlete eligibility issues related to courses in African and Afro-American Studies." The timeframe of those fall 2011 trips predated numerous vital events in the evolution of the academic scandal, however. The initial university report of the AFAM improprieties wasn't released until the late spring of 2012, where over 50 fraudulent classes would be revealed. Furthermore, the discovery of Julius Peppers' transcript, which showed likely fraud dating back to at least 1999, wasn't revealed until August of 2012. Neither of those timeline discrepancies were addressed in the school's statement regarding any potential future NCAA involvement. Moreover, it was unknown whether the NCAA official who had made several trips to Chapel Hill in the fall of 2011 was Thurnes, a co-worker of Thurnes, or someone else with a past association with UNC's new compliance officer for NCAA matters, Vince Ille. The school-released statement concluded by saying, "University officials will continue to keep the NCAA informed as developments warrant."

* * *

The essential (and unanswered) questions:

-- When already faced with heavy public scrutiny and criticism over their lax handling of the academic fraud case, why would UNC choose a person to lead an investigation who had such close past connections with individuals and aspects of the school?

-- Why had Chancellor Holden Thorp and the school refused to reveal what the reviewed athlete transcripts in early 2012 had revealed?

-- Why had the university refused to provide class and grade information for athletes, even in safely-censored formats?

-- What possible knowledge of (and/or connection to) the AFAM academic scandal was Robert Mercer associated with?

-- Since Harold Woodard has once been a lecturer in Julius Nyang'oro's department, how close was Woodard's connection to the disgraced former AFAM chairman?

-- Did UNC in part hire Vince Ille due to his close associations with current NCAA personnel?

-- Why was the NCAA still choosing to ignore the academic scandal at UNC – one which had clearly benefitted athletes and their eligibility?

Kenan Memorial Stadium
Source: Wikimedia Commons
Author: Jeick

Duke-Carolina Basketball Tip-Off 2006
Source: Wikimedia Commons
Author: Anders Brownworth

Dean Smith Center
Source: Wikimedia Commons
Author: Greenstrat

Dean Dome
Source: Wikimedia Commons
Author: Snargle

Old Well in Front of South Building
Source: Wikimedia Commons
Author: The PNM

Old Well and McCorkie Place
Source: Wikimedia Commons
Author: Seth Ilys

Roy Williams, Head Coach of the UNC Basketball Team
Source: Wikimedia Commons
Author: David Danals

North Carolina Tar Heels Men's Basketball - 1911
Source: Wikimedia Commons
Author: Unknown

Tar Heels Take Practice Shots on Flight Deck Aboard Nimitz
Source: Wikimedia Commons
Author: U.S. Navy

UNC Tar Heels Practicing on Basketball Arena Aboard The Nimitz
Source: Wikimedia Commons
Author: U.S. Navy

Smith Center Jerseys
Source: Wikimedia Commons
Author: y-its-mom

Tyler Hansbrough, Senior Days
Source: Wikimedia Commons
Author: Des Runyan

Dean Smith Center Display
Source: Wikimedia Commons
Author: Zeke Smith

Julius Peppers
Source: Wikimedia Commons
Author: D.R. Cotton

Greg Little One-handed Catch
Source: Wikimedia Commons
Author: Erik Drost

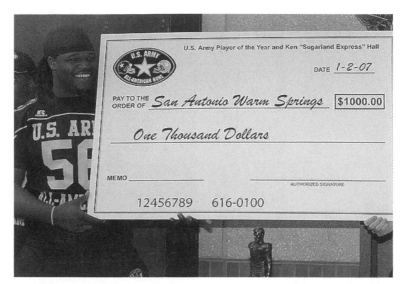

Marvin Austin at All-American Bowl
Source: Wikimedia Commons
Author: U.S. Army

Marvin Austin Selected for 2007 All-American Bowl East Team
Source: Wikimedia Commons
Author: Dennis Ryan

Sean May
Source: Wikimedia Commons
Author: Rikster2

Jerry Stackhouse
Source: Wikimedia Commons
Author: bmendez68

Vince Carter
Source: Wikimedia Commons
Author: Chamber of Fear

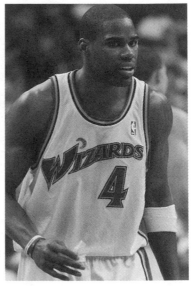

Antawn Jamison - Wizards
Source: Wikimedia Commons
Author: Keith Allison

Marvin Williams
Source: Wikimedia Commons
Author: U.S. Navy

Butch Davis, Head Football Coach at UNC
Source: Wikimedia Commons
Author: Scott Pittman

Butch Davis
Source: Wikimedia Commons
Author: Genefoto

Acc. Commissioner John Swofford
Source: Wikimedia Commons
Author: Refriedm

The unanswered question: How many of UNC's National Championships in basketball were directly affected by players who had potentially remained eligible only through deceit? Players who had likely taken countless fraudulent classes in the Department of African and Afro-American Studies (AFAM) dating as far back as the early 1990's.

University of North Carolina
AFAM
33-4
2005
NATIONAL CHAMPIONS
University of North Carolina
AFAM
34-4
2009
NATIONAL CHAMPIONS

CHAPTER TWELVE

MATT KUPEC AND TAMI HANSBROUGH; THORP'S ANNOUNCED RESIGNATION

Just after the Martin Investigation was announced in late August of 2012, yet another embarrassing episode would hit the university. While it initially appeared unrelated with the ongoing athletic/academic scandal, a closer inspection showed that there were actually several intimate ties to athletics, as well as other areas of the school that were oddly interwoven with events not only of past importance, but also some that were yet to come.

It was announced via a September 11, 2012, *News and Observer* article that UNC's chief fundraiser, Matt Kupec, had resigned two days earlier. Kupec had been the Vice Chancellor for University Advancement for the previous 16 years, and was also widely recognized as the school's most accomplished raiser of money. He was a graduate of UNC, and had been a star quarterback from 1976 through 1979. His resignation came after a brief internal investigation strongly suggested he had taken personal trips at the university's expense. An odd twist, however, was that he was accompanied on those trips by Tami Hansbrough, another university fundraiser – who was also the mother of former UNC basketball star Tyler Hansbrough.

According to Chancellor Holden Thorp, he had initially informed Kupec of findings that included trips and destinations where Tami Hansbrough's other son, Ben, had been playing. At the time Ben Hansbrough had been a star basketball player at Notre Dame. According to Thorp, Kupec offered his resignation during that meeting. "It was difficult because Matt has been such a great person for the university and has raised billions of dollars for us," Thorp said, "but I had to share with him what we had been finding and it didn't look good and that it's likely that this sort of personally driven travel was unacceptable, and we are going to need to do a pretty thorough investigation of it."

At the time, Chancellor Thorp said that he did not see the fundraising controversy as being an athletics concern. However, the presence of Tami Hansbrough in the equation made the situation ambiguous, especially considering the timeline of certain events. During her son Tyler's junior year at UNC, he won the Associated Press National Player of the Year award. Instead of leaving school early and heading to the NBA like several of his UNC teammates had chosen, Hansbrough opted to return for his senior season. Almost every underclassman who had won

that Player of the Year award in the past had left early for the
NBA. In fact, Hansbrough was the first winner since 1991 who
had opted to return to college. That decision was announced in
late April of 2008. Later that same year, Tami was hired for her
first job at UNC; that was a fundraising position in the university's dental school foundation. Her salary was approximately
$80,000 per year. Tyler Hansbrough would go on to lead the
basketball team to a national championship during his senior
year, while his mother was simultaneously employed by the
school. Chancellor Thorp confirmed that a dental foundation
audit later found that during that championship run, Tami Hansbrough had been traveling to cities in which Tyler was playing
basketball. But according to the *N&O*, Thorp said those foun-
dation-paid trips were legitimate because she was raising money for the university, and UNC fans traveling to those games
would have been good candidates to make donations.

* * *

By the time of Kupec's resignation, Tami Hansbrough had
moved on to a second and more prestigious position within
the university. She was a major gifts officer whose salary had
grown to $95,000 annually, according to the *News and Observ-
er*. She had been placed on administrative leave as of the date
of the September 11 article. Kupec declined to be interviewed.
Chancellor Thorp said the university's compliance office had
reviewed information about the travel for compliance with
NCAA regulations. That audit led to the exit of Hansbrough's
boss at the foundation, Brad Bodager. Attempts by the newspaper to reach Bodager had also been unsuccessful.

As more details emerged, it became apparent that Matt Kupec and Tami Hansbrough had been in a relationship together.

In mid-2010, Kupec had sought to hire a fundraiser. According to Thorp, he had heard that Tami (who was still working for the school's dental foundation at the time) might be interested in Kupec's new fundraiser position. When Thorp learned that she would be reporting to Kupec, he told Kupec he could not hire her because it would violate the university's nepotism policy since they were in a relationship. According to the *News and Observer* article, the position disappeared and was never filled. However, a short time later another fundraising position arose. That one was to report to Winston Crisp, who was the Vice Chancellor for Student Affairs at the time. In an article that came out on September 12 in the *N&O*, Crisp said, "Matt came to me to propose that we work together on a major gift officer for parents. That was a position that I had been interested in for quite some time but had not had the ability to fund. But it was Matt who approached me with the initial conversation of having a major gift officer for parents of children." After what Chancellor Holden Thorp said was a proper job search with multiple candidates, Crisp hired Hansbrough for the job in 2010, giving her a new position within the university and one that would ultimately allow her to be closer to Kupec. Crisp said that Hansbrough's hiring was the result of a search committee's unanimous recommendation.

* * *

Matt Kupec separated from his wife in October 2009, almost a full year after Tami Hansbrough had been initially hired by the university's dental foundation. Orange County (NC) records indicate that Kupec had committed "marital misconduct." Hansbrough, meanwhile, was also divorced from her former husband – Tyler Hansbrough's father. However, in September of 2009 she was sued in Mississippi by a woman who alleged that Hansbrough had broken up her marriage, according to a later *N&O* article. Those Mississippi court documents alleged that Hansbrough had seduced the woman's husband, leading to his separation from the woman in early 2008 and then divorce. It was during that same timeframe that Hansbrough's son Ben was beginning the transfer process to Notre Dame, and her son Tyler was announcing his intent to forgo the NBA and return to UNC for his senior season. Hansbrough would be hired at the university's dental school foundation shortly thereafter.

* * *

In a released statement after his resignation, Kupec said that, "I have been privileged to have worked with incredibly talented faculty, students, administrators and staff. I have worked with gifted Chancellors. But most of all, I have been fortunate to work with a score of passionate alumni and friends who love this University and who have paved the way through their generosity to make Carolina a true gem. I will miss you all but in my heart I will always be a part of the Carolina family."

Two of the specific chancellors Kupec had worked for were Holden Thorp, the man who was in charge at the time of Kupec's resignation, and James Moeser, who served from 2000-2008. As mentioned in a previous chapter, both of chose chancellors had served on a Board of Directors with former Governor Jim Martin (who had recently begun an investigation into the school's academic transgressions), and both chancellors' years blanketed the ongoing academic/athletic scandals.

Overall, Kupec had raised $4 billion for the university. He first joined the school as a fundraiser in 1992 and became the Vice Chancellor for University Advancement in 1995 – a position he would hold until his resignation. His most recent annual salary had been $349,800, according to school records. A look at the early stages of his employment with the university would turn up several curious connections during his time working at UNC.

* * *

As stated above, Kupec had been a mid-level fundraiser for the school beginning in 1992. In late 1994 he was the primary fundraiser involved in raising money for the university's new Sonja Haynes Stone Black Cultural Center. The funding of that Cultural Center was one of the primary topics covered at a meeting of the Faculty Council in November of 1994. According to the meeting minutes, several "experts" on the Center were assembled in order to give informational presentations to the Faculty Council about the impending project. One of the main presenters was the interim associate dean of the Office for Student Counseling. This man was the chair of the Black Cultural Center Advisory Board, and also a lecturer in the Curriculum of Afro-American Studies. His name was Harold Woodard – the same Harold Woodard who would later be head of the Academic Support Program for Student Athletes in 2012. Woodard was the eventual boss of Robert Mercer, who was discussed in the previous chapter and who had been unceremoniously removed from his job as director of that Academic Support Program. As mentioned in Chapter Eleven, Woodard stated in 2012 that he "was not aware" of what had been happening in the AFAM department during the many years of academic scandal. Yet he had at one time served as a lecturer in that curriculum, and then back in 1994 he had been the chair of the Advisory Board for a new Black Cultural Center. That same Cultural Center would eventually house the university's Institute for African American Research – an organization which Julius Nyang'oro had previously served as the executive director.

During that late 1994 meeting of the Faculty Council, Kupec spoke shortly after Harold Woodard. Kupec responded to a question regarding the fundraising for the project. Kupec said, "The project for the building is $7 million. We have raised $1.6 (million) to be exact. I've never taught and I've never coached, but on this project I can't imagine the feeling you must get in the classroom when you start to see your students get it. Or when Dean Smith's out there working with those young men, the student athletes, and bingo! Donald Williams starts drilling the 3's, and we win national championships." Kupec later touched on a number of volunteer leaders who had earlier that week met for a committee meeting regarding the fundraising efforts for the new Cultural Center. One of those volunteers at the meeting, in fact, was head basketball coach Dean Smith.

That major fundraising project for a new Black Cultural Center took place after UNC had won the national title in 1993, and also shortly after Julius Nyang'oro had ascended to become the chairman of the AFAM department. In the months closely following that late 1994 meeting which detailed Kupec's fundraising plans for the new Center, he would be promoted to become Vice Chancellor for University Advancement. As stated earlier, it was estimated that Kupec was responsible for over $4 billion in fundraising during his tenure at UNC. His intangible influence may have been even greater, though. During a speech Holden Thorp had given shortly after being hired as chancellor in 2008, he noted that, "One night eight years ago, (then-Chancellor James Moeser) and Matt Kupec took me down to Fayetteville to speak at an alumni event." That would have been in 2000, shortly after Moeser had become chancellor and years before Thorp would rise to that eventual position. Indeed, Kupec's history at the university suggested that he was close to many of its intricate workings – athletics, academics, money, and administration.

* * *

A day after the initial news story that opened this chapter which detailed Matt Kupec's resignation from the university, Tami Hansbrough resigned her position as a fundraiser at the school. A new article in the Raleigh *News and Observer* included further details about apparently impermissible trips the couple had taken while being co-workers at the school. The paper confirmed that university officials were studying at least six trips related to collegiate basketball games, but those officials had not provided any further details at that time. "We are in the preliminary stages of our review," university lawyer Regina Stabile had said. Furthermore, the *N&O* had confirmed that Kupec and Hansbrough traveled together at least 25 times from May 2010 until the time of their resignations. Some of those trips appeared personal in nature, such as a two night stay on the North Carolina Outer Banks during the July Fourth weekend in 2010. Other trips coincided with NBA games for Tyler Hansbrough.

According to the September 11, 2012, article, the *News and Observer* sought to obtain a copy of the earlier Dental Foundation audit and related expense records that revealed some of the misuse of money. However, the foundation's director at the time, Paul Gardner, said those documents were not public record because the foundation was a nonprofit and not a public agency. That request was then forwarded to UNC's legal department, but four weeks after the original inquiry the information had still not been provided to the newspaper. The Dental

Foundation's insistence on closely guarding its records would again become important almost a year later. That situation will be covered in a later chapter.

* * *

In yet another unexpected turn of events in the multi-year saga of UNC's athletic/academic scandals, Chancellor Holden Thorp announced on September 17, 2012, that he would be resigning effective at the end of the 2012-13 academic year. Multiple news entities covered the story, and also covered some of the reactions from faculty members and also students at UNC. More details would also emerge in the coming days in terms of possible reasons behind the timing of Thorp's announcement.

In a September 18, 2012, *News and Observer* article, Thorp said, "I will always do what is best for this university. This wasn't an easy decision personally. But when I thought about the university and how important it's been to me, to North Carolinians and to hundreds of thousands of alumni, my answer became clear." He said that no one had asked him to resign, but that he thought stepping aside would be best for the university and his family. "As you know it's been a tough couple of years," he said in an interview. "I've been through a lot of things I didn't imagine I'd have to go through."

He was undoubtedly referring to what the newspaper called a constant stream of damaging revelations – improper benefits for football players, academic misconduct involving a tutor, and academic fraud in the African and Afro-American Studies department. The latter had recently been punctuated by the uncovering of a former star player's transcript, which strongly suggested the fraud stretched back more than a decade. Also part of the equation was the less than week-old resignation of

Matt Kupec along with the revelation of his personal relationship with the mother of former basketball All-American Tyler Hansbrough.

According to the article, Thorp had been forced to explain that most recent university embarrassment to the UNC Board of Governors in a closed-door session the previous Friday, which would have been September 14. Members of that governing board had previously publicly supported him. UNC President Tom Ross said Thorp notified him about his resignation decision on the following Sunday afternoon.

Other quotes and bits of information were contained in a coinciding article posted on September 18, 2012, by ESPN.com. Thorp stated in that article: "It's been stressful, so I'd be kidding you if I told you I hadn't thought from time to time about whether it would be better for the University and better for me. But this weekend was the first time I really thought about it and felt like it was the right time." He said his intent was to resign effective June 30, 2013. Wade Hargrove, chairman of UNC's Board of Trustees, said in a prepared statement that the board tried to talk Thorp out of his decision. "I respect his unwavering commitment to always do what he thinks best serves the University," Hargrove said.

A wral.com article posted the mixed reactions of various students and faculty members from the school. Some felt Thorp was taking the fall for problems he didn't cause. "A few people have just ruined it for the whole bunch," freshman Savanna Fitzgerald said. "I think it is ridiculous. I think it is shocking, not on his part but the fact that he has been pushed to this, and I think a lot of it has been the negative media." Sophomore Jhenielle Reynolds said that Thorp had "done his best to show people that we are a university of academic integrity." Some students, though, felt a new leader would help the school move past the scandals. "With a new person," junior Alexander Jackson said, "we could get back to our reputation, which would be great." Mohsin Shad echoed those thoughts: "It just makes sense to me because of all the scandals he was involved in. It was probably a well-thought-out process."

Jan Boxill, a philosophy professor and chairwoman of UNC's Faculty Council, said she and many of her colleagues were in tears Monday morning when they learned of Thorp's decision. "I think he's just been beaten down," she said. Dozens of faculty members reportedly emailed Boxill to see if there was anything they could do to persuade Thorp to continue as chancellor. That persuasion would ultimately not end up being successful. Coincidentally, however, Boxill's name would arise again in the scandal the following year, and in a much less flattering context. Those events will be covered in a later chapter.

* * *

Thorp was asked in that earlier ESPN.com article if he had any regrets about how he handled any of the well-publicized issues that arose over the previous two years. He said: "Obviously, if you look back on something, it's easy to say that you wish you would have made some decisions sooner, or you had gotten some information sooner and done something with it sooner. I think once you know how things turn out, it's easy to say that. But I feel good about what I did with all the different pieces of information that came up. And I think we have reforms in place, and this is going to be a better, strong University because of it."

The end of Thorp's tenure as chancellor was a far cry from

the vision he held when first hired for the position. During a Campus Celebration Speech from May 8, 2008, then-Chancellor-Elect Thorp had made numerous remarks about his past close association with the university, and his great future plans as leader of the school. Thorp had graduated from UNC, as had both of his parents, his brother, his sister-in-law, and a cousin. He mentioned that then-UNC President Erskine Bowles had recommended him to the Board of Governors. When Bowles eventually offered the job to Thorp, Bowles essentially told him it was "the most important job offer of your life."

Other details of note were that Thorp had initially returned to Chapel Hill in 1993 as a member of the classroom faculty. He stated that the reason he went into administration was because of James Moeser, the chancellor who had preceded him – and who he also served with on a Board of Governors alongside former Governor Jim Martin. "I simply can't put into words what James Moeser has done for me," Thorp said at the Campus Celebration. "And I know that all of you here today join me in deepest appreciation and admiration for what he has done for Carolina these past eight years." Those years (and their significance) were mentioned earlier, spanning from 2000 to 2008.

Thorp went on to mention other "wonderful mentors" he'd had while at UNC, with one of the names being none other than Matt Kupec. He recounted his immediately prior job as Dean of the College of Arts and Sciences – which oversaw Julius Nyang'oro and the AFAM department. Finally, he said that some of the duties of those newest administrative jobs he held would in part be to write speeches and correspondence instead of patents and scientific publications, as was the prior case when he was a faculty member of the school's Chemistry department. "And now," Thorp said in that 2008 speech, "only a year into my new life of letters, I land a job where the last three words of most speeches have already been chosen for me: 'Hark the sound.'"

Those three words were a reference to the alma mater of UNC. Thorp expanded upon the thought, asking "But what of this 'sound'? What will Carolina's sound be in the years to come?" After making references to the Bell Tower chimes and James Taylor, he asked, "Will it be the sweet sound of a basketball hitting the net? God, I sure hope so," voicing the well-known perception that basketball was the true king on the UNC campus.

Thorp would continue with words that would end up containing a lot of irony in the future, as they would ultimately be succeeded by the numerous scandals that would punctuate his time as chancellor: "But if we do our job well, when we make a sound, we will make the sound of knowledge: knowledge that comes from an unrelenting commitment to the highest levels of scholarship. Knowledge produced when our students participate fully in research and benefit from our scholarship in the classroom. Hark the sound of knowledge." Hopefully unbeknownst to Thorp at the time, the vast athletic/academic scandal that had been prevalent at the university for years would unfortunately make a mockery of that very knowledge-based ideal.

* * *

The day after Holden Thorp announced his eventual resignation as UNC's chancellor, details emerged via a September 18, 2012, article in the *News and Observer* that showed Thorp had flown multiple times on private planes with Matt Kupec and Tami Hansbrough. Records indicated that the trips took place after Thorp had stopped Kupec from directly hiring Hansbrough because the two were dating, which suggested Thorp should have been aware of the precarious situation.

Thorp indicated that he didn't question their travel at the time, even though Kupec rarely flew with many of the other fundraisers at UNC who had higher-ranking jobs and positions than Hansbrough. The flights Thorp took with the couple weren't the only red flag he missed in a controversy that led to their resignations the previous week, the article stated. Even though Thorp blocked Kupec from directly hiring Hansbrough, he said he was okay with the eventual arrangement: Hansbrough working as a fundraiser in the university's division of student affairs, a position that was funded by Kupec's office, and which was created via Kupec's urging.

* * *

According to the *N&O*, most of the flights taken by Kupec and Hansbrough together were on private planes operated by a university-affiliated entity called Medical Air Inc. As of 2012 it was based at Raleigh-Durham International Airport, but prior to 2011 the planes were based in Chapel Hill. The primary mission of Medical Air was to ferry university doctors to rural parts of North Carolina to treat residents who could not otherwise get high-quality medical care, and/or it was to train doctors in those areas. The article said the planes were available on a limited basis for other state uses, but that medical flights took priority over others.

Kupec and Hansbrough may have taken trips to over 20 cities over two years, and a review of Medical Air flight records indicated that Kupec traveled with Hansbrough more than anyone else. In one particular instance Kupec and Hansbrough were scheduled to return from Montana on a commercial flight, but Kupec's assistant sent an email to Medical Air officials to request a private plane for part of the return trip home. "Matt and Tami will be returning from a donor visit from Montana," the assistant wrote. "There are some issues going on in the office so need to be back on Sunday." Based on further documentation, a Medical Air plane went to Chicago and brought the two back to Chapel Hill.

University officials had not provided detailed records or other information about any of the flights and billings at the time of the article. They cited an ongoing internal audit that was trying to determine whether any flights were inappropriate. Kupec continued to decline comment to the newspaper, now more than a week after his resignation. Hansbrough could also still not be reached.

The Medical Air flight manifests acquired by the *News and Observer* showed that Chancellor Holden Thorp was aboard planes with Kupec and Hansbrough in April, June and December of 2011, and then again in March of 2012. All of those flights were either going to or coming from New York. On two of the flights, Thorp's wife, Patti, joined them as the only other passenger on board the plane. Thorp said in an interview with the newspaper that at the time, he had no reason to question the travel by Kupec with Hansbrough. "The trips we went on were university business," Thorp had said. However, he had acknowledged that questions did crop up, albeit two months after that last flight together – and those questions did not come from the chancellor himself. In May, during a regular personnel review of Kupec, a review committee raised questions about Kupec's relationship with Hansbrough and their travel, according to Thorp. "Matt had his five-year review this spring," Thorp told the newspaper, "and at the end of that, there were concerns raised about Matt's travel and about whether it was appropriate and whether it was sort of personally driven or professionally driven." Thorp said he asked Kupec about it at the time of the May review and Kupec told him the travel was for university business. Thorp said he did not take any other action at that time.

The *News and Observer* said it had begun seeking travel information related to Hansbrough in mid-August of 2012. As was often the case with the paper's requests, however, those too had been denied (or at least delayed) by the university. The newspaper eventually appealed directly to Thorp. The chancellor said he had asked a university lawyer "in recent weeks" to gather information about Kupec's travel. It was after looking at that data he concluded that a deeper review was needed, which lead to his confrontation with Kupec and the latter's resignation. As mentioned earlier, approximately a week after Kupec's resignation Thorp was questioned about the situation behind closed doors by the UNC System Board of Governors. The content of those discussions had not been publicly disclosed as of the time of the news article. Board of Governors Chairman Peter Hans said that while Thorp had done well on some measures, he "needs to be successful in clearing up some lingering issues on campus." Several days later Thorp had announced his resignation.

* * *

Approximately a week later, UNC issued a news release that said an internal audit of travel and other expenses for Kupec had found nearly $17,000 in questionable personal charges, though all of which had since been repaid. The brief release mentioned some of the university policies regarding unallowable charges for a variety of endeavors, such as air travel, lodging, meals, and so forth. The release concluded by saying that no additional audit work was necessary, indicating that it was now a closed matter for the university.

Kupec released a statement that apologized for his "lapse in judgment" that led to his personal monetary charges, and noted that "Tami Hansbrough was unaware that the charges had not been reimbursed to the University." Hansbrough herself released a statement which was far less humble and apologetic. She said she "did nothing wrong in any way in the use of University or Foundation monies," and that she "was forced by the administration of the University to resign. This happened over my protest and before any substantive investigation was conducted into my responsibility related to these allegations." She went on to say her reputation had been wrongly and irreparably damaged, and that she hoped there would be "an official apology to me and my family by this (present) University administration so that my reputation and future can begin to be repaired and we all can move forward." Hansbrough was represented by lawyer Joseph B. Cheshire V, the same lawyer who had represented Jennifer Wiley, the tutor at the heart of the impermissible academic benefits provided to the football team two years earlier. UNC spokeswoman Karen Moon said of Hansbrough's request for an apology: "The University does not intend to respond."

Wade Smith, a Raleigh lawyer who represented Kupec, was referenced in an October 24, 2012, *News and Observer* article saying that he was not aware of any criminal investigation but acknowledged it was a possibility. Orange County District Attorney Jim Woodall said university officials would trigger a review if the school notified authorities of the misuse of money, much like any other embezzlement or misappropriation case involving an employer. Woodall said that as of the time of the article's release, that had not happened. Roughly one month later in a November 20, 2012, article, Woodall reiterated that university officials should request outside investigation into the nearly $17,000 in personal spending with university monies by Kupec – a request that had obviously still not been made. That November article revealed even more questionable prior spending habits by Kupec and Hansbrough that did not appear university driven. Woodall said that he had not ruled out a criminal prosecution. However, Kupec's lawyer, Wade Smith, ominously implied that bringing such charges against his client "would be unwise."

* * *

With the various scandals at UNC now well over two (documented) years old, the list of individuals whose jobs had been directly affected by it continued to grow. John Blake resigned. Butch Davis was fired. Julius Nyang'oro was essentially forced to retire. Dick Baddour retired earlier than originally planned. Robert Mercer was reassigned to a new position. Matt Kupec resigned. Tami Hansbrough was forced to resign. Holden Thorp resigned.

There was one question dealing with this most recent episode that remained oddly unanswered – and even publicly unasked. Matt Kupec had worked for the university for 20 years, the past 16 of which were in the influential position of vice chancellor. He had traveled and worked closely with multiple past leaders of the university, rubbed elbows with administrators in the prestigious South Building, and above all had raised over $4 billion for the school. When confronted with the possible misuse of university funds – which would eventually only amount to around $17,000 – he immediately resigned. The unasked question was, "why?" No criminal charges had been brought against him; the university allowed him to repay the money. The amount was a small portion of his approximately $350,000 annual salary. Even more contrasting was the minuscule percentage it was compared to the total amount he had raised for the school. Yet he stepped away from a place where he had graduated, and a position he had held for 16 years – apparently without qualm or complaint.

One general stipulation of NCAA investigations is that they have no legal/criminal jurisdiction over entities (or people) not directly associated with member schools. They can question student athletes about possible infractions, but only while they still attend school. They can question coaches, but only while still employed. And they can presumably question administrators and fundraisers and have a fair amount of leverage to coerce cooperation, but only while they still hold those jobs. Once Matt Kupec (and two days later Tami Hansbrough) resigned from UNC, those two individuals effectively removed themselves from any possible future interviews with the NCAA. Just as Blake, Davis, Nyang'oro, and Baddour had managed, in one form or another.

* * *

The essential (and unanswered) questions:

-- Was basketball star Tyler Hansbrough's return to school (for his senior season) in any way connected to his mother being hired by the university, or vice versa?

-- Should Tami Hansbrough's personal trips with Matt Kupec

that used university funds be viewed as an impermissible benefit, since some of those trips occurred while her son was still attending the school and participating in athletics?

-- What role, if any, did Matt Kupec's fundraising efforts for the Sonja Haynes Stone Black Cultural Center have in his almost immediately-following rise to the position of Vice Chancellor for University Advancement?

-- What influential role, if any, did "volunteer leader" Dean Smith play in the promotion and support of the new Cultural Center?

-- Had they not been stonewalled and withheld by the university, what would the Dental Foundation records have shown regarding the impermissible use of university funds by Kupec, Hansbrough, or possibly others?

-- Was the timing of Holden Thorp's resignation announcement in large part dictated by facts he had been made aware of by the media – facts containing the information regarding trips he took with Kupec and Hansbrough on private planes?

-- Was there a veiled meaning when Wade Smith, Matt Kupec's lawyer, said that it "would be unwise" to criminally charge his client?

-- Why did Matt Kupec resign without any apparent argument or attempt to keep his job?

CHAPTER THIRTEEN

THE ACADEMIC SUPPORT PROGRAM FOR STUDENT ATHLETES; MORE ACADEMIC FRAUD; BASKETBALL AND NAVS 302

Several major events that happened during the late-summer months of 2012 – the Peppers transcript revelation, the announcement of the Martin Investigation, and the Kupec/Hansbrough story – had effectively taken the spotlight off of an earlier topic that was still in limbo: the phone records of former football coach Butch Davis. A coalition of media entities had sued for those records to be released, and after more than a year of being entangled in legal proceedings a judge had finally ordered their disclosure. Some in the media speculated that Davis was now more apt to release them due to the effects of the Peppers' discovery, which had essentially confirmed that the academic fraud started well earlier than 2007, the year that Davis took over the UNC football program full-time.

The phone records were released in late September of 2012, though the documents were still heavily redacted due to an agreement between the lawyers of Davis and the media. Sources stated that the media's lawyers were given a choice of either receiving the names of each caller, or the number for each caller. They chose the latter. Next, all calls that were agreed upon as being clearly-personal were redacted to protect those individuals' privacy; that "deciding" process was reportedly carried out together by both law teams, according to those same sources. The resulting document totaled 136 pages and spanned calls made from March 2009 to November 2010; only a portion were ultimately deemed 100% business related. Despite the fact that Davis was hired in late 2006 and not fired until mid-2011, the range of the phone records only coincided with the date range that was requested by the media over a year earlier. Whether going back any further in time (or forward to the summer of 2011) would have made any significant difference in the discovered results is unknown.

Five calls of note were those with tutor Jennifer Wiley, the young woman who had once worked in the academic support realm for the university, and then privately for Butch Davis' family. She had been named in the NCAA's sanctions as having provided impermissible academic assistance to players, as well as money and gifts. It would later be revealed that she also passed along cash payments to players from sports agents.

According to Jonathan Sasser, Davis' lawyer, the calls from Wiley to Davis were made after she had initially been asked to meet with school investigators. Based on a *News and Observer* article from September 21, 2012, Sasser said Wiley asked Davis what the meeting was about and whether she should bring her father. Davis referred her to a school official, and Davis believed that she would attend the meeting, according to Sasser. However, Wiley later declined to speak with school officials or with investigators from the NCAA, and would later also decline all interview requests. Joseph B. Cheshire V, Wiley's attorney (and also the attorney for Tami Hansbrough), wrote in an email to the newspaper: "She, her father and I made the decision not to talk about these matters. Coach Davis had nothing to do with that decision."

As documented in earlier chapters, Butch Davis had personally hired Wiley after receiving a recommendation from a UNC official, according to a copy of a March 2008 email provided to the AP by Davis' wife, Tammy. The September 21, 2012, newspaper article said that Tammy Davis defended Wiley as someone motivated by helping others. "I said it to… anybody who would listen," she said, "in my heart and in my soul, I don't believe that young lady would do anything intentionally to break rules." A year later, however, information released in the fall of 2013 would shed new light on Wiley's potential role regarding the intentional breaking of rules.

* * *

As the month of September 2012 drew to a close and the school was still dealing with the news of Matt Kupec and Tami Hansbrough's impermissible travels, as well as Chancellor Holden Thorp's announced resignation, yet another series of troubling stories related to the schoolwork of UNC athletes would arise. In a September 30, 2012, article released by investigative reporters Dan Kane and J. Andrew Curliss of the Raleigh *News and Observer*, details were revealed that pointed to more academic fraud which the school had not earlier identified in its various internal investigations. The specific course in question was held in the spring of 2010, but had not been properly identified in the university's spring 2012 review of the AFAM department.

According to the newspaper article, AFRI 370 was an upper-level course for seniors majoring in the AFAM department, and/or for other students with a background in the study of Africa. It was touted to have "lectures, readings, and research projects" on multiple complex issues. Not only were there no lectures or readings in the class, it also never met. Furthermore, several freshman football players had been enrolled in the class – a class which was supposedly of an advanced level, and for upperclassmen. The athletes simply had to turn in a 20-page paper, often produced with extensive help from tutors.

The majority of the newspaper's information was gleaned from records obtained from UNC's Academic Support Program for Student Athletes. The records showed that the athlete support program used the no-show classes to help keep student athletes eligible to play, according to the two investigative reporters. As noted above, the documents turned up informational oversights by the university's previous in-house review. AFRI 370 hadn't been revealed as a no-show class in the school's initial probe in the spring. That led to the question of how many other fraudulent courses may have been missed in that original 2007-2011 review.

* * *

The university had long said that the academic fraud was limited to department chairman Julius Nyang'oro and department manager Deborah Crowder, but the records obtained by the *N&O* also suggested that at least one other professor in the AFAM department was aware that no-show classes existed for athletes. Alphonse Mutima taught courses in the department, and at one point he was reportedly so discouraged by an athlete's inability to grasp the content that he wanted to put the player in an "independent study paper class." That was for a Swahili class, and the "paper class" version for intermediate Swahili, or SWAH 203, was suggested to have been set up to be an easy class. That was also the particular course that football player Michael McAdoo had taken where he had eventually been caught plagiarizing a paper. University records showed that there were at least four other no-show intermediate Swahili classes. Football players accounted for seven of the enrollments in those five no-show classes, while men's basketball players accounted for three.

Certain Swahili courses held definite advantages for athletes, it was revealed. SWAH 112 combined the first two Swahili language classes into one intensive six-credit-hour course, for example. Those who passed it and the intermediate-level Swahili class would have then fulfilled their language requirement at the university. Unlike Spanish and other language courses taught more broadly at the school, there was no additional language lab required for Swahili. Records showed Swahili and Portuguese as popular languages for both basketball and football players. As noted in a previous chapter, football player Deunta Williams said that all freshmen players take Swahili. Information revealed in those new documents certainly gave

possible insight into why that was the case. Basketball players
other than Hansbrough had mentioned Swahili in the past as
well. Reggie Bullock and John Henson both made references
to classes when posting messages on the social media site Twitter. There were also instances from further back. Rye Barcott,
the founder of a group called Carolina for Kiberia, graduated
from UNC in the early 2000's. He has been quoted in numerous news articles as saying: "I was fortunate enough to take
Swahili classes with the starting lineup of the men's basketball
team at UNC. That was quite an experience." It appeared as if
Swahili had been popular with major-sports athletes at UNC for
quite some time. Whether those courses were taught irregularly
or not remained unknown. Alphonse Mutima declined to comment for the newspaper article. He was a non-tenured professor
in 2012 despite being hired in 1999, and was making $37,000 a
year.

The obtained documents also suggested that the no-show
classes were common knowledge within the athlete support
program. "Professor Nyang'oro, Chair of the AFRI/AFAM
Studies department, has been very generous in granting several
students (not just student athletes) the opportunity to do independent study papers," Amy Kleissler, a learning specialist with
the athlete support program, wrote in a February 8, 2010, email
informing tutors of the AFRI 370 paper class. "Since we have
worked with him in the past in this same manner I wanted to
let you know that his expectations are very reasonable and very
achievable for our students." "Our students" was an obvious
reference to the university's major-sports athletes.

The *N&O* article recounted other email exchanges that provided insight into the questionable actions of the athlete support
program. When one tutor told the program's assistant director,

Beth Bridger, that she was discouraged with the work one player turned in, Bridger told the tutor not to worry. "Just remember," Bridger wrote in a March 16, 2010, email, "guys are in this class for a reason – at-risk, probation, struggling students – you are making headway… keep it positive and encouraging!" As detailed in Chapter Two, Bridger had been chosen in August of 2009 to replace Cynthia Reynolds. Reynolds claimed she was moved out of her position because head coach Butch Davis wanted a younger "face" for the academic support program for recruiting purposes.

Another tutor, Whitney Read, wrote an email that showed she was concerned about papers that were largely put together with passages lifted from source materials. Jaimie Lee, an academic counselor, told her that type of work was "to be expected," as many of the athletes had "not necessarily developed the skill of critical analysis." In other documents Read noted that some athletes were rude during tutoring sessions, and did not appear to care about their classwork. Read graduated in 2009 with a degree in African Studies. At the time of the article she was no longer a tutor for the university, and declined to be interviewed. Several other former or current tutors also passed up the opportunity to talk to the newspaper about the support program. Kleissler and Lee referred questions to Bridger and other higher-ups in the program. Bridger did not return phone calls.

In a brief interview with the newspaper two days prior to the article's release, Chancellor Holden Thorp also declined to talk about the records, citing the Family Educational Rights and Privacy Act (FERPA). He said he sent copies of the various documents to former Governor Jim Martin so that he could include the data in his ongoing investigation. Thorp did not explain to the newspaper why the records had not surfaced earlier, but he did say they were "of concern."

* * *

That September 30, 2012, article covered several other angles as well. It noted the challenges that faced the Academic Support Program for Student Athletes. In particular, the program was charged with working with a group of students who ordinarily wouldn't have been admitted to the school had they not been high profile athletes. In the previous five years, records showed that 53 football players had been admitted as academic "exceptions." However, as was the university's pattern over the several months since the AFAM fraud was first uncovered, it continued to try and shield its basketball program from further scrutiny. As a result, it had chosen to not provide data from its basketball players regarding its number of academic exceptions.

Athletes typically had much greater need for classes that did not meet, the *N&O* article also pointed out. That correlated with earlier quotes given by former UNC basketball star Sean May, which were covered in an earlier chapter. Also as noted in a preceding chapter, athletes were given priority registration in terms of scheduling their classes. However, evidence showed that some non-athletes who enrolled in the classes did so unwittingly and were surprised to find the courses only consisted of a paper assignment. The article highlighted one such student who commented about the Spring 2010 AFRI 370 no-show class on a course evaluation website known as Koofers. "I am taking the course by submitting a paper with Prof. Nyang'oro and it is a bit daunting," said the unidentified student in a comment posted in April 2010, long before the scandal was publicly uncovered. "I wish I was able to take the actual course with him."

Chancellor Thorp had previously said that students who were enrolled in those types of classes were cheated out of a Carolina education. Whether he was referring to just the non-athletes who somehow managed to get into the classes, however, was unclear.

As those newest allegations of wrongdoing within the AFAM department surfaced via the *News and Observer*, university officials also admitted another troubling discovery for the first time: former department chairman Julius Nyang'oro, who had assumed that top position in 1992, had never received a review from a supervisor during the 20 years that he held the job. That would lead many to question whether the athletic/academic fraud could have been going on much further back than just 1999, which had been the current assumption based on the Peppers transcript. In a timeline of events covered earlier, Nyang'oro took over as department chairman of the AFAM department in 1992, and then multiple players on UNC's basketball national title team of 1993 were later revealed to be majoring in AFAM.

* * *

Several days later the university's basketball program would once again be thrust into the middle of the ongoing academic scandal. In an October 2, 2012, article penned by Dan Kane and J. Andrew Curliss, enrollment records that had been requested by the *News and Observer* turned up some intriguing trends – and especially in one particular course. NAVS 302 was a Naval Weapons Systems class in UNC's Department of Naval Science, which according to school documents existed in order to produce "highly qualified" officers who serve on ships, aircraft, and submarines, or in the Marine Corps. In the spring of 2007, however, the newspaper reported that 30 of the 38 students who took NAVS 302 were athletes, and six of them were members of the men's basketball team.

Bobby Frasor, one of the basketball players who took the class, said he and his teammates were placed in it after the class instructor had discussed it with counselors in the Academic Support Program for Student Athletes. "He told our academic advisers," Frasor said, "but I had never heard of the class, and basically, our academic adviser recommended it and we enrolled in it." Former All-American Tyler Hansbrough was also in the class. Records showed that it was the only NAVS 302 class over the previous six years in which basketball players had enrolled. The academic adviser that had recommended the class was Wayne Walden, who was heavily discussed in an earlier chapter as being the probable lynchpin to the scheduling of classes for Roy Williams' basketball players – first at Kansas, and then at UNC.

Hansbrough had told *Sports Illustrated* in March of 2007 that he was taking the Naval Systems class because "I wanted classes about things I wouldn't necessarily be exposed to on my own." In that same piece he said that he was enrolled in Swahili as his foreign language because he thought "it would be cool." Not mentioned, however, was the fact that Wayne Walden was actually the suspected source behind the vast majority of UNC basketball players' class selections, as noted before. Data from the earlier AFAM fraudulent courses had shown two cases where the sole enrollee in a no-show class was a basketball player. Hansbrough declined to comment for the *N&O* article.

John Infante, who helped oversee NCAA compliance at Colorado State and Loyola Marymount, told the *N&O* in an interview that UNC's support program for athletes had to be aware of the scheduling of the weapons class. "That many kids in a course which is that rare for athletes to take, you can probably assume – or at least say – that academic support staff should have known," he said. "They should have noticed that." The key question from an NCAA viewpoint, Infante said, would be how lenient the professor was with athletes once they enrolled and whether there was special treatment.

The professor for the class in question was Lt. Brian Lubitz, and according to UNC records he taught it only that one time. He was also earning his MBA from the school's Kenan-Flagler Business School at the time. By October of 2012 when the article was released, Lubitz had left the school and was working in the private sector. Several attempts by the newspaper to reach Lubitz over the previous two months had been unsuccessful.

The syllabus for the NAVS 302 class showed that it was a different type of course than in other years, according to Curliss and Kane's article. It had no required exams or quizzes and no major research paper. Students received much of their grade from a short midterm paper and a group project. Lubitz spelled out in his syllabus that he reserved the right to have quizzes and tests, but the syllabus said, "At this time none are anticipated." The class's average grade that semester was a 3.63, or slightly better than a B-plus. That was apparently so misaligned from past NAVS 302 results that the work requirements for the course would eventually be changed.

The head of the Naval Science department at UNC at the time of the October 2012 article was Capt. Doug Wright. He said the course work requirements in that particular class had troubled his predecessor, Capt. Stephen Matts, so much so that Matts told instructors who took over after Lubitz that he wanted the requirements changed, as mentioned above. Indeed, later course outlines showed quizzes, tests, and papers or presentations. Capt. Matts, the head of the department when Lubitz taught the course, could not be reached by the reporters for comment.

Capt. Wright backed Matts' assessment. Wright said he would have made the same changes because the class (as set up under Lubitz, and as taught to the 30 athletes) would make it difficult to determine whether students were actually learning the material. "It would make it harder to... figure out how they are doing," Wright said. "Could it be done? Sure. Is it 'illegal?' No. But I wouldn't have done it and apparently my predecessor didn't approve of it either because they changed it." Since Wright took over the department, the weapons class average grade had dropped to roughly a C.

Chancellor Holden Thorp said in an interview that the class looked like an example of clustering, which was covered in an earlier chapter when referencing the chosen majors of several of UNC's basketball players. The article noted that universities often try to track clustering to make sure classes and majors had not become easy spots for athletes trying to keep their grades up to stay eligible for sports. However, the data strongly suggested clustering wasn't an area which UNC placed great importance upon in the past.

Thorp went on to tell the paper that he had since sent the information on the Naval class to former Governor Jim Martin to be included as part of his review. Efforts by the newspaper to reach other members of the 2006-07 basketball team were unsuccessful, and Bobby Frasor declined to say which of his teammates attended the class. Only one player on that year's team, Wes Miller, had a grade-point average of 3.0 or better for the year, according to an analysis the *News and Observer* did of Atlantic Coast Conference data.

In an editorial that appeared in the newspaper the following day, questions were again raised about the true intentions of certain aspects of UNC's athletic/academic infrastructure: "Once again, here is an example of an 'academic support program' being aimed at keeping the stars on the field – or on the court. That is not, or should not be, the purpose of a counseling program supposedly aimed at helping people achieve in the classroom on their own. And yes, once again, the question is raised: Why should athletes, already isolated enough thanks to their practice and game schedules, have their own adviser system? Finally, why would such a specialized course aimed at future Naval officers even be open to other students? One hopes Chancellor Holden Thorp, who is resigning to return to the faculty, could get to the bottom of that on his own, without waiting for reports from ongoing investigations related to the previously disclosed academic fraud."

* * *

Head basketball coach Roy Williams held a news conference on Thursday, October 11, 2012, to discuss the upcoming season. According to a corresponding article in the *News and Observer*, he was also faced with questions related to his past players taking the unusually easy Naval Weapons class. His overall message was that he saw no issue in six of his players having enrolled in a class that was filled mostly with athletes, and that had no quizzes or exams. "I would have loved to have taken something like that (on naval weapons)," Williams said, "and I don't think it's an aberration."

Regarding his opinion that the lack of exams and quizzes were a non-issue, he offered that when he was a student at UNC he took a guidance counseling class in which the grade was based on "participation in class and role play," and that they didn't have any tests, either. "I don't know what (Lubitz's) deal was," Williams said. "If he felt like he was teaching something and they were learning what he wanted, then he must have felt good about doing it that way, just like me." Williams also said he did not have a problem with academic counselors responsible for helping athletes get their class work done also recommending classes for them to take. He did not, however, mention Wayne Walden's potential role in that process.

The article also stated that Williams offered little new information regarding the many known no-show classes. Instead, he repeated earlier statements that acknowledged that mistakes were made, but he had all along avoided giving many specifics about basketball players' involvement in those courses. This, despite data that showed some of the classes contained only basketball players. "I've said thousands of time – no that's an exaggeration – but several times that, you know, the investigation has brought up some things that we're not proud of, that we're not happy about," Williams said at the press conference. "But I think it is a very small problem that we've got to take care of, and I think we are doing it. But to answer your question, I'm sort of tired of answering those questions."

* * *

Three days after news surfaced of the basketball players' enrollment in the Naval Weapons class, the *News and Observ-*

er published an article that showed that multiple experts felt it was past time for the NCAA to return to UNC. Mark Jones, a former director of the NCAA's infractions section, acknowledged in an interview that academic concerns covered a wide spectrum, and that definitions of what might trigger sanctions were not always clear-cut. However, many of the events that had taken place at UNC seemed to plainly call for a closer look. "One of the things the NCAA wants to make absolutely clear is that whenever you have a staff member at a school who is doing anything to substitute their work for a student athlete's work," Jones said, "or is doing something improper to change a grade or arrange a fraudulent credit, then that's a violation." Those were some of the exact occurrences that had happened within the fraudulent AFAM courses identified earlier in 2012, where grade changes were made without authorization and through forgery. Furthermore, documents that had recently been released from the school's Academic Support Program for Student Athletes indicated that tutors and academic advisors likely provided an impermissible level of paper-writing for athletes spanning a number of years.

Other experts weighed in on the issue, as well. Gerald Gurney was a professor at the University of Oklahoma, and had also previously been the 2010-11 President of the National Association of Academic Advisers for Athletics. He said that what had happened at UNC with African Studies and other courses was "a classic pattern of an endemic problem in academic support. This has all of the ingredients of a major academic violation because it is so systematic over a long period of time. I feel certain that the NCAA is planning on inviting themselves back. They simply can't let this go."

The article noted that NCAA President Mark Emmert had

told CBSSports.com in a radio interview earlier that week that his organization was closely monitoring the unfolding situation in Chapel Hill. A UNC spokesman said that the university had been in contact with the NCAA and that there was "ongoing communication." That was a slight shift from five weeks earlier, when the school had said that the fraudulent African Studies classes were not subject to NCAA sanctions simply because they had included non-athletes as well as athletes – an announcement that had drawn national criticism of the NCAA.

Allen Sack, who was a professor of sports management at the University of New Haven and was the head of the Drake Group, said that there had always been "easy" classes at universities. But he told the *N&O* that the various recently-released documents showed something different that fans might not fully understand: Athletes were not supposed to get the kind of extra help from the athletics support program that was shown in the documents. "This is a major scandal because it raises serious questions about athletic counseling as a cottage industry," Sack said. "I certainly suspected this stuff was going on (around the country), but the documents (the paper is) disclosing are convincing me that the NCAA should come into UNC and that the time for a congressional hearing of the NCAA itself has arrived."

David Ridpath was a professor at Ohio University at the time of the article, and had formerly worked in athletics compliance at Marshall University when it faced NCAA sanctions. He reviewed a draft of a research paper that a UNC athlete had worked on with a tutor. Ridpath said the player's paper was "about 90 percent plagiarized" and that the athlete was getting improper help. He said what had been happening at UNC certainly "meets the NCAA's academic fraud bylaws." Chancellor

Holden Thorp simply said the latest document disclosures were all under review, and acknowledged that they were a "concern" for the university.

* * *

An article by Rachel George of *USA Today* Sports appeared on October 10, 2012, and gave more fuel to the "NCAA should return" fire. At one point it referenced the Naval class data that had been revealed by the *News and Observer*, and said the new information in conjunction with the eventual findings of the Martin Investigation could prompt another visit from the Association. Jo Potuto, then Nebraska's faculty athletics representative to the NCAA and previously a member of the Committee on Infractions for nine years, confirmed to *USA Today* that it was her experienced opinion that the Association's enforcement staff could revisit the school as more details emerged. Speaking generally and without particular knowledge of the UNC case beyond media reports, she said, "You're typically more likely to go back and revisit the more serious the charges are. That being said, academic integrity issues are pretty large violations."

Very few UNC faculty members other than history professor Jay Smith had spoken out during the scandal, but Lewis Margolis, an associate professor in the school of public health, talked to *USA Today*. He expressed his frustration that public records requests and reporting had forced the university's hand. "If UNC were more transparent, those stories would not be there," said Margolis, likely referring to the myriad of angles the Raleigh *News and Observer* had been covering for the past several years. "(The reporters are) doing their job. We, the university, should be doing its job." A coalition of local North Carolina media outlets had filed a lawsuit against UNC in 2010 seeking records related to the NCAA investigation. Citing federal privacy laws, university officials resisted the release of many, wrote Rachel George. A judge, however, had recently ordered the release of several of the records sought by the group, which had resulted in the recent series of new stories.

Still up for debate was whether the wide-ranging problems were limited to the actions of only a few employees who didn't follow procedures, or whether they were a byproduct of a systemic issue, the article stated. Many within the school's administration, athletics department, and faculty held fast to the mantra that the issues were caused by a very small number of people on campus. And as was usually the case, any talking points from the university made sure to deflect attention away from the school's basketball program, as well as to try and downsize the scope of the academic fraud in general. New Athletics Director Bubba Cunningham said in the article, "The major infractions were in football. And then I think in that discovery process, we saw we had a little bit of a lack of oversight in a certain department. But I do think that the issues are very, very isolated."

The public-relations talking points seemed to be working, however, as many in the general public who were not aware of the exact details of the scandal appeared to believe whatever quotes they read. William Brader, a freshman UNC student, said: "It seems kind of unfair because there are a lot of other universities doing it and we got caught." Professor Jay Smith, however, remained a strong – albeit virtually lone – voice of reason: "What has been most troublesome to me about this entire scandal, if we're going to call it that, over the last two years, is that it has called into question our institutional decision-making and our priorities."

* * *

The UNC System Board of Governors had assigned a five-member academic review panel to look into the latest troubling reports out of Chapel Hill. According to a sidebar article that appeared on October 11, 2012, in the Raleigh *News and Observer*, Chairman Louis Bissette of Asheville said it was clear that more needed to be done to get to the bottom of the problems at the school. University staffers and faculty members met with the panel on that date. One person in particular who was questioned by the panel was the dean who was in charge of the Academic Support Program for Student Athletes, Harold Woodard. His program had come under heavy scrutiny due to its role in helping athletes. At one point, according to the *N&O* article, Dean Woodard told the panel that tutors had in the past provided athletes with what he called "overhelp." Woodard, as recounted earlier, was a former lecturer in the African curriculum at UNC, played a major role in securing a new Black Cultural Center for the school (which had ties to Julius Nyang'oro), and was formerly the boss of Robert Mercer, who had overseen the athlete support program for the vast majority of the years when the academic fraud had occurred. Woodard said in an interview that his office had not provided any records to any outside reviewers to date, but that they had them. Louis Bissette, the chair of the special Board of Governors panel, said that any competent review of the school's scandal would have to include scrutiny of the tutor documents.

* * *

On October 16, 2012, former Governor Jim Martin stopped by the *News and Observer*'s office to provide an update on the status of the investigation, according to an article published by tarheelblog.com. Amongst the various points disclosed by Martin were that the original goal was to have the investigation finished by October 11th, but that the new target date was the end of the month – and it could quite possibly take even longer. Martin indicated that according to data the AFAM classes were not the easiest at UNC, but rather other departments had higher grades on average. He did not divulge which departments those higher grades belonged to. Earlier articles from other news entities had pointed out that while a decent percentage of UNC basketball players had majored in AFAM, it was not the top choice – that distinction belonged to Communications.

Another vitally important disclosure was that neither Julius Nyang'oro nor Deborah Crowder had spoken to members of Martin's team, and Martin said he did not expect the pair to, either. Again, he did not expand on the point at all. That lack of explanation would end up being the most important aspect of the topic. It was well known from earlier university reports that Nyang'oro and Crowder were heavily suspected of playing a vital role in much of the academic fraud. It would be a logical assumption that once a person with unlimited investigative lee-way and privileges (such as Martin supposedly had) concluded that those two key individuals would not talk, he would have used ancillary methods to gather information. Namely, the emails and/or phone records of Nyang'oro and Crowder. History would ultimately show, however, that Martin and his team did little to none of that. It would be yet another strong sugges-tion that the university apparently secured a figurehead to do a façade of an investigation, as opposed to hiring a true investiga-tor to get to the bottom of the fraudulent athletic issues.

Next, Martin said, "I haven't found anyone that knew that the courses were phony." The obvious yet unspoken response was, who would have actually admitted that fact? If students who took the classes did, then they could risk losing credit for a course. If faculty members did, they could risk losing salary and/or their jobs. And if people associated with athletics and who made sure players were in those no-show classes admitted it, then victories could be vacated. But again, that line of reasoning had apparently not been pursued by the former governor or his team. Martin was, however, asked by the *N&O* whether the AFAM classes were a "scheme to keep athletes eligible." His response was that tutors simply worked to help athletes into courses they could handle.

Martin's brief update to the newspaper left more questions unanswered than solved. Based on the lack of answers (and investigating) into issues that appeared to be obvious problems to the casual observer, the public's faith in Martin and his team getting to the true root of the scandal was beginning to fade. Whether that was due to a lack of investigative skills, a lack of desire, or both, was a matter of debate.

* * *

The month of October would draw to a close with yet another embarrassing anecdote of plagiarism from UNC athletes. An October 21, 2012, article in the *News and Observer* revealed that Erik Highsmith, a then-current football wide receiver, had written two blog posts for a class that were copied almost exactly from a passage on an education website written by four 11-year olds. Furthermore, information surfaced that the instructor of the course had reported the infraction, but there was little evidence that any concrete action had been taken against the athlete.

J. Nikol Beckham, the instructor of the spring 2011 course

in question, told the *N&O* that she had spotted the plagiarism and reported it to the academic support program for student athletes. Since it was in the midst of other examples of tutors providing improper help to athletes that an NCAA investigation had turned up, she was concerned the plagiarism went beyond Highsmith and her class. "I suggested that they consider that this isn't an isolated incident," she said, "and I expressed my disappointment considering everything that had been going on for the last year. And I received a great deal of assurances that it would be handled."

Someone at the support program told Beckham that they would talk to the student, "but after that, I never heard anything," she said. She was no longer teaching at the university as of the date of the article, having moved to work at a school in central Virginia. Highsmith declined to be interviewed, according to Steve Kirschner, an associate athletics director for communications at UNC. Other academic officials did not respond to numerous requests for comment by the *N&O*. As was the status quo for the past several years of the scandal, UNC officials declined by citing the Family Educational Right to Privacy Act (FERPA).

One thing Kirschner did do, however, was dispute that the plagiarism found to date suggested a systemic problem. "Faculty, advisors, counselors, coaches and staff interact with our student athletes daily and often remind them of the responsibility they have to do the right thing in all aspects of their lives – academically, athletically and socially," Kirschner said in a written response. "And we believe our student athletes meet those responsibilities the overwhelming amount of time."

It was unclear what grade Highsmith received in that

COMM 350 course, the *N&O* reported. He was not the only athlete to plagiarize in the class, however. The blog entries showed Donte Paige-Moss, a defensive end who left the team after his junior season, copied a comment from the Collegiate Times website and posted it as a comment for the blog. No apparent action was taken against Highsmith upon the public revelation of the plagiarism. That October 21 article also told of a 19-page draft of a paper in an African Studies no-show class that was turned in to a tutor by a different football player. It consisted of little more than a string of copied passages, and was discovered when the newspaper obtained records from within the Academic Support Program. That particular player had also declined to be interviewed, and had not been suspended from any games since the draft paper became public.

* * *

When an internal investigation of the many AFAM no-show classes was released back in May, the authors had stated that "no instance was found of students receiving a grade who had not submitted written work," the *News and Observer* pointed out on October 21, 2012. What was noticeably missing from that report, however, was whether the students' submitted work had been tested for plagiarism. The university also later acknowledged that the reviewers did not see every paper turned in because of a one-year retention policy of student assignments that the university held itself to. Like aspects of the Martin Investigation, they seemingly ignored the digital element and its implications. If students had emailed papers as attachments (as was the case with many classes in the current century), then those digital copies would still exist on the university's vast computer servers.

To reiterate the above confounding technical limitation, the newspaper said that none of the investigations that were underway at the time appeared to have a goal of determining how often athletes were committing plagiarism. Former Governor Jim Martin said earlier in the week that he and Baker Tilly, the national accounting firm hired for the probe, simply did not have the time to take on a task like that.

* * *

Jay Smith, the UNC history professor who had been one of the few faculty members to be outspoken about the scandal's impact on the university's academic integrity, told the *News and Observer* that the Academic Support Program needed a thorough review, regardless of what Martin found. "It's painfully obvious to anybody who had been paying attention for the last couple of years that plagiarism seems to be widely accepted among at least a certain subsection of athletes, and, it would seem, within a certain number of counselors and tutors," Smith said. "And that is a problem. That is a huge problem." After over two years of scandal, Smith would finally get vocal support from another faculty member in the near future that actually contained substance. That will be detailed in the next chapter.

* * *

The essential (and unanswered) questions:

-- Would Butch Davis' phone records have shown other anomalies and their timeframe included his full tenure at the school?

-- How had the university managed to overlook the no-show AFRI 370 class in its earlier internal review, and how many other courses were similarly missed?

-- Historical evidence showed that not only did Swahili have multiple fraudulent courses in its curriculum, but also the strong tendency of basketball and football players to take it in order to fulfill their Foreign Language requirement. Considering that evidence, why wasn't a closer look taken in order to determine if Swahili was an aberrant curriculum that existed at least in part for the benefit of UNC's athletes?

-- Why would virtually every current and former tutor within the Academic Support Program for Student Athletes (that was contacted by the press) decline to publicly comment on his/her past interactions with athletes?

-- Despite "clustering" being a major red flag to most universities with regards to their major-sports athletes, why hadn't UNC shown concern when six of its men's basketball players all enrolled in a Naval Weapons class that had apparently never been taken by any members of the basketball program in the past?

-- Did the fact that an instructor was getting his MBA degree from UNC have any bearing on his teaching an overly lax course at the same time, which also happened to contain nearly 80% athletes and almost half of the school's basketball team?

-- Despite quotes from numerous experts on NCAA matters that said the Association should return and reopen its investigation of UNC, why did that not happen after the most recent athletic/academic discoveries?

-- Why were the emails and phone records of Julius Nyang'oro and Deborah Crowder never meticulously examined by former Governor Jim Martin and his team?

-- Despite those early, clear signs that Martin may have lacked the investigative skills to adequately determine the true depth of the fraudulent issues at UNC, why didn't the school, its Board of Trustees, or the System's Board of Governors step in to correct the mistake of whom UNC had chosen to lead the review?

-- Why was no eligibility action ever taken against Erik Highsmith even though there was a documented case of him committing plagiarism?

-- Despite multiple past examples of UNC athletes plagiarizing their school work, why didn't any of the various ongoing investigations feel a need to gather more data on that important issue?

CHAPTER FOURTEEN

MARY WILLINGHAM; AFAM INDEPENDENT STUDIES; THE FACULTY COMMITTEE ON ATHLETICS

The previous chapter ended with UNC history professor Jay Smith once again speaking out against some of the reported actions of the university, and the apparent lack of concern school officials displayed towards the indiscretions that continued to damage its reputation. As had been the case for almost the entire multi-year scandal, Smith was virtually the only UNC staff member who had been vocal about his displeasure regarding the events that had transpired. Considering the university had an academic staff numbering well over 3,000, and that a large part of the school's mantra was that it did things "the Carolina way," the fact that he stood alone was rather astounding. Why had so many others remained quiet? Was it because they possibly feared for their jobs should they speak out against the university and its athletics program? Did they perhaps not care about the school's (and their own) academic reputation? Or did some of them actually value the national title banners that hung from the rafters of the Dean Smith Center as much as the casual, everyday fans of the school did? As 2012 drew near an end, though, a separate voice of displeasure finally stepped forward to join Smith and admonish the past academic indiscretions.

* * *

Mary Willingham was a reading specialist at UNC. She graduated from Loyola University in 1994 with a BS in Psychology, and then completed the LD Certification Program at UNC in 2003. She began working at the school in October of that same year as a tutor in the Academic Center for Student Athletes. In January of 2010 she transferred to the school's College of Arts & Sciences and became an Assistant Director for the Center for Student Success and Academic Counseling. According to the university's website, the Center was "dedicated to promoting academic excellence to assist students in achieving their academic goals while enrolled at Carolina."

Willingham came forward with an exclusive media interview by way of a November 17, 2012, article in the Raleigh *News and Observer*. Being the first person from inside the academic support program to go public with details about its operation, Willingham told the newspaper that many past UNC athletes had stayed eligible to play sports because the academic support system had provided improper help and tolerated plagiarism. Even worse, when she raised questions or made objections to the cheating she saw, she said that no one at the university took her concerns seriously – much like teacher J. Nikol Beckham and the Erik Highsmith case from the previous chapter.

In the article that was a front-page feature, Willingham said she lodged complaints at least two years before UNC's academic problems erupted into a full blown scandal. She would eventually focus some of her thoughts on the matter into a thesis for her master's degree, which was based on the corrupting influence of big-money sports on university academics. Willingham kept her complaints in-house for a while, but a recent event had been the last straw for her. After attending the funeral of former UNC System President Bill Friday, a huge supporter of Carolina yet also a prominent critic of revenue-driven college sports, Willingham saw that no one within the university was willing to admit that they had been aware of an athletic/academic problem. It was then that she decided to go public via a series of interviews with the *News and Observer*.

Willingham clearly stated that there were numerous people in the academic support program who knew that what was going on was wrong, but they looked the other way, helping to protect one of the nation's most successful (and previously respected) athletic programs. She said that no-show classes had been offered by the chairman of the AFAM department at least as far back as 2003, when she had begun working for the support program. Despite being billed as lecture classes, they were commonly known within the program as "paper classes." However, those classes never met. Willingham learned of the irregular courses when she had been asked to work with an athlete on a paper. She said it was a "cut-and-paste" job, but when she raised questions about it, staff members told her not to worry.

The student later received a grade of B or better. Ever since the uncovering of Julius Peppers' transcript there had been strong suspicions that the problems within the AFAM department had spanned further back than 2007. Through Willingham, confirmation of that hypothesis from someone with direct university knowledge was finally provided.

Willingham also stated that members of the men's basketball team took no-show classes until the fall semester of 2009, at which time the team had been assigned a new academic counselor. It was discussed in a previous chapter that Wayne Walden, the long-time academic advisor for basketball coach Roy Williams at both Kansas and UNC, had left the program in mid-2009. Willingham said the new counselor was "appalled" to learn of the fraudulent classes, and wanted no part of them. Willingham declined to name the new counselor, but university records showed that Jennifer Townsend was hired as an associate director in August 2009 and took over the role that Walden had vacated for the men's basketball program. According to the newspaper article, the new counselor (Townsend) told Willingham that she would not enroll the players in the no-show classes, stating, "I didn't come here... to do this. Everything has to be on the up and up."

Townsend's past work history had indirect connections with prior NCAA violations, so it was likely that she knew fraudulent classes and actions when she saw them. Her profile on UNC's website showed she was formerly the academic counselor for men's and women's basketball at the University of Minnesota. She worked there after the school went through one of the most notable scandals in college basketball history, the *N&O* said. In 1999, the St. Paul Pioneer Press uncovered a cheating scandal involving a former university office manager who had written papers, filled out take-home exams and done other course work for 20 basketball players over a five-year period. The NCAA responded with numerous sanctions for the school, and perhaps more importantly erased a 1997 Final Four appearance from the record books. In comparison, the events at Minnesota at the very least appeared to be on par with some of what had happened at UNC. At the worst, the events at Minnesota paled in scope with UNC's infractions, as the events at Minnesota covered a shorter stretch of time and dealt with far less affected athletes. However, the NCAA had still not revisited UNC to reopen an investigation – one which could potentially cause the erasure of not only Final Four appearances from the record books, but also multiple National Championships won by the school's basketball team. Jennifer Townsend, the former Minnesota employee and then-current academic advisor for Roy Williams' program, did not return messages left by the newspaper.

* * *

Willingham made other assertions in her interviews with the *News and Observer*. She stated that some of the athletes she had worked with told her they had never read a book or written a paragraph, but were placed in no-show classes where the only required assignment was a 20-page paper – and yet they came away with grades of B or better. Willingham did say that most of the athletes in the nonrevenue sports were capable of doing college-level work. However, the lowered academic standards for football players and men's basketball players – known as "special admits" – brought in athletes who lacked the academic ability, while still being expected to devote multiple hours a week to their sports. She said that was a dynamic destined to produce cheating. The special admissions for football and basketball players went back at least as far as the early 1990's, according to the article. An earlier chapter noted that UNC had refused to release data on the number of special admits its basketball program had allowed. "There are serious literacy deficits and they cannot do the course work here," Willingham said. "And if you cannot do the course work here, how do you stay eligible? You stay eligible by some department, some professor, somebody who gives you a break. Here it happened with paper classes. There's no question."

Other information she told the *N&O* was that roughly five years ago, Bobbi Owen, the senior associate dean who had oversight of the Academic Support Program, tried to get control over the number of independent study classes offered by the AFAM department. At the time they had averaged nearly 200 such classes a year. Independent studies required no class time and often not much more than a term paper. Past data showed that they were immensely popular with basketball and football players. The transcript of Julius Peppers, for example, showed that he had taken four such courses, and former star basketball player Sean May had also mentioned taking courses where he didn't actually have to be in attendance.

* * *

According to the November *News and Observer* article, in October of 2012 Mary Willingham had started a blog called "Athletics vs. Academics, a Clash of Cultures." Former Governor Jim Martin and a representative of the accounting firm Baker Tilley interviewed her a few days later. Martin declined to talk about what she said, but he was no longer standing by what he had stated prior to her interview: that no one in the program had seen a problem with the no-show classes. Instead, his new stance was that he couldn't comment.

When questioned about Willingham's assertions, Chancellor Holden Thorp declined to discuss them. He said, "I'm not going to talk to you about this stuff because we've got this thing going on with Governor Martin, and that's where our focus is right now, and these are the kinds of matters we're working on. That's all I've got to say about it right now." Calls and emails from the newspaper to other university officials, former and current Academic Support Program staff and others to address Willingham's claims were either not returned, drew no comment, or no response.

As pointed out earlier, Steve Kirschner, an athletics department spokesman, had said in prior email messages that the last basketball player to major in African and Afro-American Studies graduated in 2009. He said interest had declined in the department's majors after 2005, and chalked it up to "different players have different interests." However, what he failed to mention was that 2009 was also the year that men's basketball academic advisor Wayne Walden also left the program. And as Willingham asserted, that was the year that the new counselor (Jennifer Townsend) refused to take part in the AFAM no-show classes that had long littered the schedules of UNC's basketball players. UNC officials continued to claim that coincidence was the root of many of their athletic/academic problems, but the data and details continued to strongly suggest otherwise.

* * *

After her early negative experience with an athlete's paper, Willingham told the *News and Observer* that she avoided papers from the African Studies department by spending most of her time working with athletes in the nonrevenue sports. The issue of plagiarism arose again, however, when she was asked to look at a history paper for a football player. She said it, too, did not look like the student had written it. Willingham believed the athlete's tutor had done the work, and she told the program director about the issue. The program director was Robert Mercer, and the tutor was Jennifer Wiley. Mercer would eventually refer Willingham to another academic counselor, who denied a problem and took no action, Willingham said.

After that frustrating episode of non-action, Willingham told the newspaper that she began seeking jobs outside of the academic support program. It was in early 2010 that she began working for another learning center at UNC that served non-athletes. Two years later, the NCAA would find that Wiley had written parts of papers for three football players. One of those athletes, Willingham said, was the same player she had previously reported. Jennifer Wiley had long refused to comment on any news articles, and Robert Mercer – who had been moved out of the academic support program earlier in the year – could not be reached for comment, either.

Willingham said she met with UNC attorneys at their request in mid-2010. That was during the NCAA investigation, and the meeting was to discuss what had happened in 2008. Afterwards she said they thanked her for coming, but never talked to her again. Furthermore, Willingham said she never heard from the NCAA at all during the entire time the Association was on campus looking into the athletic/academic scandal. It was unknown whether the NCAA had even been made aware of Willingham and her claims. Since that knowledge would likely have been relayed to the NCAA via university officials, there was significant doubt of it conveyance.

The bombshell November 17, 2012, *N&O* article closed by saying that for the most part Willingham did not blame the athletes. She conceded that some were uncooperative and troublesome, but many wanted to succeed on the field and in the classroom. "It's not right," she said. "It's the adults who are not doing what they are supposed to do."

* * *

An article appeared in *USA Today* a few days later on November 20, 2012. It covered some of the fallout from Willingham's claims about the depth of UNC's past knowledge regarding its own athletic/academic indiscretions. The article noted that all of the recent revelations had yet to spark a new probe from the NCAA, but that one state senator would like to see an actual criminal investigation, as well. Republican State Senator Thom Goolsby had recently written on his blog, Carolina Columns, that UNC's continued academic integrity issues merited a tougher approach than had been taken up to that point. "The reputation of the state's flagship university is at stake and someone must take this matter seriously," Goolsby wrote. "Any prosecutor worth his salt would turn detectives loose on staff and administrators involved in the fraud and subsequent cover-up. If necessary, the General Assembly could consider legislation to make prosecuting this type of academic fraud easier."

Goolsby, who had received his law degree from the very school he was admonishing, continued with his blunt comments. "The UNC academic fraud scandal is like a pesky staph infection that just won't go away for university officials – nor should it. As reporters at the Raleigh *News and Observer* continue to dig, they uncover more and more dirty little secrets. The latest problems swirl around a pus pocket called the Academic Support Program."

He would end his diatribe by stating what many in the public had long wondered: why had several of the applicable governing bodies not stepped forward and demanded the truth? "The UNC Board of Governors should seriously consider asking for the resignations of current UNC Trustees who failed to safeguard academic integrity," wrote Goolsby. "They have shown little willingness to get to the truth of this scandal and cure the infection. When UNC comes to the General Assembly for more funding, university officials should expect that legislators charged with representing the taxpayers will demand answers."

* * *

What initially seemed to be a minor article appeared in the *News and Observer* on December 1, 2012, regarding the resignation of UNC's Associate Athletics Director for Compliance, Amy Herman. According to school officials, her move was not related to the ongoing problems within the athletics department. Instead, Athletics Director Bubba Cunningham and athletics department spokesman Steve Kirschner both said Herman was resigning for personal reasons. Despite those claims, there were past connections between Herman and the ongoing issues plaguing the athletics department.

The *N&O* article said that Cunningham had reorganized the compliance department in August of 2012. It was then that he had hired Vince Ille to lead it. Ille was covered in an earlier chapter, and his connections with current NCAA officials were detailed at that time. Since that August reorganization Herman had reported to Ille.

Herman's tenure coincided with the initial NCAA investigation that had found impermissible benefits involving agents and academic fraud within the UNC football program. In a September 2011 deposition, Herman said that she had been inexplicably advised by school officials to avoid creating documents that would have been subject to North Carolina's open records law, meaning that they could later be legally requested by the media.

* * *

Following Mary Willingham's mid-November assertions that academic staffers at the school had known all along about the fraudulent courses, more information would eventually surface to back up those claims. A December 8, 2012, article in the *News and Observer* reported that various documents and interviews suggested some faculty and athletic officials were aware of higher-than-expected Independent Study enrollments by athletes in the African Studies department. The dates of the knowledge were as early as mid-2006, but the voiced concerns apparently never reached top academic officials at the school.

The article stated that from 2001 through 2006, independent study courses offered by the Department of African and Afro-American Studies showed up with regularity on the schedules of men's basketball players. In one year alone, in fact, basketball players accounted for 15 enrollments. That particular year was when the team won the 2005 NCAA Championship. Two years later, athletes from the basketball program all but disappeared from those independent study classes – classes which did not meet and typically only required a paper for credit.

A university athletics department spokesman attributed the decline in enrollments to a waning interest in African Studies among basketball players, wrote the *N&O*. Evidence had recently emerged that suggested there may have been other reasons, however. Those documents of evidence showed that officials within the department and within the Academic Support Program for athletes started having concerns about independent studies in 2006, which coincided with a lengthy story in the New York Times about an independent study scandal involving athletes at Auburn University.

The *News and Observer* article indicated that Robert Mercer, the former director of the Academic Support Program, and John Blanchard, a senior associate athletics director who oversaw academics, said they saw higher-than-expected independent study enrollments from athletes in the African Studies department. UNC records showed more than 1,400 enrollments of athletes and regular students in that department from fall 2001 to summer 2006, with some professors listed as teaching dozens of students at a time. Blanchard and Mercer reported the enrollments to Dick Baddour, the athletics director at the time. They said they and Baddour then took the information to the Faculty Committee on Athletics, but the committee told them there was nothing to be concerned about. That appeared to be where the momentum stopped for a deeper look into the enrollments and the African Studies department, the article said. It is important to note that there would later be significant concerns raised regarding the accuracy of those recollections. Namely whether those athletic officials truly raised "red flags" to the Faculty Committee on Athletics.

Members of that Faculty Committee on Athletics, which had oversight of athletic matters on campus, told reporter Dan Kane that they did not recall such a warning. Committee minutes from 2006 reflected some discussion about independent studies and included a reference to the New York Times report, which was published on July 14, 2006. In that Auburn University case, many athletes had used the independent studies courses to boost their grade point average.

Regarding that 2006 meeting of UNC's Faculty Committee on Athletics from November, "The committee has conducted a review of student athletes' registrations in independent study courses and has an interest in receiving current information in this regard," the minutes said. Two months later, the committee inexplicably reported: "No sense exists of a current problem." Robert Mercer was then tasked with tracking independent studies, the discussion apparently never went beyond the faculty athletics committee, and the African Studies department was not looked at any further.

The Faculty Committee on Athletics appeared to be comprised of eleven members in 2006, and several athletics department personnel also attended many of its meetings. There were several interesting ties between some of the committee members and UNC's basketball program. Barbara Wildemuth was a professor and associate dean for academic affairs at the School of Information and Library Science. She was also the academic advisor and a former teacher of Byron Sanders. Sanders was a member of the 2005 National Championship team. Committee member Rachel Willis was an American Studies professor, and on a university webpage she was pictured posing with star basketball player Shammond Williams in 2003. English professor George Lensing was featured in an article from the university's General Alumni Association website. It said, "Former UNC men's basketball coach Dean Smith asked Lensing to talk with his players each year during a break in practice." Whether those various past connections contributed to the quick absolving of any problems within the basketball program is unknown.

* * *

The December 8, 2012, article in the *News and Observer* went on to say that the university did eventually launch a formal probe into the AFAM department in August of 2011 – but that was five years after the Faculty Committee on Athletics was first notified of concerns. Furthermore, the 2011 probe was only initiated after the *News and Observer* had obtained a transcript for football player Marvin Austin, which showed that he received a B-plus in an upper-level African Studies class before beginning his first full semester as a freshman at UNC.

The new information about the events of 2006 raised more questions about how much concern some university officials and faculty had about academic standards being lowered to help athletes remain eligible to play sports, reporter Dan Kane wrote. It also raised serious questions about the willingness of university officials to report what they knew about the problems in the African Studies department, and potentially other curriculums, as well.

Considering that the May 2012 internal probe was conducted by academic officials within the College of Arts and Sciences, which was home to the African Studies department, it would have stood to reason that the 2006 independent studies issue would have been included. No mention was made that there had been prior concerns about the department, however. At the very least that oversight suggested a lack of record-keeping and/or communication; a worst-case scenario would be that there had been a deliberate withholding of information.

A report was released in late July of 2012 from a special faculty subcommittee. A reference was made in the report about Robert Mercer and John Blanchard meeting with the Faculty

Athletics Committee all the way back in 2002 to discuss the teaching of independent study courses. The two athletic leaders were told that "faculty members have great latitude to teach courses as they see fit." The report also stated that academic counselors who worked with athletes therefore concluded that it was "not their responsibility to question decisions made within academic units about specific courses." Minutes from that meeting did not, however, show concern about the independent study courses. Also, for some reason they did not show Mercer in attendance, either. As mentioned before, the legitimacy of certain claims would be questioned in the future. Was "red flag" information truly passed on to the Faculty Committee on Athletes on various occasions?

* * *

As mentioned earlier, the December 8, 2012, *N&O* article reported that the years of 2001 through 2006 had a high volume of independent studies enrollments in the AFAM department. Records show that there were 1,433 in five years, with huge numbers of the enrollments being for particular professors. In spring 2002, for example, one African Studies professor was listed as having 70 independent study students under his guidance. The documents say the instructor of record was "not necessarily (the) instructor of supervision." In at least 20 other circumstances, either a professor or staffers in the department were assigned 20 or more independent study enrollments in a semester. Often those were for sections that had originally been listed during the registration period as having a maximum limit of one student.

During that time period, the newspaper said, football players accounted for 172 enrollments, or 12 percent. Basketball players accounted for 39 enrollments, or 3 percent. While those were a relatively small percentage of the overall number of students signed up for the classes, they were much higher than either team's representation of the entire student body. The basketball breakdown can be taken even further. During the five years in question (2001-2006), the basketball team had less than 30 different scholarship players. Based on the fact that basketball players had accounted for 39 enrollments, then it is possible that every single player who was on scholarship from 2001 to 2006 took a fraudulent independent study course. Even if the 39 enrollments were limited to a smaller pocket of individuals, the odds that at least one player from each season took a course is mathematically high. Furthermore, an earlier chapter established that seven players from the team's 2005 National Championship team was majoring in AFAM, and earlier in this very chapter data revealed that 15 independent study courses were taken by basketball players during that title year.

Julius Peppers played basketball for the last time in 2000, just before the search parameters of the above data. His transcript that was inadvertently made public, however, gave an idea of how the independent study courses may have benefitted star athletes at UNC. His transcript showed that he was allowed to enroll in four independent studies within the AFAM department – the first of which was in the summer after his freshman year in which he had received an F, two D's, two D-pluses, two C's and one B. On the verge of not having a high enough GPA to participate in sports in the fall, he got a B in his summer independent study course, a class that was supposed to have been available only to "advanced undergraduate and graduate students," according to UNC registration records and the *N&O*. Peppers would go on to receive a B and a B-plus in two other independent studies, again allowing his GPA to rise about the bare minimum that was needed to continue playing sports at the school. His transcript showed that he was enrolled in the fourth class, but he would ultimately leave for the NFL without graduating.

* * *

James Moeser, UNC's chancellor from 2000 to 2008, told the *N&O* that the high enrollment numbers in the independent study courses were clearly an indicator of a problem and should have been brought to the attention of the dean of the College of Arts & Sciences. "That's excessive, and it's not normal," he said. The dean during the time period in question, Madeline Levine, said no one came to her about the issue. She reiterated that the concerns of Mercer, Blanchard, and Baddour should have come her way. "I would have expected them to go to a particular senior associate dean, or to have gone to me, or to simply call the college and say, 'We've got a problem,'" said Levine. "If it had gone to one of the senior associate deans, then I would expect that that dean, with something as irregular as that, would have let me know."

The *N&O* had sought explanations for the independent study enrollment decreases since receiving the data more than a year earlier, the newspaper said. Chancellor Holden Thorp and other administrators declined to talk about it. Thorp was Madeline Levine's successor as dean of the Arts & Sciences College, but said he was unaware of any problems with the independent studies until 2011. Attempts to reach the professors in the African Studies department who had the highest numbers of enrollments were unsuccessful. Former Governor Martin had been scheduled to present his findings at a UNC Board of Trustees meeting less than two weeks from the time of the *N&O*'s

early December article. He said he was trying to pinpoint what the discussion was back in 2006 and determine if it was the cause of the enrollment drop. "I think you can expect that that's something that we have to pursue," Martin said, "even if it takes us past December 20." A closer look must not have happened, however, as Martin's findings would ultimately be released on the 20th as earlier planned.

* * *

The essential (and unanswered) questions:

-- Why had virtually every member of UNC's faculty and academic staff, which numbered over 3,000, chosen to remain silent regarding the ongoing athletic/academic scandal that had encompassed the school for more than two years?

-- Why had no one at the university taken Mary Willingham's initial claims of plagiarism seriously?

-- Despite apparent attempts to change the academic culture within UNC's basketball program and to do things on the "up and up," why had Jennifer Townsend refused to comment for any of the *News and Observer*'s articles?

-- The NCAA never spoke to Mary Willingham during its 2010 investigation into the school. Did university officials even tell the NCAA about her past observations of cheating?

-- Why were so many associated with the UNC Board of Governors and the UNC Board of Trustees unwilling to publically demand answers to the roots of the ongoing scandals at UNC?

-- Why had Amy Herman been advised by school officials to avoid creating documents that would have been subject to the state's open records law?

-- In 2006, did the Faculty Committee on Athletics take a true and thorough look into the high number of independent study enrollments? And if so, then how did they apparently miss the disproportionately large number of basketball players who were taking those questionable courses?

-- Did the connections between some members of the Faculty Committee on Athletics and the school's basketball program have anything to do with the lack of attention that was drawn to the independent study courses?

-- The preceding two questions are both based on assumptions that the Faculty Committee on Athletics had truly been informed of concerns regarding athletes and independent studies. Was that the actual case?

-- Were players enrolled in the possibly fraudulent independent study courses solely for the purpose of raising their GPA's – so that in turn they would remain eligible to compete in athletics?

-- Players from UNC's 2005 National Championship basketball team took 15 independent study courses that year. How many of those 15 courses were potentially fraudulent, yet kept them eligible to compete athletically?

-- Despite the abundance of information from Mary Willingham and also the independent study data from 2001-2006, all of which pointed to direct cheating meant to benefit athletes and potentially their eligibility, why had the NCAA still refused to address the matter?

CHAPTER FIFTEEN

MARTIN REPORT RELEASED; IMMEDIATE CRITICISM AND DEBUNKING; BAKER-TILLY'S RETRACTION

On **December 20, 2012,** former Governor Jim Martin released a report of the findings that resulted from a three-plus month investigation into academic fraud at UNC. The basics were that more than 200 lecture-style classes were either confirmed or suspected of having never met; dozens of independent study classes had little or no supervision; and ultimately there would be 560 suspicious grade changes revealed that dated as far back as 1994. The biggest – and most important to UNC – proclamation by Martin, however, was that it was not an athletics scandal, but an academic one.

That infamous quote would be well documented in the days and weeks to come: "This was not an athletic scandal. It was an academic scandal, which is worse." What was not addressed was "for whom" it was worse. The school's academic reputation? Perhaps. But worse for the school's athletics programs? Definitely not. The atmosphere in the room when Martin made the statement told unaffiliated onlookers all they needed to know. There were smiles around the table amongst the school's Board of Trustees, and congratulations could be heard. Athletics Director Bubba Cunningham said, "I feel like it's now complete. This report has been very thorough, an exhaustive study. From that standpoint, we've been looking for closure, and I hope this gives us the closure we've been looking for." Just how exhaustive and complete the report actually was, however, would soon be brought under scrutiny.

An article that appeared on ESPN.com on the afternoon of Martin's report provided more details of his findings. The investigation conducted by Martin and members of the Baker Tilly company found 216 classes with proven or potential problems. Both athletes and non-athletes benefitted from those classes, Martin said, which would ultimately be a convenient way around certain NCAA bylaws. "The athletic department, coaches and players did not create this," the former Governor told the UNC Board of Trustees. "It was not in their jurisdiction, it was the academic side." Martin also told the board he found no evidence that any coaches knew anything about the irregularities. However, it would later be shown that very little research was done to that end. An NCAA spokesperson did not immediately respond to an ESPN email seeking comment on the matter.

* * *

The Raleigh *News and Observer* published an article of its own late on the day of Martin's report, and immediately began to question some of the findings. The title of the article was "In the wake of Martin report, what will the NCAA do?" and it provided insight from several experts with deep knowledge of the NCAA and its rules. Up to that point NCAA officials had taken no action following a string of athletic/academic-related revelations encompassing the university, instead having only said that they were monitoring the developments. Athletics Director Bubba Cunningham said, "(The report) showed the same irregularities that went back further, but it didn't show that there was anything directly related to athletics." He was then quick to point out one of the university's oft-repeated talking points: "Certainly there were student athletes involved in classes as were a lot of other groups."

While Martin and those associated with the school were telling all who would listen that it "was not an athletic scandal," parties not affiliated with the university were not so sure. David Ridpath, an Ohio University professor, was a former university compliance officer and an expert in litigation involving college sports issues. In an email he wrote to the *News and Observer* he said that the NCAA's inaction at UNC had been "unconscionable." Ridpath continued, "I go back to the 'but for' test. This fraud would not have happened but for the athletes, many of whom were not prepared to do college level work." As documents released several months later would reveal, athletes likely were the reason the fraud was originally conceived. Those were documents Martin and his team had apparently missed, though.

Michael Buckner was a Florida lawyer who advised universities in NCAA probes. He said that NCAA rules were broken if an athlete was kept eligible through any type of academic fraud. "The NCAA may request specific information on the involvement of student athletes in the illicit activities," Buckner said. Martin's report, however, didn't show how many unauthorized grade changes benefitted athletes, for example. Chancellor Holden Thorp declined to address whether UNC had examined whether any of its athletes were kept eligible as a result of the grade changes and other misconduct. He would only say that Martin's report had been sent to the NCAA. Ridpath and Buckner were only two of several experts that the *N&O* asked to evaluate the report. All said that the NCAA should look deeper, but they expressed some doubts whether the Association actually would.

Gerald Gurney, a professor at the University of Oklahoma and the past president of the National Association of Academic Advisors for Athletics, told the newspaper: "The findings show that these 'anomalies' existed over a long period of time, covered basketball as well as football, was systematic and pervasive. I was also struck by the number of grade changes. Did the changes help to establish athletic eligibility?" Dick Baddour, the school's former athletics director who had resigned earlier in 2012, continued to convey some of the school's PR messages, though. "Given the thoroughness of (the report), it's time to move on," Baddour said. "I don't expect (the NCAA) to raise additional issues."

* * *

The *News and Observer* released two more articles – one feature and one editorial – the next day, December 21, 2012. More questions were asked, and more doubts were raised. The feature article, written by investigative reporter J. Andrew

Curless, said that Martin's report was notable for what wasn't in it, as there were gaps and unanswered questions because the scope of Martin's work was limited. Furthermore, Martin said that he and two consultants who had assisted him had run out of time. This was a peculiar statement for him to make, because there had never before been a specified time limitation on the investigation. In fact, when data was brought to his attention two weeks earlier by the newspaper, Martin said it would likely be information he would pursue, "even if it takes us past December 20," That certainly did not sound like the type of quote that would come from someone who had a strict time limit put upon his work.

There were numerous seemingly vital topics that were not covered in depth in his report. He got no information from the people he held responsible – Nyang'oro and Crowder – simply because they refused to speak to him. Martin said he checked some of their email messages, but that he did not review phone logs. In terms of investigative protocol that was an odd course of action, as those two supposedly held the answers to years of academic fraud. Why would one not thoroughly check the records of a man who had since 1992 been the chairman of the affected department, or the records of a woman who had since 1979 worked at the university and been close to athletics?

According to the *News and Observer* article, Martin did not interview any current or former basketball players or coaches – despite the fact that there were more independent study courses taken by basketball players in the years 2001 through 2006 (39), than there were actual scholarship players on the team. And despite the fact that Roy Williams had brought his own academic advisor from Kansas – Wayne Walden – who had personally overseen the scheduling of courses for all the basketball players. And despite the fact that Walden's replacement – Jennifer Townsend – had been appalled at the no-show courses that the basketball team had been taking a part of, according to insider Mary Willingham. Instead, Martin said he didn't think he would learn information from talking to others that hadn't been obtained elsewhere, or that wasn't already known.

Martin's review also didn't include inspection of individual student transcripts – even though the effects of the fraudulent courses on an athlete's eligibility could have easily been determined through those reviews. He gave only brief mention to questions of plagiarism, saying: "This review was not intended to make academic judgments about whether plagiarism occurred." Furthermore, Martin said he did not study the actual work of students in the courses he identified as irregular. He noted in his report than an earlier university review of suspect classes had not found instances of students receiving grades without doing work, and that was "an aspect that was outside the scope of this review." Essentially, while there may have been fake grades, plagiarism, and no legitimate work turned in, the message was that those weren't things his review team had been interested in.

As was pointed out in various realms of online media, the report was received warmly by many members of the school's Board of Trustees. The *N&O* also mentioned Joy Renner, the chair of the Faculty Athletics Committee. She said, "I'm a very skeptical person by nature, so I kind of like to see data, and I like to know what's real and not real. So I think I can feel good about moving forward, that this was more isolated." Unfortunately, some of the data she referred to was incomplete and/or erroneous, as would be shown in the near future.

Mary Willingham, the UNC academic support employee who had come forward a month earlier with assertions of long-time cheating within athletics at the university, told the *News and Observer* that she was disappointed that Martin's report never addressed why athletes were in those classes. She sat in the room as Martin spoke to the trustees, the paper wrote, but walked out when he started talking about the broader topic of grade inflation at UNC and other universities. "He did the who, what, where, I guess, but he never answered the why," Willingham said. "He had the opportunity to expose that, and I think intentionally he chose not to do it because I don't think he wanted to expose the corruption of the NCAA and the athletic program."

Raina Rose Tagle, a partner in the firm Baker Tilly which assisted Martin, spoke to members of the Board of Governors. She said, "We did what we could. And now that we've reached our conclusions, I think it could sound like we are championing on behalf of the university. But I think what we're doing is, we're saying 'This is what we did, and this is what we found. And it is what it is.'" Just over a month later, however, Ms. Tagle and her firm would alter their official stance.

* * *

The editorial that was featured in the *News and Observer* on December 21, 2012, was similar in theme. Written by staff columnist Luke DeCock, it pointed out the narrow scope of Martin's review. It stated that "Martin did not discern any connection to athletics despite considerable anecdotal evidence, but given the methods used (by Martin), that was unlikely anyway." As mentioned earlier by Thorp and other university officials, Martin supposedly had "unfettered access to University systems, records, and personnel." However, Martin chose to use very few of those resources, and instead "relied heavily and almost exclusively on statistical analysis and interviews with cooperating parties." Martin inexplicably rejected the analysis of phone records, dismissed any thorough examination of email correspondence, and declined to interview any current or former basketball players. As stated earlier, Martin had said, "My opinion was basketball players wouldn't tell us anything we didn't know from other sources." As the editorial pointed out, that wasn't exactly leaving no stone unturned.

The editorial also pointed out another instance of the "looking forward" talking point the university continued to employ. It said that Martin and the members of Baker Tilly were able to give the university a blueprint for corrective action and prevention. However, the real questions – those with serious implications – remained: Who orchestrated the fraud? Why did it happen? And how did so many athletes end up in the suspect classes? "You can have a lot of theories and hypothesis about this," Martin said, "but in order to come up with some kind of condemnation you have to have some evidence." Such evidence, unfortunately, was not aggressively sought by Martin and his team. Whether that was by design or due to a lack of investigative prowess was a matter of opinion.

* * *

An article from the *News and Observer* on December 22, 2012, highlighted a "battle over two cultures" at UNC – academics and athletics. The media had begun to pick up on the public-relations messages coming from the school. The article observed that after the release of Martin's report, the mantra of everyone at UNC was "moving forward". While seemingly every leader at UNC wanted to avoid uncovering too much about the past, not all of the power figures within the school agreed upon the specifics of the forward motion, however. Chancellor Thorp had said several months earlier that the university would look to implement plans for tougher admissions standards for athletics. A few weeks following that proclamation, though, men's basketball coach Roy Williams had contradicted Thorp's statement when he said he did not think UNC would jump ahead of others. Apparently Williams objected to holding a certain subset of athletes to lofty new guidelines. Following the difference of opinions, Thorp said only, "We're working on a plan we can all agree on."

* * *

The local North Carolina media wasn't the only faction to cry foul after the release of Martin's limited analysis of UNC's athletic/academic scandal. Across the nation multiple national media entities conveyed similar feelings. One in particular came from David Whitley of sportingnews.com. In a December 22, 2012, article, he decried Martin's report as being every bit as scandalous as the actual events that had transpired at UNC for years. It portrayed what many across the country were saying, and often did it in a mocking fashion.

Whitley said, "If you guys ever take another look at North Carolina's academic scandal, don't ask school investigators about (Julius) Peppers or any other player. Based on the latest report, sports had nothing to do with the scholastic shenanigans." The article continued with its condemnation of the Martin report, repeating the former Governor's proclamation that it was not an athletic scandal, but an academic one. "UNC would like you to believe you can have one without the other," Whitley wrote. "It is determined not to look like some Jock Factory that cares more about dunking than microbiology. It sure doesn't want the NCAA back sniffing around. Though all noses shut down whenever they get within a mile of (the) Dean Smith Center."

Like the local *News and Observer* newspaper, Whitley also pointed out that Martin failed to look for true evidence, and that the report failed to address key questions that had circulated since the scandal had expanded earlier in the year. Martin's report said that athletics department counselors didn't knowingly funnel athletes into the fraudulent courses. Whitley then chided that they probably never noticed how players like Peppers would get F's in other departments, but suddenly "turned into an Academic All American" once they enrolled in AFAM courses. Again stating the painfully obvious, the writer said there was no telling how many other "Peppers" there had been over the past 15 years, as Martin's team didn't check athlete transcripts or interview any current or former players.

Whitley said the results of Martin's limited review "means UNC can now try to put a neat bow on the scandal and tell everybody to just move along." He closed by giving some pointed comparisons to UNC's situation and a previous academic scandal at Florida State University, one which included far fewer athletes over a much shorter time frame. Whitley said, "It doesn't take a rocket scientist to see that's an academic and athletic scandal (at UNC). … Peppers did not major in rocket science. Neither, it seems, did UNC investigators."

* * *

On December 29, 2012, just over a week after the review's release, a fact-based debunking of some of Martin's findings would begin. An article that appeared in the *News and Observer* reported that minutes from several Faculty Athletic Committee meetings failed to confirm details that were included in Martin's review. Martin had said athletics officials had tried to raise red flags about questionable AFAM courses in both 2002 and 2006. That apparently was not the case. Dr. Stanley Mandel, a medical school professor who was committee chairman in 2002, said: "You won't find any reference to it in the committee minutes because there was no reference to it. There was no discussion. Nothing was brought up." Furthermore, Dr. Desmond Runyan, a former social medicine professor who was on the committee in 2006 and 2007, said he never heard anything negative regarding athletics and academics. "It seemed like everyone around the table was congratulating themselves about what a squeaky clean program they had," he said.

The lack of confirmation from both the meeting minutes and also from actual members of the committee had major implications. Martin's stance that athletic officials tried to alert the committee was critical to the university's efforts to convince the NCAA that there were no violations related to an academic fraud that had spanned over 15 years, the newspaper said. In essence, such a claim would have protected the athletics department, as they would have (presumably) raised concerns only to be told not to worry about them. Now, however, data had been produced to directly counter those statements by Martin and his team.

Upon a closer inspection of Martin's report, it was discovered that his team had only interviewed one person who had been on the Faculty Athletics Committee – business professor Jack Evans, who was ironically the university's long-time faculty representative to the NCAA. The newspaper said Evans took the minutes of the meetings in 2002, 2006, and early 2007. He declined to talk to the *N&O* about what happened on the committee, or what he told Martin. The former governor said in an interview with the newspaper that he had based his findings on interviews with Evans, the former director of athletics, Dick Baddour, and associate athletics director, John Blanchard, former academic director, Robert Mercer, Chancellor Holden Thorp, and faculty member, Laurie Maffly-Kipp. Five of those six people had direct ties to UNC athletics and/or the NCAA. Maffly-Kipp, the sixth, was one of three faculty members who authored a special report on academic fraud that had been released earlier in 2012.

It would eventually be revealed that Maffly-Kipp received much of the information that had been included in that July, 2012, report not from the actual minutes from the 2002 and 2006/07 meetings, but instead the information was "paraphrasing what we heard from Thorp that had transpired there," according to email correspondence with the newspaper. So while she was the lone interviewee by Martin who was not directly connected to athletics, she had apparently gotten her information second-hand – directly from the chancellor. Thorp could not be reached for comment, but a spokeswoman said Thorp provided the meeting minutes to Maffly-Kipp's committee. Along with Evans and Thorp, none of the others— Mercer, Baddour, or Blanchard could be reached for an interview, either. The contradictions were puzzling, to say the least. With members of UNC's leadership refusing to speak and clear up the matter, it was hard to know who was being truthful.

Despite all of the contradictions to a very key component of his report, Martin told the *N&O* that he still stood by his findings. He offered one additional vote of support: Law professor Lissa Broome, who replaced Evans as the NCAA faculty representative in 2010, was chairman of the Faculty Athletics Committee in 2006, and was also a member in 2002. Martin did not interview Broome for his report, but said she came up to him after his presentation to the Board of Trustees and told him he was "on the mark." That would again prove to be the beginning of a contradiction, however. Broome had told the *News and Observer* in early December that she did not recall any specific warnings or concerns in the FAC meetings. Also, on the same day that Martin said she gave him the supportive endorsement, the paper again asked about the committee meetings. "I just don't recall myself," Broome had said. "I wish I did."

* * *

Following the various national media articles mocking his report, and specifically the late-December piece from the *News and Observer*, former Governor Jim Martin wrote a "letter to the editor" that was published by the *N&O* on January 2, 2013. He made several claims in an effort to justify his work and counter the newspaper's assertions, and did so in a sometimes condescending nature.

Martin said that regarding many issues, he and his team dug "as far as our powers allowed." He did not, however, discuss the fact that he virtually ignored the emails and phone records of not only former UNC athletic coaches and support personnel (such as Wayne Walden), but also the key figures of Julius Nyang'oro and Deborah Crowder. Regarding those latter two individuals, Martin said he did not interview them, but "neither did (the *N&O*'s) excellent reporters." He also tried to downplay the potential usefulness of Professor Jay Smith, who had complained of not being asked back for a second interview with Martin. "My judgment," Martin said, "was that he was not a useful source". In closing, Martin said he had found "answers to the issues we were asked to investigate," a statement which may have held the key to many of the issues at hand. What, exactly, had they been asked to investigate – and by whom? Or more importantly, were there aspects of the scandal they had been told to avoid? A day later aspects of the former governor's work – in this case, his letter to the editor – would again be debunked by the newspaper.

* * *

The rebuttal to Martin would appear on January 3, 2013, from the investigative reporter who had spent the most time on UNC's past issues: Dan Kane. Virtually all of the major points that Martin had raised in his letter were countered with facts and data. On the charge that the newspaper only found three members of the committee who denied concerns were raised by athletic officials, Kane had this to say: "Readers should know that our stories don't always include every interview that we do for our reporting. In this case, we interviewed five members of the 2002 committee who said they either did not recollect such a warning or say it never happened." A sixth member briefly said he had no recollection before his wife hung up the telephone. Regarding the 2006 and 2007 committee meetings, Kane said the newspaper interviewed three faculty members at a November 2006 meeting, as well as the then-Chancellor, James Moeser. He said four faculty members who were present at a January 2007 meeting were interviewed. "None remembered being warned about suspect classes," Kane wrote. He then clearly re-stated that Martin had interviewed none of those people – not the six from 2002, or the seven different individuals from 2006-07.

The issue of Laurie Maffly-Kipp getting her information second-hand from Chancellor Holden Thorp was reiterated. Regarding John Blanchard, whom had said he twice raised concerns to the committee in 2006 about the independent studies courses (and presumably told Martin those same things), the newspaper asked Blanchard if he had any records or correspondence to back up that assertion. "He said he had none," wrote Kane. In closing, the newspaper posted the minutes of the committee meetings online for its readers to judge for themselves. That two-day exchange would essentially mark the last major involvement Martin would have in terms of conversing with the media.

* * *

A brief update on UNC's scandal was given by NCAA President Mark Emmert in mid-January in response to questions he was asked at the Association's annual conference. Based on a January 19, 2013, article in the *News and Observer*, Emmert said that NCAA interest would hinge on whether the fraudulent scheme particularly benefited athletes. He did not say, however, whether the NCAA would actually be looking to determine that information itself.

Emmert said he was troubled by many aspects of the scandal, such as freshman athletes being enrolled in African Studies classes that had been billed as being for experienced students and which did not meet. "Sure it does," Emmert said when asked if those types of activities raised a red flag. "And we will continue to talk more with North Carolina." Again left unanswered, though, was why the NCAA would not simply investigate the matter themselves and get the answers firsthand.

As had been parroted by the university leaders for the prior six months, their various in-house reviews had claimed the scandal was not about athletics because non-athletes had been enrolled in the bogus AFAM classes as well. Critics, however, said the NCAA was being shortsighted in ruling out academic fraud investigations based on that point. Those critics told the *N&O* that it sent the message that those who want to cheat on academics to help athletes stay eligible to play sports merely need to enroll non-athletes as well. Gerald Gurney, an expert with various past experiences with academic matters who has been quoted in earlier chapters, said: "If I were to be an athletic academic counselor trying to keep an impact player eligible I would make sure that some equipment manager or some non-athlete were in a course. That's a ridiculous argument."

The conflict in reports between athletics officials, Martin, and the Faculty Athletics Committee had also sparked a new controversy. According to the *News and Observer*, some faculty members had become concerned that the university had made them scapegoats to prevent the NCAA from investigating. Lloyd Kramer, the history department chairman who attended the meetings in question, had asked the university's Faculty Council to take up a resolution that disputed Martin's finding.

* * *

Following the tense exchanges between the *News and Observer* and Martin and the various contradictions of information that were exposed, an article appeared on January 25, 2013, that made an important announcement. Baker Tilly, the management consulting firm that had helped Martin in his review, withdrew its assertion that athletics officials had raised concerns about independent study courses during meetings in 2002 and 2006. As stated before, that earlier finding had been significant to Martin's report because it indicated that those athletics officials had tried to fix what later became known as a major part of an academic scandal. Raina Rose Tagle of Baker Tilly told a UNC Board of Governors panel that she wanted to "clarify" that finding. She said the athletics officials "asked a question of the Faculty Athletic Committee as a whole but sort of offline." As a result, one of the most significant findings of Martin's report was deemed incorrect, and was officially no longer included.

* * *

The essential (and unanswered) questions:

-- Why hadn't Martin's report shown how many of the 560 unauthorized grade changes since 1994 had benefited athletes and their eligibility?

-- Why did Martin say he and his team had "run out of time" for their investigation, yet only days earlier there hadn't been any indication of a time limit?

-- Why didn't Martin thoroughly check the email and phone records of the two individuals he presumed were the cause of the academic fraud? Was it to avoid discovering intent?

-- Was that the same reason why he didn't interview any current or former basketball players or coaches?

-- Was that the same reason why he hadn't inspected any individual student transcripts?

-- Why had Martin interviewed only one member of the past Faculty Athletic Committees, despite meetings from those committees being vital to the validity of his overall findings?

-- There were several stark contradictions between UNC administrators and faculty members. Who was telling the truth?

-- What, exactly, had Martin and his team been asked to investigate – and by whom? And more importantly, were there aspects of the scandal they had been told to avoid?

-- Why had the NCAA opted to "continue to talk more with North Carolina" as opposed to simply reopening an investigation and getting some factual answers for itself?

CHAPTER SIXTEEN

FURTHER DEPTH OF THE ACADEMIC SCANDAL; ROBERT MERCER; BOARD OF GOVERNORS; SACS

Shortly following the late-January retraction by Baker Tilly, an editorial would appear in the *News and Observer* written by John Drescher. That piece would be important for a variety of reasons. It mixed data and facts with numerous hard-hitting statements about the questionable thoroughness of the Martin investigation. Of equal importance was the identity of the writer himself. Not only was Drescher the executive editor of the *N&O*, but he was also a graduate of UNC. As a result, he had proven himself to be one of the few individuals with any sort of past association with the school who was not afraid to decry the athletic/academic scandals as a

series of deplorable acts which had resulted in little to no consequences.

Drescher's editorial recounted the events that led Baker Tilly
to drop one of its key findings: that athletics officials and academic support officials had raised questions and concerns with
the Faculty Committee on Athletics about certain courses. That
had been one of the main presumed "facts" within the Martin
report that had tried to free athletics from taking primary blame
in the scandal. However, it was later shown to have never been
the case.

Prior to the retraction, former Governor Martin had written:
"I believe that findings and conclusions should be based on
evidence, not hearsay and imagination." Drescher's editorial
responded with, "If only that were what Martin's report did."
Drescher talked about his past experience as a reporter on the
Capitol beat, which coincided with the time when Martin was
governor from 1985 to 1993. Drescher had interviewed Martin
several times, and indicated that Martin was smart and capable.
"But he's an inexperienced investigator," Drescher wrote, "and
it showed in his report. After athletic department officials told
him they had raised red flags with the faculty committee, neither Martin nor Baker Tilly interviewed any of the faculty committee members, except for the NCAA representative. That's
right: Gov. Martin never talked to the people he blamed for
dropping the ball."

Drescher's editorial went on to state that Martin and Baker
Tilly were obligated to interview several members of the faculty committee for two primary reasons. One was to make every
effort to get to the truth. The second was to give members of
the committee a chance to respond to charges that they had

heard concerns about possible academic abuse. "There's no acceptable explanation for why Martin and Baker Tilly didn't interview these faculty members," Drescher continued. "Martin and Baker Tilly seemed more determined to absolve the athletic department of blame than to get to the bottom of what went wrong."

Despite members of the UNC System's Board of Governors not thinking that the retraction damaged the rest of Martin's findings, UNC Professor Jay Smith felt otherwise. "The importance of this event cannot be overstated," Smith wrote in *The Herald-Sun* of Durham. "The validity of Martin's interpretation of UNC's troubles as 'not an athletics scandal' hinged on the anecdote about the FAC; the discrediting of that anecdote undermines the interpretive thrust of the entire report."

With Baker Tilley's retraction, Drescher wrote, Martin had painted himself into a corner. As noted in the previous chapter (and reiterated in the editorial), the only officials Baker Tilly had found who knew about the fraudulent classes, other than the department head and his assistant, were from the athletics department and the faculty representative to the NCAA. "In trying to get to the bottom of the scandal," Drescher said, "it's helpful to ask the basic questions... What did he know? When did he know it? I'd pose a third question: When he knew, what did he do about it? Martin and Baker Tilly tried to show that the UNC athletic department was pure. Instead, cornered by the facts, they've unintentionally shown that athletic department officials suspected academic fraud years ago and did little or nothing about it."

* * *

Months later the true cost of the Martin investigation would be revealed. According to a copy of UNC's agreement with Baker Tilly, the firm was to provide five employees at a combined cost of $1,520 per hour for the work. Martin himself had reportedly volunteered his services to the university, only being reimbursed for approximately $5,000 in expenses. Baker Tilly, however, had charged UNC a total of $941,000. Karen Moon, a university spokeswoman, would later tell the *News and Observer* that all of the money paid to the firm had come from a university foundation that took in private donations, so no taxpayer dollars had been spent. And despite the fact that Baker Tilly had been forced to retract one of the most vital claims in the entire report that had aimed to absolve athletics of any wrongdoing, Moon said: "Their analysis was independent, objective and thorough."

* * *

Just as Baker Tilly was retracting its earlier backing of that key component of the Martin report, updated data on the scandal was released regarding the information that was uncovered. In a January 25, 2013, article in the *News and Observer*, it was revealed that athletes who took a subset of 172 fraudulent classes within the AFAM department had an average grade of 3.56, which was between a B-plus and A-minus. Those classes had also accounted for 512 total grade changes during the time period that had been examined. The period covered in the new data did not extend prior to the fall of 2001, because the report indicated that information did not exist in electronic format beforehand. In all, 216 suspect courses were identified back to 1997, with 560 grade changes that lacked proper authorization.

The extremely high average grade for athletes in the fraudulent courses should have raised a major red flag. The transcript of Julius Peppers showed that his grades in AFAM courses were considerably higher than in his other subject areas, and essentially had kept him eligible to participate in sports. An average grade of 3.56 amongst athletes for over a decade likely had similar effects for some – if not all – other cases involving football and basketball players. Yet once again, that line of investigation was inexplicably not pursued by Martin or Baker Tilly.

* * *

On February 7, 2013, the UNC System Board of Governors' special panel released its own report. It largely accepted the findings of Martin and Baker Tilly, even after the vital retraction and the updated data that had been released. The report was met with criticism by some BOG members, and other details emerged from the findings that added more questions to an already ambiguous scandal.

Articles were released from various local sources on February 7, including wral.com, wncn.com, and several by the *News and Observer*. Multiples quotes and valuable pieces of information came forward as a result. The special panel had been selected by the Board of Governors itself, which as previously noted had a heavy percentage of UNC graduates as members. In fact, one portion of the report seemed to echo the sentiment that many of UNC's leaders had been loudly stating over the previous six-plus months: that they would try and make sure nothing of the sort ever happened in the future. "This panel acknowledges the open question about what might have occurred years ago," the report said, "but believes that it is immaterial to its focus on current practices in both Academic Affairs and the (academic support program) that reduce the risk for any such anomalies occurring in the future." Essentially, they conceded that they didn't know why the past indiscretions happened, and they weren't overly concerned with those reasons, either.

Some of the same types of contradictory remarks that had dotted the Martin report also showed up in the BOG panel's report. In the wral.com article, it stated that the panel told the rest of the board that it may never know if athletes were steered to bogus classes, but added that there was no evidence to support a conspiracy between the athletics department and the AFAM department. Louis Bissette, the board member who led the panel, said: "We are not an investigative body. We are a review panel." That would lead to the same unanswered questions that plagued the Martin report. Why not look at past email and phone records to determine if there had been collusion between athletics and academics? And if the BOG (and apparently Martin and his team) were not investigative bodies, then why not hire a real investigative team with experience in that realm?

There were other factual and data-driven inconsistencies. Bissette was told that there were no records that could show how many freshman non-athletes were able to enroll in and complete African Studies courses designed for upper-level students. As detailed in earlier chapters, past transcripts of UNC students would have clearly shown that distinction. So in that regard there definitely were records that could have provided that data – though it would have been a time-consuming process to accumulate the information. Apparently that was not the meticulous type of approach the panel wished to take, even though it would have provided accurate results.

Board of Governors member Jim Deal called the scandal embarrassing and inexcusable. "The chairman had a fiefdom and he was the king and nobody ever looked at what the king was doing," said Deal. However, he stopped short of questioning the findings of the panel's review. Other board members were not as forgiving, though. Member Fred Eshelman of Wilmington expressed his incredulous doubts by saying: "This stuff was propagated for 14 years basically by two people without additional collusion?"

Burley Mitchell, a former State Supreme Court Chief Justice, was even more outspoken. According to the wncn.com article, he blasted the consultants who provided much of the legwork for Martin's report, saying they relied on incomplete statistical evidence and failed to interview key people involved in the scandal. "It was inconceivable that it was two people who did this. You have 172 fake classes. Forty-five percent of the students in there are athletes. That is way disproportionate for their number on campus, which was less than five percent who are athletes. Somehow they are being directed to those courses," Mitchell said. "There is, to my mind, a good deal of evidence throughout this campus there were a large number of people, particularly in athletics, who knew that these courses did not amount to anything."

Mitchell continued by alluding to the allegations that academic counselors had steered athletes to certain courses. "It was clearly also an athletic problem to an extreme," he said. In support of Mitchell's point, an article appeared in the New York *Times* during the same timeframe. In it, former UNC player Michael McAdoo alleged that he and other athletes got special treatment while at UNC. According to the article (and a recap later published by wralsportsfan.com), McAdoo claimed that despite wanting a different major, counselors at UNC selected AFAM for him because it worked around the Tar Heels' practice schedule. He said that he was "assigned" a Swahili course, never attended it, and never met the professor. That was also the class where (with the help of tutor Jennifer Wiley) he plagiarized a paper and lost his NCAA eligibility.

A spokesperson at UNC said in reply to McAdoo's claims, "Number one, I cannot comment on any student's academic record. Number two, I cannot comment on Michael's situation because of ongoing litigation. As far as the counselors, I would refer you to the Martin report for what counselors did or didn't do." McAdoo's disdain for the university and how they treated him was clear, though. He was quoted in the New York *Times* as saying, "I would still like to get a college degree someday. But not at the University of North Carolina. They just wasted my time."

McAdoo's assertions were yet another piece of anecdotal evidence of counselors steering athletes to fraudulent courses, and they supported the stance of Burley Mitchell and others that the reviews by Martin and the BOG special panel had not delved deep enough into the issues in question. When asked whether the NCAA should be investigating above and beyond what the Martin report and the BOG panel had reported, Mitchell said, "Hell, yes." Steve Kirschner, a UNC spokesman, said after the panel's report: "We do not comment on the specific details of our daily operations."

* * *

More damaging information was revealed on February 7, 2013, which dealt with what at first appeared to be a side note of the Board of Governors' report, but eventually raised more serious questions. The limelight was once again directed back towards some of the fraudulent courses, and the past lack of action that leaders within the school had taken in terms of identifying and potentially stopping the offering of those courses. The *News and Observer* reported that according to university documents, the former director for Academic Support for Athletics had been instructed in previous years to track independent study courses to make sure there were no improprieties. But Robert Mercer, that former director, had apparently not followed through with that task.

The initial request of Mercer had been made by the faculty committee following an independent study scandal at Auburn University in 2006-07. The committee had wanted to be sure that something similar was not happening at UNC. However, officials from both the school and the overall UNC System said that they could find no evidence that Mercer had followed up. "He was asked to provide reports, but he did not provide written reports, is all I can tell you," said BOG member Louis Bissette. "It's another failure."

As thoroughly discussed in the previous chapter, Mercer was one of four officials with athletics ties who claimed that he raised concerns to the Faculty Athletics Committee in 2002 and 2006 about independent studies classes. That claim was at the center of the Martin report's findings and overall validity. The *News and Observer*'s Dan Kane pointedly asked in a February 7, 2012, article: If Mercer was concerned about those classes, why hadn't he been tracking them as he had been asked? Chancellor Holden Thorp said, "That should have been followed up on. I wish it had been, because we would have caught all of this stuff." As was often the case with UNC employees during the ongoing scandal, Mercer could not be reached for comment.

Thorp said he didn't know whether Mercer's apparent lack of action on the issue of the independent studies casted doubt on Mercer's assertion that he raised concerns about them, the *N&O* article stated. Burley Mitchell, the Board of Governors' member who had been so outspoken about the lack of a true investigation into the university's issues, said the revelation made Mercer's assertion look like a "smokescreen."

* * *

The university attracted negative attention from the Southern Association of Colleges and Schools (SACS) several days later. According to a February 12, 2013, article in the *News and Observer*, SACS was an agency that monitored the academic quality of schools and colleges across the South. Its board could issue colleges a warning, or worse, probation. If a school on probation did not clearly address problems, it could lose accreditation.

In a notice from the accrediting agency, UNC had been told that it must ensure the legitimacy of degrees awarded to an unknown number of graduates who took bogus classes going back to the 1990's. One possible solution proposed by SACS president Belle Wheelan would have been for the school to offer those graduates with free courses to take the place of the fraudulent ones. When asked why any former student would return for an extra course, Wheelan said: "Integrity. Honesty. Fairness. You know, all those things we like to think they learned as part of that academic program in the first place." A team assembled by the accrediting agency was scheduled to visit UNC in April.

As an embarrassing byproduct of the warning from SACS, approximately two weeks later UNC officials confirmed that administrators were performing visual inspections of classes across campus to make sure they were taking place. The spot checks were part of the university's efforts to assure SACS that there would be no need for a sanction against the school in the wake of its various academic fraud scandals.

* * *

As March got underway, there were finally some minor rumblings from UNC's faculty with regards to the stigma the academic scandals had placed on the university. According to a March 8, 2013, article in the *News and Observer*, Professor Jay Smith was again at the vocal forefront. As a leader of a professors' coalition known as the Athletics Reform Group, Smith had spoken at a Faculty Council meeting and called for a multi-year, wide-ranging series of town hall meetings to "debate openly and honestly" the university's commitment to NCAA Division I athletics. In calling for a faculty-led debate, the news article reported, Smith read an email from an unnamed colleague that ran down a series of events that began as a scandal in the football program and led to the discovery of major academic fraud.

At the same meeting, Chancellor Thorp had announced that an outside panel led by Association of American Universities President Hunter Rawlings would hold its first meeting on April 19. Thorp had asked Rawlings to lead an effort to examine the balance of athletics and academics at the school. That led to tense moments during the meeting, however, as the article stated that Thorp bristled when Jay Smith suggested the Rawlings panel was "not going to serve the function that most of us hoped."

Some professors at the meeting took issue with Smith's overall proposal, suggesting that faculty had been concerned all along and the administration had launched reforms to deal with the problems uncovered. However, the past record of printed comments seemed to speak for itself: other than Smith and Mary Willingham, virtually no other UNC faculty members had been willing to publicly decry the prominent role the school's athletics programs had played in the ongoing scandals. Greg Copenhaver, a biology professor, argued that Smith cast athletes in a bad light, even though the vast majority of which were "good actors." Almost as if scripted, Copenhaver then suggested that the faculty focus on moving forward, rather than looking back – one of the oft-repeated PR sentiments from those at UNC who seemed to want to avoid uncovering any dark athletic secrets of the past.

* * *

The essential (and unanswered) questions:

-- Through the use of nearly one million dollars from private donations, had UNC essentially paid Baker Tilly to try and absolve athletics from primary responsibility in its academic scandal?

-- Considering that athletes received an average grade of nearly an A-minus in 172 fraudulent courses, why hadn't further research been conducted to determine the effects of those fictitious grades on those athletes' eligibility?

-- Like Martin and his team, why had the Board of Governors also neglected to closely scrutinize the email and phone records of Julius Nyang'oro and Deborah Crowder?

-- Once the BOG conceded that they were not an "investigative body" and were unable to uncover the answers to key questions (just as Martin and his team had been unable to do), why wouldn't they insist on the hiring of a true, skilled investigator to look into those matters?

-- What possible motive would Robert Mercer, at the time the director for Academic Support for Athletics, have for failing to track independent study courses as he had been asked to do?

CHAPTER SEVENTEEN

PUBLIC DOCUMENTS; SUNSHINE DAY

The Raleigh *News and Observer* had never come right out and blatantly said it, but there were certain suspicions that had long been asked via several social media sites: Had UNC intentionally delayed and/or stonewalled the release of certain public documents that could have provided insight into the various scandals, and which also could have caused further damage to the school's reputation? Based on the university's extremely negligent response to numerous document requests that seemed to clearly fall under the Freedom of Information Act, the idea of an orchestrated delay certainly appeared to have merit. That topic of freedom-of-information laws would arise in early March of 2013 due to the long delays some in the media had been subjected to by UNC.

A "Sunshine Day" event was scheduled for Monday, March

11 in Raleigh. A panel of individuals would be there to discuss public records. An article ran in the *News and Observer* two days prior to the event, highlighting the frustrations that some in the media had felt over the previous year. Written by reporter Dan Kane, the article stated that in the 18 months since UNC had first acknowledged academic fraud had permeated its campus, there had been several public reports and open meetings about the issues. However, Kane noted that much remained unknown, in large part because the university had either not responded to numerous requests for information, or had outright rejected them.

Kane pointed out that the work of Baker Tilly and Jim Martin did not closely examine paper records of enrollment in more than 40 fraudulent classes identified before the fall of 2011, nor did they identify how many of the 560 overall suspected grade changes involved players on the school's football and men's basketball teams – data that could have retroactively affected the eligibility of some athletes. The newspaper filed a records request with UNC to obtain that information, and got a less than cooperative response: If Baker Tilly and Martin didn't do the analysis, then it wasn't going to be made available. The *News and Observer* stayed above the belt and didn't ask an obvious question, but many in social media did: UNC paid Baker Tilly nearly one million dollars, yet the firm couldn't find the time to sit down and closely examine some paper records? According to State Senator Thom Goolsby, the lack of information about the scandal was one reason that the university's academic reputation continued to suffer. "If the answers had been forthcoming in this, the story would have been over," he stated.

In all, university officials said they had received over 900 information requests in the three years since the first stages of the scandal become public, with roughly half coming from media entities. Chancellor Holden Thorp attempted to address some of the "delay" concerns in a written statement. "On the whole, we have made what I consider to be extraordinary efforts to provide the public with information about these issues," Thorp said. "We continually strive to improve our internal processes and the University's capacity to respond to and communicate with those who are requesting public records, including members of the news media. The principle of openness is important, and one about which we can all agree."

That "principle of openness" would seem to be a grey area, however, as evidenced by the amount of time it had taken to fill certain requests. For example, the *News and Observer* had submitted information requests on various topics pertaining to the school's scandal on the following dates: June 11, 2012; October 22, 2012; October 25, 2012; and February 14, 2013. All of those had remained unfilled until just days prior to the March 9, 2013, article – and it was likely not a coincidence that they were filled just days prior to the Sunshine event where the importance of public records would be discussed. Another request that was noted in Kane's article – one asking for correspondence, supporting documentation and drafts related to an internal probe of academic fraud, which was submitted on June 20, 2012, remained unfilled. Almost nine months had passed since its initial request.

* * *

The March 9, 2013, article said that the newspaper had filed dozens of public records requests related to the scandal. In some cases, the university had responded by providing revealing information. For example, certain documents had shown

the number of enrollments of football and men's basketball
players in certain no-show courses spanning as far back as 10
years. Specific information was also revealed about the AFAM
independent studies program. However, despite the media
having requested, received, and reported that information prior
to the release of the Martin report, the Baker Tilly consultants
and Martin excluded virtually all of it from their submitted report – for reasons unknown. Or, at least, for reasons that could
only be murmured by the media, but not proclaimed as outright
accusations.

In the many instances where the university had not filled the
requests, however, often the school had not responded at all.
Some of those requested documents included records turned
over to the State Bureau of Investigation, as well as documents
that may have been generated when former AFAM chairman
Julius Nyang'oro first spoke with university officials before
he resigned from his position. The article said that the lack of
response on some requests troubled Wade Hargrove, chairman
of UNC's Board of Trustees. A lawyer who specialized in the
media business and public records, Hargrove said he had told
university officials to be forthcoming and timely in responding
to public records requests. "On its face, it's hard to understand
why it takes this long to respond to some requests," he said.
Yet the trend continued. And if the chairman of a university's
Board of Trustees had no real influence to put an end to potential stonewalling, then that was very telling with regards to the
pecking order of leadership at the school.

Many critics continued to indicate that the lack of information from UNC suggested that the university was trying to keep
the scandal from prompting a second NCAA investigation. A
follow-up visit by the NCAA, Kane wrote, would likely focus

on men's basketball – the school's holy grail and the commodity it was most closely associated with in the public eye. Gerald Gurney, a professor and former head of Academic Services for Athletes at the University of Oklahoma, said as much: "It is clear to me that the university does not wish to seek the truth because they are afraid of what the answer might be, and how it might affect their premier athletic program, which is men's basketball."

The *News and Observer* reported that it had requested all correspondence between the NCAA and the university as it related to the academic fraud scandal. As of the article's press time, that request had only been partially fulfilled. Senator Thom Goolsby said the UNC scandal was a big reason he was pushing legislation that would have created a misdemeanor crime for public officials who refused to provide public records. Goolsby said he hoped the SBI investigation would answer how the scandal happened, who knew about it and why it took so long to become public. He conceded, however, that it may not happen, since the SBI investigation pertained to criminal matters and not the extent (and initial intent) of the academic fraud. "I know that there's a lot of people in the legislature who are looking out for this, listening for this," he said. "We want answers, and I hope we're going to get them." But like UNC's Board of Trustees chairman Wade Hargrove, apparently state senators didn't have much influence over the university's actions, either.

* * *

Two days later the "Sunshine Day" event panel discussion was held, and the *News and Observer* provided a recap article of several of the key points. The March 11, 2013, article's lead-in tied the topic to the piece that had been released two days earlier, which had detailed how UNC had long delayed the release of certain public documents. Part of the Sunshine event dealt with discussing the Family Educational Rights and Privacy Act, known as FERPA, which the university had long tried to use as an all-inclusive shield to keep from having to release information. Many of those documents eventually became public anyway based on a judge's ruling, saying that FERPA had its limits. "A lot of times, FERPA is used as an excuse not to release anything," said Lucy A. Dalglish, the journalism dean at the University of Maryland. "But there is a lot of information that is release-able. It can get tricky, but I don't think FERPA protection extends as broadly as a lot of schools interpret it."

Dalglish was among several speakers at the N.C. Sunshine Day event. Others included Amanda Martin, general counsel for the N.C. Press Association; Dick Baddour, the former UNC athletics director; Kevin Schwartz, the general manager for *The Daily Tar Heel* newspaper; and Jon Sasser, attorney for former UNC football coach Butch Davis. *News and Observer* reporter Dan Kane also had the opportunity to touch on several topics during the event.

During a panel discussion on the UNC case, Schwartz said he believed the school had used the Federal Education Privacy Act as a tactic to stall media interest in the story, a sentiment long shared by most everyone not associated with the school. Dick Baddour objected, however: "I don't think there's any evidence that the university was hiding behind FERPA." Baddour pointed out, though, that he was not speaking for the school; a representative for UNC was invited to join the panel but had declined.

Despite having possibly been forced into an early retirement from the school, Baddour was still doggedly supportive of his former employer. He criticized the *News and Observer* for publishing the transcript of UNC football player Julius Peppers. Following a moment of stunned, flabbergasted silence by nearly all in attendance, reporter Dan Kane stated the obvious: the transcript had essentially already been "published" by the school itself, as UNC had allowed it to be publicly housed and viewed on its website for years. Kane also reiterated that he had asked the university several times about a "test transcript," giving officials a chance to remove it from public view before it was identified and eventually connected to Peppers by fans of N.C. State University.

The Sunshine Day event brought more attention to the UNC scandal, and also the institution's practices of withholding information that would likely further damage the school's athletics programs. It showed that Baddour stood by the school's past actions, but also that Kane and others in the media would continue to pursue the truth. Despite being a graduate from UNC's School of Law, Amanda Martin, the lawyer representing the N.C. Press Association, said in reference to the past (and continued) legal pursuit of those public records: "I didn't relish suing my Alma Mater, but sometimes people just need suing." Since a formal representation from UNC had declined the invite, an official response from the university on the event's various topics was left to guesswork.

* * *

More than a month later two articles came out on April 18, 2013. The first appeared in the *News and Observer* and focused on Chancellor Holden Thorp, who would soon be stepping

down at UNC and taking a job at Washington University in
St. Louis. The article in part talked about the overwhelmingly
negative effect dealing with athletics could have on a university
leader. Thorp went as far as to suggest that dealing with intercollegiate athletics was the most important part of the chancellor's job. "That's not right that it's that way," Thorp said. "We
should try to figure out a way to change that. But for the time
being, if you're running a school that has big-time sports, if
there's a problem, it can overwhelm you."

Thorp said he had been so distracted by athletics that it was
difficult to accomplish other priorities. The article said that
when he became chancellor five years earlier, he never would
have dreamed of the problems he would face in athletics. One
of the biggest ongoing issues was the massive academic fraud
scandal that was heavily centered around athletics. Thorp acknowledged that he was caught up in the egotistical thought
that an athletic scandal could never happen in Chapel Hill. "In
order to be vigilant you can't be telling yourself, 'Oh we're one
of the places that never gets in trouble,'" he said. "That's part
of what hurt us."

* * *

The second *News and Observer* article released on April 18,
2013, focused on university employee Mary Willingham. She
had come forward the previous November to reveal a pattern of
athletic/academic cheating that she had observed over multiple
years. Despite the fact that much of her information had been
inexplicably ignored by former Governor Jim Martin and the
Baker Tilly review team, Willingham still won the Robert May-
nard Hutchins Award from The Drake Group – validating her as
a reputable source. It was given annually to a university faculty

or staff member who defended the institution's academic integrity in the face of college athletics.

In her comments after receiving the award, Willingham spoke more about how athletes stayed eligible at UNC, and how many of them were ill-prepared for college level work. "Many athletes told me what they would like to study," she said. "And listen to what we did. Instead, we directed them to an array of mismatched classes that have a very, very long history of probable (athletic) eligibility. And sadly, it's still happening."

Willingham went on to talk about her struggle to combat the system at UNC. She said that NCAA paperwork would arrive annually that required a signature and promise that she hadn't seen cheating, or been a part of it. "I've got to tell you that most of the time, I scribbled my initials on it," she said. "So yeah, I lied. I saw it – I saw cheating. I saw it, I knew about it, I was an accomplice to it, I witnessed it. And I was afraid, and silent, for so long."

Perhaps it was that fear and silence that had long kept almost every other member of UNC's faculty from speaking up about the academic scandal, and the role that athletics had played in it. Allen Sack, a member of the faculty at the University of New Haven and the president of The Drake Group, said that faculty members should stand up and say, "No, we're not going to tolerate this anymore." That had clearly not happened at UNC, though.

The article stated that during her 20-minute speech, Willingham strongly criticized the NCAA – calling the organization a "cartel." At the time of the article it had been nearly a year since reports of widespread athletic/academic fraud within the school's AFAM department had arisen, yet the NCAA still hadn't returned to reopen a formal investigation. Willingham also expressed frustration at the amount of money the school had paid on consultants and reports related to the various scandals; consultants and reports that had also largely tried to turn the focus away from athletics.

* * *

On April 19, 2013, the Raleigh *News and Observer*'s investigative reporting was honored with recognition in two national journalism contests. In a staff report posted by the newspaper, it stated that the *N&O*'s reporting on academic and athletic scandals at UNC had won first place in the education writing category of the National Headliner Awards, which had been announced by the Press Club of Atlantic City. The award honored three staffers – Dan Kane, J. Andrew Curliss, and Andrew Carter. The UNC reporting also finished third in the investigative reporting category in the annual Associated Press Sports Editors contest.

* * *

The essential (and unanswered) questions:

-- Had UNC intentionally delayed and/or stonewalled the release of documents in an attempt to limit the damages caused by the ongoing scandals?

-- Despite charging UNC nearly one million dollars for its services, why had Baker Tilly not been able to find the time to closely examine paper records that existed prior to 2001?

-- Why had UNC continued to delay and withhold public documents, even after the chairman of its own Board of Trustees told university officials to be forthcoming and timely in responding to records requests?

CHAPTER EIGHTEEN

CAROL FOLT; JAN BOXILL; JAMES MOESER; NYANG'ORO AND CROWDER EMAILS; PUBLIC RELATIONS FIRMS

As the date drew nearer when Holden Thorp would be stepping down as Chancellor, his eventual replacement was announced. Carol Folt, an environmental scientist who had worked for 30 years at Dartmouth College (including nearly a year as interim president), was tabbed to take over UNC's top spot. Based on quotes and details in an April 13, 2013, *News and Observer* article covering a reception held in Folt's honor, she indicated that she was excited about her new duties. "It's the honor of a lifetime," she said. "I just can't tell you how it feels. It's a little bit of a dream state." Folt said she had been on a tour of the campus, and that she and her husband had caught "Tar Heel fever" when they attended a Duke-UNC basketball game the previous month. She did, however, allude to some of the issues that had plagued the school over the prior several years. Referencing perspective, optimism, and opportunity, she said: "That's what will carry us through the tough times." Indeed, she wouldn't have long to wait for more "tough times" to surface.

* * *

The previous chapter discussed requests for public documents, and the often difficult obstacles the media had faced to get many of its requests fulfilled. Several documents were released in May, however, and they led to more discoveries of possible improprieties. According to a May 18, 2013, article in the *News and Observer*, a key UNC report from a year earlier had purposely omitted substantial information that would have painted athletics in a much more critical light.

In July of 2012 a special faculty report on the academic fraud (initially discussed in Chapter Eight) suggested that academic counselors may have steered athletes to fraudulent classes in the AFAM department. A request by the newspaper for emails and other correspondence related to that report had finally been filled by the school, and the details revealed some interesting final-day edits. Earlier drafts of the report (but not the final version) had specifically mentioned Deborah Crowder, the former assistant in the AFAM department, and also noted her connections to athletics.

The earlier draft had the following statement: "Although we may never know for certain, the involvement of Debbie Crowder seems to have been that of an athletic supporter who managed to use the system to 'help' players; she was extremely close to personnel in athletics." However, documentation showed that Jan Boxill, chairwoman of the school's Faculty Executive Committee and also a former academic counselor for athletes, wanted the statement cut because in her opinion it amounted to hearsay. She told the authors of the report that other professors, whom she did not identify, raised that concern. The final version did in fact make a change and read as follows: "Although we may never know for certain, it was our impression from multiple interviews that a department staff member managed to use the system to help players by directing them to enroll in courses in the African and Afro-American Studies department that turned out to be aberrant or irregularly taught." The final version had no specific mention of Crowder, and more importantly no mention of her being "extremely close" to athletics.

The May 18 *N&O* article went on to make it clear that the information about Crowder was not hearsay. Crowder's ties to the athletics department had been reported by the paper in June of 2012, and were also later acknowledged in the Martin report. As mentioned earlier, Martin never interviewed Crowder. He had, however, received both versions of the faculty report in question. Why no mention of Boxill's requested edit was ever made in his report is unknown. Furthermore, other records showed numerous bogus classes that appeared to have been set up by Crowder. Athletes accounted for all but eight of the 56 students enrolled in nine specific classes. Those enrollments included 31 football players and eight basketball players, all of which further cemented the "not hearsay" stance of the newspaper. It was extremely unclear, therefore, why the authors of the faculty report gave in to Boxill's request. More details on the matter would surface several months in the future, however.

* * *

As Holden Thorp's tenure as chancellor continued to draw to its end, more controversy arose, but this time by his own doing. He had said in April of 2013 that he felt college presidents had pressing demands and therefore should leave sports to athletics directors. That rubbed many people the wrong way, especially at UNC. Hodding Carter III was a UNC professor and former Knight Foundation president. The goal of the Knight Commission on Intercollegiate Athletics was to ensure that intercollegiate athletics programs operated within the educational mission of their colleges and universities. In a May 19, 2013, *N&O* article, Carter acknowledged that college sports can take a leader down fast, but said that Thorp's proposal was way off base. "You really have got to get control of (big-time college sports), but you don't get control of it by letting the guy who raised Godzilla become the person who now is supposed to supervise Godzilla, and that's what the athletic directors are, and the conference guys."

Thorp indicated that he knew his suggestion would cause waves. "Bill Friday's ghost and Hodding Carter and all those people are ready to kill me," he said. "They don't admit that their presidential control idea didn't work." It certainly hadn't worked in the case of Thorp, the newspaper wrote, who said he took the job with no idea about the athletics minefield ahead. Too often, Thorp said, he found himself in front of microphones trying to explain the various scandals and pledging to fix them.

Looking back, Thorp said he would have done some things differently. "But it's always easy to see those things at the end," he said. "It's real easy to look at somebody else's crisis and know what to do. It's a whole different deal when you have a big bureaucratic organization, trying to make quick decisions and getting people on board." And "a big bureaucratic organization" was a good analogy for UNC's leadership over the previous three years of problems.

The academic scandal in the African Studies department was perhaps the most embarrassing episode to Thorp, but it did have one good result, he said: that a myth had been deconstructed. "It was a failure of lots of people over a lot of years to detect it," he said. "I think that was fueled by this notion that these kinds of things didn't happen here." As for Carol Folt, the woman who would be taking over his position in a couple of months, Thorp had a specific suggestion for her: Watch the TV drama "Friday Night Lights." Thorp said he wished he had watched it five years ago, because an education about athletics would have come in handy.

* * *

During this same timeframe Holden Thorp's predecessor also spoke up. James Moeser was chancellor at the school from 2000 to 2008, which incidentally happened to be some of the prime years of the athletic/academic scandal. Displaying an obstinate loyalty to his former employer, Moeser voiced his displeasure over the media's coverage of the academic scandal that had involved countless UNC athletes.

In a mid-May interview in the *Chapel Hill Magazine*, Moeser said: "I'm really angry about (the media). I think they target people, and they take pleasure in bringing people down. I think their real goal here was to remove banners from the Smith Center." As the complaints were seemingly directed at the Raleigh *News and Observer*, which had been unyielding in its coverage of UNC's various athletic scandals over the previous three years, Moeser's interview was given attention in a May 20, 2013, article by the newspaper. The remarks were part of a short article in which Moeser defended "The Carolina Way," wrote reporter Dan Kane. That term had become a motto for the university and had formally been a source of pride and chest-thumping from both its alums and nonaffiliated sports fans. It had recently taken a beating amid the various scandals, however.

When Moeser referred to the "banners" in the Smith Center, he was undoubtedly talking about the three National Championships that were won by the men's basketball teams – teams which featured numerous players who majored in an African and Afro-American Studies department that had been proven to be rampant with academic fraud. Despite the apparently obvious connections between those championships and the proven bogus classes and degrees, Moeser seemed more concerned with defending an ideal. "I think (the media) has really put a target on the university," Moeser had told the *Chapel Hill Magazine*, "and they've treated The Carolina Way in a very cynical fashion, trashing it, really, and indicating The Carolina Way was always just a fiction, a façade we put in front of misbehavior. I really resent that. I think The Carolina Way is genuine, I think it's real."

John Drescher, executive editor of the *N&O*, disputed Moeser's take on the media coverage. He provided several quotes for Kane's article, and would follow up with an editorial the next day. In Kane's May 20 piece, Drescher said, "We weren't trying to get anybody, but we were trying to get to the bottom of what happened at UNC. Most of our readers understood that and appreciate the digging we did." Others in the media also supported the *N&O*'s work. John Robinson, the former editor of *The* (Greensboro) *News & Record*, wrote in his blog, "Media disrupted," that Moeser didn't understand the media's job in an open society. "What actually has happened is that the *N&O* discovered some rot in the internal workings at UNC in athletics and academia and, like an infection in the body, you have to keep going after it to get rid of it all," Robinson wrote. "That's what the *N&O* has done and is still doing."

Even some of the faculty at the university said Moeser's remarks were misguided, Kane's article stated. Michael Hunt, a history professor emeritus, said Moeser may have been reacting to the criticism leveled by rival fans. "He may be reflecting the embattled feeling that the administrators are feeling," Hunt said. "The problem is they are dragging this out, and I don't think anybody is saying – I haven't heard a word saying – 'Oh, the *N&O*'s persecuting Chapel Hill.' Nobody is saying that except for the people who are trying to keep the lid on." Moeser himself could not be reached for comment.

A scathing and direct editorial by executive editor John Drescher came out a day later. In it he countered Moeser, and said the former chancellor had taken up a tactic usually preferred by losing politicians: saying "they're out to get us." When responding to the accusation that the media was trying to bring people (and banners) down, Drescher had this to say: "Moeser's wrong, obviously. If the media were any good at targeting people, they would have targeted him. His successor, Holden Thorp, took over before the scandals broke and ended up taking the heat (and the fall) for problems that festered under his predecessor."

Drescher went on to allude to the "Carolina Way" that Moeser had opined about. "UNC's reputation for academic quality

and aboveboard athletics has taken a hard hit. The damage
has been made far worse by the failure of university leaders
to admit problems and search relentlessly for where the trouble began and where it spread." Finally, the executive editor
reached the heart of the matter by way of a statement that could
have been said about countless UNC, Board of Trustees, and
Board of Governors leaders over the past three years: "But
what is Moeser angry about? Not about what happened or how
it has been handled. He's angry about what got reported. He
thinks reporting that seeks to find the extent of the problems is
a mean-spirited effort to strip a proud university of its greatest
athletic laurels, the banners from its national men's basketball
titles. No, it's an attempt to do what universities also should
do: Seek the truth."

* * *

More damaging information would surface less than three
weeks later, and again it was due to the school (finally) releasing public information that they had long tried to conceal. A
set of newly released emails was the focus of a June 8, 2013,
article in the *News and Observer*, and a key confirmation was
the very close relationship former AFAM chairman Julius
Nyang'oro had with the program that tutored athletes. The
emails in question were released by the university as part of a
public records request that had been filed nearly a year earlier.
Inexplicably, none of the details within the correspondence had
shown up in the numerous investigations conducted since the
school confirmed the existence of the fraudulent courses in May
2012, the paper wrote. That was once again proof that Martin
and Baker Tilley either never checked the emails of Nyang'oro
and Crowder, or that the emails were checked and summarily
ignored.

UNC Chancellor Holden Thorp and other officials had long said that the Academic Support Program for Student Athletes had not collaborated with anyone in the AFAM department to create the classes that helped to keep athletes eligible to play sports. Some of the emails strongly suggested otherwise. One of the exchanges was between Nyang'oro and Jaimie Lee, an academic counselor for athletes. "I failed to mention yesterday that Swahili 403 last summer was offered as a research paper course," wrote Lee. "I meant to (ask), do you think this may happen again in the future?? If not the summer, maybe the fall?" To which Nyang'oro responded: "Driving a hard bargain; should have known... :) Will have to think about this, but talk to me...." Nyang'oro did not schedule the Swahili class, but he did create another one for the summer. Later that day he emailed Lee informing her of the new class. Those discussed courses had shown up as ones that should have been taught lecture-style, but had instead been turned into "paper" classes that only required a term paper at the end.

One of the university's long-standing talking points was that non-athletes took the fraudulent classes as well, which should keep the scandal out of the NCAA's realm. School officials said that it wasn't only athletes who benefitted from the bogus classes. However, other parts of the email records may have provided a clue as to why non-athletes were in some of the classes. In early 2005, administrative assistant Deborah Crowder raised concerns that too many students were seeking to enroll in independent studies within her department. She had told one advising official that word about the department's independent studies "had sort of gotten into the frat circuit." That would seem to imply that the preference was for the courses to be reserved for a very specific subset of UNC's student population, because as the records showed, the largest percentage taking the courses was athletes. Considering Crowder's close ties to athletics (and especially the men's basketball program), the emails show the distinct possibility that "regular" students signed up for multiple fraudulent AFAM courses against the preferences of athletes at UNC.

As usual, school officials largely chose to avoid the newly uncovered revelations. Attempts by the *N&O* to reach Thorp and Karen Gil, dean of the College of Arts & Sciences (which oversaw advising and the African Studies department), were unsuccessful. A UNC spokeswoman, Karen Moon, said the newly released correspondence contained no "new information" about the Academic Support Program for Athletes. But Peter Hans, the chairman of the UNC System Board of Governors, disagreed. "This is additional confirmation that there was far too cozy a relationship between the academic advisers in the athletic department and Nyang'oro and Crowder," Hans said.

Jaimie Lee still worked for the school's support program at the time of the article, but could not be reached for comment. Like Deborah Crowder, Lee also had interesting connections. Before joining UNC as a counselor, she worked for a charitable nonprofit founded by former UNC basketball players, the newspaper reported.

The new emails also showed that a tutor, Suzanne Dirr, had drawn up "topic" papers for athletes that were virtual outlines of papers they would have to write for classes. Interestingly, Dirr submitted her suggested topics to Crowder for approval – despite the fact that Crowder was not a faculty member, but only an administrative assistant. Crowder's importance to the AFAM department (and the UNC athletic infrastructure) continued to become more and more evident with each new set of released information. Dirr died in 2008; Crowder continued to decline numerous requests for interviews.

Madeline Levine, a former interim dean of the College of Arts & Sciences, said she was appalled to see how much work the tutors had done for the athletes in those classes. "It looks really corrupt, academically corrupt, to me," said Levine, who is now retired. She was also troubled by the tone of the emails between Nyang'oro and various academic counselors. Levine said that while some of it might have been in jest, it suggested a relationship in which Nyang'oro was doing favors for the counselors. In one email from September 2009, Cynthia Reynolds, a former associate director who oversaw academic support for football players, told Nyang'oro in an email that "I hear you are doing me a big favor this semester and that I should be bringing you lots of gifts and cash???????" She also suggested that she and Nyang'oro talk about students' assignments via "phone call, meeting or drinks, whichever you prefer."

The article reported that on three occasions the records showed that Nyang'oro and his family were offered football tickets and food. In one email, Reynolds told the former AFAM chairman he would be "guest coaching," which meant that he could watch the game with the team on the sidelines. Reynolds left the program in 2010. An earlier chapter recounted her claim that she had been the victim of age discrimination. She could not be reached for the article.

The "no comment" approach continued to be the status quo, as was the practice of dodging questions by university officials. Beth Bridger, who replaced Reynolds and also showed up in emails, could not be reached for comment. UNC spokeswoman Karen Moon would not specify who among the various investigators into the academic fraud scandal had received the Crowder and Nyang'oro correspondence given to the *News and Observer*. Moon said it was "considered during past investigations, in which the university cooperated fully." She also did not explain why it took nearly a year to produce the emails for the *N&O*.

Perhaps the most important aspect of the new emails was that they did not represent the entire record. Karen Moon said other correspondence had been withheld because of student privacy concerns or because it was a personnel matter. The university could have released additional correspondence with redactions to protect student identities, the newspaper pointed out, or UNC could make the personnel information public under a provision in state law that allowed its release to protect the integrity of the institution. The school chose to not make those efforts, however. That was likely as telling as the actual emails that were released.

* * *

Signs had long pointed to a unified "public relations" front by the school, as officials associated with UNC (and even entities such as the System's Board of Governors) had parroted some of the same catch phrases when commenting on the athletic/academic scandals. An article published by the *News and Observer* on June 8, 2013, finally gave some clear evidence as to why those talking points had been so similar. Public documents that had been released showed that there had been a dedicated PR and communications effort over the previous two years that had cost the university more than $500,000.

The breakdown of those bills was as follows: The Fleishman-Hillard firm received $367,000 for 22 months of work;

Doug Sosnik, an NBA consultant, received $144,000 for 10 months' work; and Sheehan Associates of Washington, D.C., received nearly $20,000 for work performed on "two occasions," a university official said. As was the case with the nearly one million dollars that was paid to the Baker Tilley firm during the Martin investigation, the university's privately funded foundation paid for all of those PR costs.

Some of the specific correspondence between Sosnik and the university was especially revealing. A former counselor to President Bill Clinton during the Monica Lewinsky embarrassment, the key message Sosnik wanted reinforced at UNC was that the school's scandal was in the past; the university had made reforms and would become stronger as a result. Records also showed that UNC administrators, with the help of Sosnik and a member of Fleishman-Hillard, fought back when Mary Willingham told the *News and Observer* that school staff had used no-show classes to keep athletes eligible. The school administrators and public relations consultants reviewed and offered edits to a letter to the *N&O* editorial page written by Steve Kirschner, an athletics department spokesman. The letter sought to refute Willingham's claims. Furthermore, some of the correspondence showed that UNC trustee Don Curtis and Athletics Director Bubba Cunningham didn't think the NCAA would dig into the academic fraud after former Governor Jim Martin's investigation concluded that it was an academic scandal and not an athletic scandal.

* * *

According to a June 20, 2013, article in the *News and Observer*, UNC was handed down a lenient response from the Southern Association of Colleges and Schools Commission on

Colleges (SACS), which had earlier been on campus following the revelation of academic fraud within the AFAM department. It was announced that the school would be monitored in the future, but not sanctioned. Other details were that 384 students who took fraudulent classes from 1997 to 2009 would be given the opportunity to "make whole" their academic degrees. Specific information regarding the method of completing those degrees was said to be forthcoming.

Some on campus were appalled by the lack of action by the accrediting agency, the paper noted. "It's amazing. I guess the flagship gets off the hook," said Mary Willingham, the UNC reading specialist who used to work with athletes and who had been outspoken about the problems at the school. "For me, it's getting to the point where power is so much more important than justice."

* * *

As the month of June slowly came to an end, one more important article was released regarding the academic situation at UNC. A June 29, 2013, piece by *N&O* reporter Dan Kane focused on the academic performance by the school's athletes, and the stark drop that had happened over the previous several years. According to recent academic progress statistics from the NCAA, the paper reported, UNC's men's basketball team – at one point the best in the Atlantic Coast Conference with a near perfect Academic Progress Rate (APR) score – had fallen to eighth place. The school's football team had recently been just a few academic points away from losing postseason eligibility. Both teams had just scored their all-time lows on the APR. UNC Athletics Director Bubba Cunningham and other officials declined to be interviewed for the article. Not surprisingly, the years that UNC's basketball and football teams scored well on the APR were ones in which athletes had been taking dozens of fraudulent classes within the AFAM department. With that in mind, it could hardly be considered an unexpected coincidence that the APR score dropped following the exposure of the university's athletic/academic scandal.

* * *

The essential (and unanswered) questions:

-- Why did the faculty authors of a July 2012 report allow their wording (in reference to Deborah Crowder) to be changed?

-- Other than free tickets and food, did Julius Nyang'oro receive any other gifts from athletic personnel in exchange for academic favors?

-- Why would Crowder be concerned that frat students were signing up for AFAM independent studies courses?

-- Why did athletic tutor Suzanne Dirr submit paper topics directly to Crowder – who wasn't even a faculty member?

-- Why did none of the school's prior investigations mention the revealing and damaging email exchanges conducted by Nyang'oro and/or Crowder?

-- Why did the university refuse to release the remainder of the Nyang'oro and Crowder emails, even in redacted form?

TARNISHED HEELS

CHAPTER NINETEEN

PJ HAIRSTON AND IMPERMISSIBLE BENEFITS; CONNECTIONS BETWEEN BASKETBALL PLAYERS, FELONS, AND UNC ALUMNI

As **covered in** the beginning of the book, in early January of 2010 a number of Tar Heel star football players announced they would forgo the NFL draft and return to school. The majority of them would eventually lose their NCAA eligibility due to accepting impermissible benefits. Fast forward to April 12, 2013. P.J. Hairston, the basketball team's leading scorer the previous season, announced he would return to UNC for his junior year instead of entering the NBA draft. Hairston released a statement at the time of his decision: *"I value the experiences I have had over the past two years in Chapel Hill and hope to continue to grow under Coach Roy's guidance. Coach always says when you focus on the team during the season, he will support us in the offseason – this is my way of supporting coach, my teammates and the Tar Heel community. Go Heels!"* Unfortunately for Hairston, his career would take a very similar turn as some of those other gifted UNC athletes who chose another year of school over a guaranteed professional payday. And as was the case with the football players who elected to stay in *Chapel Hill*, perhaps there was an underlying reason for them returning, after all.

On May 13, 2013, Hairston was caught speeding in Durham County in a 2012 Camaro. Not much was said about the event, despite the fact that the vehicle was on the expensive end of the spectrum for many college students. A few weeks later, however, Hairston had another run-in with the law. On June 5, 2013, he was stopped in Durham and charged with possession of marijuana. The initial details were limited, but the vehicle that was cited at a Durham traffic stop was a 2013 Yukon, and was reported to be a rental.

A June 6, 2013 article by *USA Today Sports* recounted some of the information from the traffic stop. According to police, Hairston was stopped at an intersection for a license check at 10:20 p.m. the prior evening. He and two other passengers faced misdemeanor drug charges, the article said. Hairston also was charged with driving without a license. Steve Kirschner, UNC's senior associate athletic director for communications, said in a statement: *"Coach Williams and Bubba Cunningham are aware of a situation that took place last evening with P.J. Hairston. We're currently looking into it to gather the facts. We will issue a statement when we have enough information to do so."*

* * *

For several weeks the story remained dormant. The rumors were plenty, and were mostly discussed through social media: Hairston apparently didn't have a license; a gun had been found outside the vehicle; the Yukon was a rental. Little official confirmation, though, could be found from media (or university) sources. That would partially change on June 30, 2013, as information from what had become a reputable non-media source emerged. As had been the case on several occasions over the previous few years, it came via the *Packpride.com* website. The details were from the same message-board user who had broken the story about the transcript identity of Julius Peppers the previous summer, as well as several other key aspects of the ongoing athletic scandal. Based on internet archives of the *Packpride.com* website from the evening of June 30, people from multiple sites across the internet immediately took serious notice of the claims the board user was making – largely because of his accurate informational track record.

Parts of the post said: *"The renter of the vehicle Hairston was driving on the night he was arrested was Haydn 'Fats' Thomas of Durham, 39 years of age. [Thomas] has prior arrests on a variety of counts, but more recently (and most notably) on drug and weapons charges."* The post gave further background information on Thomas, including links to his past criminal history. It closed by referencing the potential NCAA impact of Hairston's actions: *"What is no longer in question is whether [Hairston] accepted a "gift" (in the form of a rental vehicle) from someone. What is in question, is why that gift was made. And who at unc (other than Hairston himself) had knowledge of it."*

A free-flow of information would begin to gather on the
Packpride.com website over the next few days as the story
began to pick up steam on the internet. The information was
finally confirmed by a mainstream media source several days
later. In a July 3, 2013 article from *USA Today Sports*, college
basketball writer Eric Prisbell presented the first of numerous
eventual blows to UNC and Hairston that would be seen nationwide. It stated that the newspaper had obtained a rental receipt
showing that Haydn Thomas had indeed rented the 2013 Yukon.
In the article, Thomas said he had rented the car for himself
and that a friend, Miykael Faulcon of Durham, had borrowed
it to go to a store when the arrest occurred. *"I don't know P.J.
Hairston,"* Thomas said. *"I know Miykael, his friend. I don't
know anyone at Carolina. I don't even like the Carolina team.
Look at the age disparity between me and those boys. I could
be their father."* Despite those bold statements of denial, in the
coming days they would be shown to be false.

Other specific details from Prisbell's article on July 3 were
that the Yukon was rented at 10 p.m. June 2 at the Hertz location at Raleigh Durham International Airport, and was returned
at 10:30 p.m. June 5. The charge was $1,261.64. The license
plate number on the rental receipt matched the one listed on
the police report of Hairston's arrest, as did the year, make
and model of the vehicle. The police report revealed that a
9-millimeter handgun was seized during the traffic stop that led
to Hairston's arrest on possession of marijuana charges. The
handgun was found outside the vehicle, according to the limited
report. Thomas went on to say that he knew Faulcon from
"partying at clubs." He seemingly went out of his way to add
that he was not a University of North Carolina athletic booster

nor was he connected to a sports agent. *"Why am I being persecuted?"* Thomas asked. *"I did not rent nobody a car."*

Following Hairston's arrest in June, UNC basketball coach Roy Williams had told *USA Today Sports* that he was waiting for more information before making a decision about Hairston's status with the team. *"The good thing is,"* Williams said, *"I don't have to make a decision right now because we're in summer school, fall semester has not started, basketball has not started. We're going to wait and see what happens. I've got some ideas, but right now those ideas are staying in my mind. I am waiting until all the facts come in and then I will take care of everything that needs to be taken care of."* As of July 3, some very specific facts had been revealed. Yet at the time, Williams – and UNC – remained silent on Hairston's status with the team, taking no punitive action against him.

* * *

Three days later more news would emerge, much of which debunked some of the quotes that Haydn Thomas had given just a few days prior. Based on more receipts that were obtained by *USA Today*, Eric Prisbell wrote on July 6, 2013 that the Camaro that Hairston was driving on May 13, 2013 when he received a speeding ticket was also a rental. That Camaro had been paid for by a woman who shared a Durham address with Haydn Thomas, seemingly eliminating the claim that Thomas did not know Hairston, as well as the possibility that the Yukon rental had been a one-time type of event.

The woman's name was Catinia Farrington, and the address she listed on the Hertz rental receipt matched the address Thomas listed on his voter registration. The Camaro had been rented from April 25 through June 17 of 2013, a period of 54 days. The bill for Farrington was $3,249. In addition, Thomas himself had rented the same vehicle from March 25 through April 15, for charges of $2,468.47. Corresponding information indicated that receipts were only available from Hertz for a six month period, so whether the Camaro had been rented earlier than January was unknown. Calls to both Thomas and Farrington prior to the second story by Eric Prisbell were not returned.

* * *

By this time two major stories had come out regarding a star UNC basketball player and almost certain impermissible benefits, yet Roy Williams and UNC maintained their silence. Unfortunately for the school, even more information would continue to surface that connected Haydn Thomas to Hairston and the university. In a *USA Today Sports* article from July 10, 2013, it was reported that four rental vehicles linked to Thomas had received a total of nine parking citations on the school's campus since February. The citations were all issued between February 21 and May 28, 2013, and were for vehicles that either Thomas or Farrington had rented from the Hertz location at the local airport.

The vehicles included both the aforementioned 2013 Yukon and 2012 Camaro that Hairston had been driving during run-ins with the law. The other vehicles were a 2013 Chevrolet Tahoe and a 2013 Mercedes Benz. An interesting sidenote was that while the Mercedes had received four tickets between May 8 and May 30, a peculiar message had actually been sent out a message via the Twitter social media site on December 20, 2012 from an acquaintance of Hairston named Jarrett Ballard. The tweet said, *"So pj comes to pick me up in.. 2012 Benz 2door"*.

While vague in nature, given the latest revelations the tweet at least hinted at the possibility that Hairston had been driving high-end vehicles for some time. The article said that unpaid fines for the tickets totaled $315. The newspaper contacted UNC's department of public safety seeking more information about the citations, but was referred to the university's general counsel's office.

Some conflicting quotes were given in the article regarding the relationship of Haydn Thomas with Hairston and another of the young men who had been involved in the June 5 traffic stop in Durham. Thomas had earlier stated that he didn't know Hairston, but was acquainted with Mykael Faulcon – and it was Faulcon for whom the vehicle had been rented. Writer Eric Prisbell spoke with Trudy Ransom, Faulcon's mother, who said that her son and Thomas had no relationship. *"I don't know why (Thomas) says he has a relationship with my son,"* Ransom said. *"I won't comment about P.J. Hairston. I will let this play out in court and I hope the innocent will remain innocent."*

Another potential ramification of the parking tickets dealt with the time frame of the dates. The earliest on-campus citations were issued on February 21st, which was still during UNC's 2012-13 basketball season. The Tar Heels would go on to win four more regular season games, two ACC Tournament games, and one NCAA tournament contest. If Hairston had indeed been driving one of those rental vehicles when it was ticketed on February 21st, that would constitute an impermissible benefit – and make him ineligible for the remaining games on the team's schedule. That would also retroactively vacate those seven victories should the NCAA choose to pursue the matter.

* * *

The next big revelation would come two days later, and it would almost completely shatter the earlier statements given by Haydn Thomas. The felon's contention was that the rented Yukon had been for Mykael Faulcon, and that Thomas did not know P.J. Hairston. The Raleigh *News and Observer* entered the fray in a big way via a July 12, 2013 article, providing evidence that discredited those earlier statements.

The newspaper had obtained a detailed police report into the Durham traffic stop and arrest of Hairston, which also included interviews with Hairston and the two other young men who had been with him at the time. The report revealed that Hairston told police he had switched places with a passenger to try to avoid a citation of driving without a license; he admitted to being a "recreational" marijuana user; and perhaps most importantly he said that he had been given the rental car to go to Atlanta and see friends. As the paper pointed out, the details within the police report directly countered claims by Haydn Thomas. In it, Hairston admitted via interviews with the police that he received the vehicle "from Fats".

The detailed report revealed numerous contradictions from earlier statements, and also pointedly confirmed (by Hairston's own admission) that the vehicle had been rented for him, and not Mykael Faulcon. Haydn Thomas had told *USA Today* a week earlier that he didn't know Hairston, but he later told the *N&O* that he knew UNC athletes through parties. Thomas could not be reached for comment for the July 12 article. Considering the multiple contradictions that were now on record, any statements by him likely would have been viewed as extremely questionable, regardless.

* * *

Just over a week later it was announced that all charges against Hairston related to the arrest in Durham had been dismissed, with no further explanation given by the police. In a July 22, 2013 article in *USA Today Sports*, UNC athletic director Bubba Cunningham said that the school had no update on Hairston's status with the program in light of the charges being dropped. At the time the university had still taken no disciplinary action against the star player. In a written statement by head basketball coach Roy Williams, he said: *"Other issues have been written about recently that are disturbing and bother me deeply. Our basketball program is based on great ideals and these issues are embarrassing. These are not common in my 10 years as head coach at UNC and they will all be dealt with harshly and appropriately at the correct time to ensure that our program will not be compromised."* Oddly, the charges against Hairston's two passengers during the June 5 arrest apparently weren't dropped. Furthermore, Haydn Thomas told *USA Today Sports* that he had yet to be contacted by either the NCAA or UNC.

* * *

Despite somehow escaping any legal consequences from the drug and gun incident in Durham, less than a week later Hairston found himself in trouble with the law yet again. On July 28, 2013, he was pulled over for travelling 93 mph in a 65 mph zone and cited for speeding and careless and reckless driving. Following Hairston's third legal infraction in just over three months, UNC apparently could no longer dodge taking disciplinary action. Basketball coach Roy Williams announced later on the evening of the 28th that he was indefinitely suspending

Hairston. According to a July 29, 2013 article by *USA Today Sports*, the university's three-sentence press released cited only the most recent traffic citation, as opposed to including the other questionable events that had festered since late May.

More troubling connections emerged in August regarding Hairston and his possible impermissible use of vehicles, further clouding the guard's future eligibility at UNC. In an August 9, 2013 article by Associated Press writer Aaron Beard, university records that had been recently released showed that a rental car driven by Hairston also had a dozen campus parking citations over a two-month period. The vehicle was the 2012 Camaro in which Hairston had been charged with speeding in May. The parking violations stretched as far back as April 1, 2013. Additionally, the majority of the violations were new information, and above and beyond what *USA Today* had reported in its July 10 article.

As if there were any questions whether Hairston (or another basketball player) had accumulated the tickets, three of the citations were issued while the Camaro was parked near the Smith Center and Hairston's dorm, the A.P. article stated. In addition to the tickets for the Camaro, a 2009 Porsche Cayenne registered to Catinia Farrington was twice cited for campus parking violations. As noted earlier, Farrington, who shared an address with Haydn Thomas, had been the official renter of the Camaro when Hairston had received his first speeding ticket in May.

* * *

By mid August there was little doubt that Hairston had received impermissible benefits. The biggest unanswered question was why, and whether there was the possibility of a deeper and more coordinated system of benefits for UNC athletes.

Possible theories began to take shape based on several sources of information. The first clue initially seemed unrelated. Pictures of fellow basketball player Leslie McDonald had surfaced over the summer showing him using a custom mouth guard in UNC basketball games. Upon further inspection, his name had also appeared on the website of "Iceberg" mouth guards. When information of this potential impermissible benefit began to show up on social media sites, UNC sent a "cease and desist" order to the company, telling it to not reference McDonald on its website. Interesting connections would then be pieced together via public records, however.

The parent company of the custom mouth guards, ICEBerg Holdings LLC, had filed its Articles of Organization in the state of North Carolina in April of 2013. The executors were Lee Gause and Spencer Howard. Gause was a New York based dentist, and Howard was a dentist working in Durham, NC. Gause earned his undergraduate degree from UNC, while Howard was a graduate of the university's School of Dentistry.

Further background on the two men showed that Spencer Howard was associated with several other businesses in NC. Howard was a co-incorporator of the Durham business Kairobi Exotic Rentals and Transport, Inc. The man who was the other co-incorporator was Haydn Thomas – the convicted felon who was tied to P.J. Hairston and the multiple rental vehicles. The connections did not stop there, however. Haydn Thomas was also the registered agent for the then-dissolved business Six Sigma Consulting. Public documents showed the business's address as 415 Dunstan Avenue in Durham. Various online references showed that address as also being associated with Spencer Howard. Furthermore, Haydn Thomas was also listed as the registered agent for the "Spencer B. Howard Dds Pa

401k Profit Sharing Plan and Trust," and Thomas also showed up in various online pictures of Howard's Durham office, with the felon appearing to have an on-site desk and work area.

The connections, all verifiable through public documents, were potentially damning. P.J. Hairston, who chose to return to UNC for his junior season instead of entering the NBA, on multiple occasions used rental vehicles connected to Haydn Thomas, a convicted felon. Hayden Thomas had multiple business connections with UNC Dental alumnus Spencer Howard. Howard was co-executor of the Iceguard company with Lee Gause, another UNC alumnus. The Iceguard company had not only supplied UNC basketball player Leslie McDonald with benefits, but also used his name on its website – while McDonald was an amateur NCAA athlete.

Speculation on social media began to ask questions of the UNC School of Dentistry, and what role (if any) it and some of its other alumni might have played in the providing of benefits to UNC athletes. As was covered in an earlier chapter, Tami Hansbrough had first worked for the Dental Foundation before getting a more prestigious job by way of Matt Kupec. However, as was also importantly noted in that chapter, the Dental Foundation had refused to release certain documents under a public request law, saying that it was a private entity. So whether there was any level of corruptness with regards to the foundation, its alumni, and athletes would remain unknown – unless the NCAA chose to piece together the evidence and find out for itself.

* * *

The essential (and unanswered) questions:

-- How long had Hairston – and potentially other UNC basketball players – been using rental vehicles supplied by boosters?

-- Why did the NCAA choose to not pursue the possibility of vacated wins from UNC's 2012-13 basketball season, despite strong evidence that eligibility rules had been broken?

-- Why did the Durham police department drop Hairston's charges, but apparently not those of his two passengers?

-- Based on business connections with felon Haydn Thomas, was there a deeper connection between UNC athletes and university alumni Spencer Howard and Lee Gause regarding impermissible benefits?

CHAPTER TWENTY

JAN BOXILL AND ATHLETIC-MINDED EDITS TO A FACULTY REPORT

As discussed in Chapter Eighteen, wording in a UNC internal academic report released in late July of 2012 had been changed at the last minute prior to its release. The changes were initiated by Jan Boxill, chairwoman of the school's Faculty Executive Committee. When the *News and Observer* first reported on the changes in mid-May of 2013, some details were lacking as to why the edits were requested. However, newly released correspondence led to a new *N&O* article on July 20, 2013. The apparent motivation behind Boxill's requests seemed to fall in line with the university's perceived "athletics first" mantra that had become apparent over the years of scandals.

The July 20 article, penned by Dan Kane, focused on emails between faculty leaders at the school. The specific requested change by Boxill was in reference to Deborah Crowder, the long-time administrative assistant in the scandalous AFAM department who also had very close ties to the men's basketball program. With regards to why Crowder's name and specific connections to basketball were being eliminated from the report, a past email from Boxill to the faculty authors of the special internal probe stated: "The worry is that this could further raise NCAA issues and that is not the intention." Essentially, it appeared as if the school (and its leaders) were specifically trying to avoid more attention from the NCAA, and they felt that if too many specifics were included in the report, then the Athletic Association might return and open a new investigation.

John Thelin, an education professor at the University of Kentucky and author of "Games Colleges Play," indicated that rewriting a sentence that carried the suggestion of an athletic motive behind the scandal should not have been the mission of a member of the faculty. "The faculty committee should not anticipate the audience or implications," Thelin told the newspaper, "but rather fulfill the charge they undertook." Jay Smith, the UNC history professor who had long been one of the athletic/academic scandal's most vocal critics, said of Boxill's meddling: "It seems consistent with what I have taken to be the university's strategy all along, which is they wanted to come up with findings that seemed frank and candid, but which also carefully exclude any further NCAA investigation." That would be an important strategy indeed, as the article noted that the NCAA typically did not involve itself in academic fraud cases unless there was an intent to assist athletes above other students.

Oddly, the change in the faculty report was made after Boxill and several committee members had praised previous drafts, Kane wrote. Boxill said in an earlier email to the *N&O* that some faculty committee members objected to describing Crowder as "extremely close" to athletic personnel. Boxill called it "vague without definite boundaries." Seven of the faculty members on the committee in a position to review the report said they did not make the suggestion; the other five who were not authors of the report could not be reached. Boxill claimed others on the committee had suggested the change, but who those people were remained unknown. Boxill did not respond to interview requests from the *N&O* for the July 20 article.

Along with Crowder having many earlier-documented ties to athletics, Boxill herself was in a similar position. She was a former women's basketball coach at another university, and had worked in broadcasting with UNC's women's basketball team. She also had extensive academic ties to UNC athletics. For over 20 years – starting in 1988 – Boxill had been an Academic Counselor in the Student Athlete Development Center. Other positions she had held in that Athlete Development Center in the past included the Learning Skills Coordinator, the Freshmen Academic Success Program Coordinator, the Tutor Coordinator/ Supervisor, and the Intern Supervisor. This begged a clear and obvious question: had Boxill used her position as chairwoman of the school's Faculty Executive Committee to influence the 2012 internal report in an attempt to protect athletics? Boxill was the first non-tenured faculty member elected to the chairman/woman's post. Ironically, the subject of one of her philosophy courses at UNC was ethics in sports.

* * *

The authors of the 2012 faculty report were Laurie Maffly-Kipp, Steven Bachenheimer, and Michael Gerhardt. According to the *N&O*'s article, correspondence among the three showed that they were worried that Boxill would try and dilute the findings of the report prior to its release. They sent drafts to her in Portable Document Formats (PDFs) so she could not easily alter them. After a draft of the report had been discussed in a Faculty Executive Council meeting, Gerhardt wrote in an email: "It seems to me that we might need to tell Jan that there is a line we hope she does not cross." Maffly-Kipp also questioned the need for the late changes. "Why is it a good thing to remove Deborah Crowder's name from the report?" she asked. "The fact is, she was close to people in athletics." Gerhardt, a law professor, wrote: "(Boxill) is free to disagree with the report as anyone is, but i (sic) cannot believe she has the authority to change what it says. Indeed, apart from her lack of authority to do this, it strikes me as very poor political judgment. Just imagine what the papers will do with that."

* * *

An editorial was released in the *News and Observer* on July 24, 2013, by staff writer Luke DeCock. Following the story of Boxill's role in the final faculty report, the editorial was largely directed at the faculty in general. DeCock said that one of the most surprising developments in the three years since the school had admitted academic fraud was the role the faculty had played. Specifically, "the faculty has been almost entirely absent. Complicit, by collective silence. Complicit, in the case of Jan Boxill, by action."

When referencing past half-hearted attempts at reform by the university, the editorial mentioned Thorp and his commission of the Martin report. "Jim Martin, an honorable, respected, dignified man of distinguished service to the state of North Carolina, ended up the figurehead of a report that posed few legitimate questions and answered fewer, a whitewash." At the same time, however, DeCock said the faculty's silence along the way may have been somewhat understandable – if not justifiable. "It's not hard to understand why some faculty may not have thought it worth speaking out. Many had confidence in Thorp, a longtime colleague, and taking a more aggressive public stance would have meant crossing him." A year earlier while speaking at a forum on the future of intercollegiate athletics in Chapel Hill, Professor Hodding Carter III made reference to faculty inaction. "As far as I can see, on one campus after another, the silence of the faculty is very much the silence of the lambs," Carter had said, "allowing the slaughter of the integrity of the institutions they serve to go forward." As was widely known at the time of DeCock's editorial, essentially the only two UNC faculty members who had shown any sort of displeasure in the university's handling of the scandal were Jay Smith and Mary Willingham.

The piece ended by referencing the late Bill Friday, a long-time academic leader in the state who was associated with UNC. Also included was a pointed condemnation of the school's storied reputation: "Perhaps the disclosure of Boxill's role will serve as a catalyst for more decisive action on the part of her colleagues, because North Carolina is making a mockery of Friday's dream. That's no way to honor the legacy of a man who deserves better, or a school that once stood for something more."

* * *

In an interview almost 10 days later, Boxill finally spoke about the changes she had made to the 2012 faculty report. In a July 30, 2013, article in the *News and Observer*, Boxill said her suggestion for a revision came from other committee members who, during a session to review the draft, did not like the phrase "athletic supporter" (when referencing Deborah Crowder), partly because of its alternative meaning as a "jock strap". Boxill said she did not remember which members had uttered the concerns in the committee meeting. As noted in Kane's article from a week and a half earlier, all of the members he had spoken to had denied making the suggested changes. Not surprisingly, also left unaddressed in the new article was why Crowder's name had been completely removed from the report.

* * *

The essential (and unanswered) questions:

-- Did Jan Boxill change the wording of a 2012 academic report with the specific intent of trying to keep the NCAA from returning to campus?

-- Given Boxill's close ties to UNC athletics for over 20 years, had she used her then-current position of leadership to purposely try and shield the school's athletic programs from additional scrutiny?

CHAPTER TWENTY-ONE

SECRETARY OF STATE FOOTBALL/AGENT INDICTMENTS

In early October it was announced that an Orange County (NC) grand jury had handed up five indictments related to the UNC football scandal from three years earlier. According to an October 1, 2013, article posted by the local ABC station WTVD, the indictments were sealed and the names and charges were redacted in court documents that had been obtained. The names would eventually be revealed in the coming weeks.

The first indictment was for the UNC tutor who had been one of the centerpieces of the football academic scandal, Jennifer Wiley. Now going under the married name of Jennifer Lauren Wiley Thompson, she had been one of 10 people found by the NCAA to have provided impermissible benefits – both academic and financial – to members of the UNC football team. The WTVD article stated that in the course of a criminal investigation, agents with the Secretary of State's office searched Wiley's phone records – finding "extensive contact between Wiley and UNC-CH student athletes" and "direct contact between Wiley's number and (sports agent) Peter Schaffer."

The second indictment, which was announced on October 9, was for a Georgia-based sports agent. Terry Watson was indicted with 13 counts of providing cash or travel accommodations to former UNC players Marvin Austin, Greg Little, and Robert Quinn valued at nearly $24,000 in an effort to sign them, according to *USA Today*. Watson also faced a count of obstruction of justice for not providing records sought by authorities.

The third indictment was for Patrick Mitchell Jones, a real estate agent from Cartersville, Georgia, reported wncn. com on October 14, 2013. He was indicted with one count of athlete-agent inducement for providing money in May 2010 through a woman identified as Constance Orr to entice Robert Quinn to sign with agent Terry Watson. Orr was a student and softball athlete at UNC at the time.

The final two indictments were for Willie James Barley, who was indicted on four counts of athlete-agent inducement, and Michael Wayne Johnson, who was indicted on three counts of athlete-agent inducement. According to a November 14, 2013, article in *The Daily Tar Heel*, Barley was employed by Watson Sports Agency. Johnson was a graduate of Durham (NC) Hillside High School and was a former quarterback at

N.C. Central University. Johnson later worked for Rosenhaus Sports Representation, but his biography had been taken down from the agency's website by the time of the indictment.

* * *

An article on chapelboro.com from October 10, 2013, warned that the initial five grand jury indictments might not be the end of the matter, as Orange County District Attorney Jim Woodall had said there were other ongoing investigations involving UNC. Of note was an investigation into the school's AFAM department, which potentially held both academic and athletic ramifications. Woodall had not announced who he and the SBI had been investigating on that front, but a question remained as to whether Julius Nyang'oro and possibly other members of the AFAM department had committed fraud by collecting paychecks for classes that were not taught. More information on that front would surface in the coming months.

* * *

The essential (and unanswered) questions:

-- Had the athlete-agent aspect of the scandal been initiated completely from the outside, or had university representatives within the UNC infrastructure known about the ongoing impermissible benefits?

CHAPTER TWENTY - TWO

NCAA STAYS AWAY; NYANG'ORO INDICTED; HAIRSTON DISMISSED

The final months of 2013 would contain a flurry of articles spanning nearly every aspect of UNC's multiple scandals. On September 27 the men's basketball team began preseason practice. Both P.J. Hairston and Leslie McDonald were present, but word was circulating that if the season had started that day, neither would be on the court. It remained to be seen if that would truly be the case once the team played its opening game in six more weeks. Meanwhile, more news emerged on other fronts.

An October 7, 2013, article in the *News and Observer* provided an update on the AFAM department and the students who had been affected by fraudulent classes. As of the article's print date, only one student had enrolled in a make-up course and only one alumnus had inquired about the possibility, according to university officials. UNC spokeswoman Dee Reid said that 46 people were at risk of not graduating unless they completed an extra course. Reid said she didn't know what year of study the 46 affected students were in or how many of them were athletes. The offer of free courses was part of an arrangement the school made with SACS, the accrediting body of the university. The academic degrees of 384 students and alumni were said to have been affected between 1997 and 2009, according to UNC. Future data presented by the *N&O*, however, would show that the numbers were likely much higher: as many as 4,200 students could have ultimately been affected by taking fraudulent courses.

Of the 384 people officially identified, 80 were current students and 304 were alumni. There was no mandate for the alumni to return to campus to retake a class, however. The article said that because university policy required that transcripts be sealed one year after graduation, there would be no way to award credit or a grade for a new class. The university had said it would cover the cost of the extra courses and textbooks with private funds. It remained unclear whether more students would feel obligated to do the extra work for a problem that was essentially caused by factions within the university itself.

* * *

That same day a report came out stating that a longtime UNC tutor had quit, and done so in the form of writing a letter to basketball coach Roy Williams that was published in *The Daily Tar Heel*. Jack Halperin's short message said: "Roy, after 23 years as an academic tutor, and after going through the devastating football scandal, I am resigning in protest of your disgraceful decision to allow P.J. Hairston to remain on the team. If I were arrested driving with no license, illegal drugs and a gun in a felon's car, my employment at this University would end immediately. Hairston's DTH quote was, 'I will play this season.' Since when does the criminal decide his fate?"

* * *

An article appeared on October 11, 2013, on insidehighered. com detailing a new documentary film called "Schooled: The Price of College Sports". It was based on the widely read Atlantic article "The Shame of College Sports" by historian Taylor Branch. Multiple people involved in varying aspects of college sports – both past and present – spoke in the documentary. Two of particular interest were UNC learning specialist Mary Willingham and *News and Observer* reporter Dan Kane.

"It's the adults that are failing the students," Willingham said. She also recounted a sobering conversation with a top UNC athletic official, the article detailed. The official acknowledged that investing millions to boost the school's mid-level football team to the elite level in the late-1990's would mean recruiting academically unprepared students. "I just felt like I was drowning," Willingham said of the "drastic drop" in athletes' academic preparation that followed. Some students who had been recruited couldn't even read, and she recalled three in particular with whom she had to work on "letters and sounds."

When the article (based on the corresponding documentary)

mentioned the fraudulent AFAM classes which displayed multiple signs of being a vehicle to keep athletes eligible, it observed that the NCAA declined to investigate UNC because athletes were not the sole beneficiaries of the classes. "If the NCAA doesn't want to look at this," Dan Kane said, "you could argue they just sent a message to everyone across the county." He was likely referring to a "blueprint" that other schools could follow if they wanted to provide impermissible academic assistance to their athletes without garnering unwanted attention from the Athletic Association.

* * *

UNC began its basketball season on November 8, 2013, and both P.J. Hairston and Leslie McDonald sat out the contest. No official word was given for their absence other than there being "eligibility concerns." There was another equally big story on that day as well. A *News and Observer* article was released that stated the NCAA was unlikely to punish the school for the widespread academic fraud in its AFAM department.

Information had been discovered once again through public records requests by the newspaper that had finally been filled. According to the *N&O*, newly released email correspondence revealed that the NCAA still did not see the school's athletic/academic fraud as a concern. Writer Dan Kane said that in late September, Vince Ille, a UNC senior athletic official who had first been discussed in Chapter Eleven of this book, asked the NCAA to confirm that it had no plans to further investigate the fraud. "It is my understanding that, based on the available information, no additional investigation regarding these issues is being contemplated by the NCAA enforcement staff, nor does the staff believe that any modification of the infractions case that was complete on March 12, 2012 is necessary," Ille wrote. "Can you please confirm or correct this assessment?" Less than an hour later, Mike Zonder, the NCAA's associate director for enforcement, responded: "You are correct in your assessment regarding the situation involving the AFAM department."

Zonder and NCAA President Mark Emmert did not respond to interview requests from the *N&O*. A spokeswoman for the NCAA, Emily James Potter, said in a short statement that Zonder's email was "correct." Ille and other UNC officials also declined to be interviewed. An ambiguity was where Ille had initially gotten the impression that led to his email to Zonder: that it has been his "understanding" that nothing additional would happen to the university. One possibility for that impression (which was hinted at in the article) could have come from Jackie Thurnes, Ille's former co-worker when he was at the University of Illinois. After working with Ille on that collegiate campus, Thurnes would leave Illinois to become an enforcement official with the NCAA.

Overall, the article's effect on the watchful public was one of stunned disbelief. Over a year earlier in September of 2012, UNC officials had released a statement saying that the NCAA had thus far found no evidence of violations. A vast amount of incriminating news had emerged since then, however, detailing multiple connections between athletics and the academic fraud. So it was no surprise that onlookers were left dumbfounded by the NCAA's continued indifference to the events in Chapel Hill.

* * *

It was detailed in an earlier chapter the vast amount of

money UNC had spent on outside public relations assistance – a known total in the half-million dollar range. With that in mind, an early-November employment announcement from the school made an ironic bit of sense. A release from wral. com on November 11, 2013, said that Joel Curran, a senior executive in a public relations agency and fittingly an alumnus of UNC, had been named the school's first vice chancellor for communications and public affairs. Curran was the managing director of the New York office for MSLGROUP, described in part as the world's fourth largest public relations and engagement agency. The news release added that he had worked at public relations agencies across the country. Some people in social media speculated that if UNC felt the need to continue to spin stories and craft a certain message, they might as well hire someone full-time to help with that task.

* * *

On December 2, 2013, an Orange County grand jury indicted former AFAM department chairman Julius Nyang'oro on a charge of obtaining property by false pretense. More importantly, his lawyer – Bill Thomas of Durham – said that his client intended to fight the charge filed against him. "Dr. Nyang'oro is presumed to be innocent under our law," Thomas said. "There's been one side of this story that has been put forth in the press, but he's going to have an opportunity to present his side. We intend to present his case in court. He is going to contest these charges." Those statements held some large ramifications, as Nyang'oro could possibly divulge a massive amount of as-yet-unreleased information about the AFAM scandal if put on the stand.

An article on December 3, 2013, by the *News and Observer*

also had further insight from Jim Woodall, the Orange County District Attorney. Woodall had indicated that a second individual could face charges in the case, but he would only say that person was not a current UNC employee. Widespread speculation was that he was referring to Deborah Crowder, the longtime AFAM department manager who had also been extremely close to factions within the school's men's basketball program. Crowder had retired in 2009.

* * *

Yet another embarrassing episode would hit the school's basketball program a few days later. On December 6, 2013, a former UNC player was found to have marijuana and drug paraphernalia inside a house he had been renting from head basketball coach Roy Williams. According to a follow-up article from the News & Observer on December 13, Will Graves was the former player in question. Police had found 4.4 grams of marijuana, eight marijuana seeds, three blunts, and two "burnt marijuana blunts" inside the rented house.

Steve Kirschner, a UNC athletics department spokesman, said Graves had been renting the house from Williams while Graves took classes at UNC during the fall semester. Graves had played for the Tar Heels from 2007 through 2010, but had actually been kicked off of the team by Williams for a violation of team rules. Despite that prior conflict, Graves had been serving as a part-time video coordinator for the men's basketball team at the time of the drug discovery. Property tax records showed that the house had an assessed value of over $600,000. In a separate article, Kirschner had told the Associated Press that Williams had allowed people to stay at the home periodically.

* * *

On December 18, 2013, basketball player Leslie McDonald was cleared by the NCAA to return to the team. He had missed a total of nine games due to receiving impermissible benefits. Among them had been the use of cars associated with Haydn Thomas, the use of a custom mouth guard, and also an iPhone. He was ordered to repay $1,783 to a charity of his choice before the end of the regular season.

Fellow player P.J. Hairston was not as fortunate. The school announced two days later that Hairston would not return to the court that season, as the university had decided against seeking his reinstatement from the NCAA. UNC Athletic Director Bubba Cunningham gave more insight into the matter in a December 20, 2013, *News and Observer* article. "We've all been hopeful the entire time that he would be able to play again," Cunningham said. "But by the time we gathered all the information and worked with the NCAA, it just wasn't there." Cunningham declined to detail the exact monetary value of the impermissible benefits Hairston had received.

When news began to spread that the school hadn't even asked the NCAA to look at Hairston's situation, many in social media began to speculate whether there was a deeper reason for that inaction by the university. Some wondered if the purpose was to keep from having to release information to the NCAA that might have uncovered even more issues within the basketball program. Or, in Hairston's specific case, might have spanned back to prior seasons and forced the vacating of wins.

Hairston's family released a statement in which it criticized UNC's decision not to seek reinstatement, the *N&O* article reported. "We are displeased with the University of North

Carolina's decision not to submit the necessary paperwork to the NCAA requesting to have P.J. reinstated," the statement read. "This process has been long, and for (it) to end without having a final decision from the governing body is a shame."

The Associated Press had earlier reported that Bill Thomas, a Durham lawyer representing Haydn Thomas, said his client had met with school officials in early December for "an in-depth interview… to clear up any misconceptions about the relationship between Haydn Thomas and Mr. Hairston." As an interesting and somewhat odd side note, Bill Thomas was also the lawyer representing former AFAM chairman Julius Nyang'oro in his grand jury case.

Not really mentioned by the media at that time, but still an issue of great importance, was the school's ongoing NCAA probation. Athletics Director Bubba Cunningham had made the following statement in early 2013 when discussing the release of the Martin report: "There's no denying that we've got major violations and we're on probation. We didn't go to a bowl game, and we're under the repeat violator clause for the next five years." The infractions incurred by McDonald and Hairston would clearly appear to be a violation of the school's probation. Once again, where was the NCAA?

* * *

As December would near its end, an article appeared on the website bleacherreport.com titled "Inside Roy Williams' Most Trying Season." It talked of the effects the various scandals had had on the 63-year-old coach, with Williams saying, "I never in my life thought I'd have these kind of things happen. It's cast a light on our program that I don't like, and it's cast a light on me that I don't like at all." Scott Williams, the coach's son, actually had some very telling comments in the article – some of which could have even been considered Freudian slips. "It's not that Carolina's record is spotless," the younger Williams said. "No one's record is spotless. But in the past it was much easier to get things taken care of and not have everything play out in such a public forum."

* * *

With 2013 drawing to a close, it had ultimately proven to be another year of scandals surrounding the athletic/academic infrastructure of UNC, and another year of the university's leadership refusing to come clean and show full transparency. Public records and documents continued to be withheld from the media, which only prolonged the likely eventual emergence of more damning information in the future. As it was, the tide would take a major turn when the calendar rolled over to 2014. Once relegated to the local North Carolina sports and academic scenes, the story garnered national attention in a big way as the New Year began.

* * *

The essential (and unanswered) questions:

-- Even with a prodigious amount of new and incriminating evidence that clearly suggested widespread athletic/academic fraud, why was the scandal at UNC still not a concern to the NCAA as 2013 came to an end?

-- Did UNC not seek reinstatement for P.J. Hairston in an attempt to specifically avoid further scrutiny from the NCAA – scrutiny which might have spilled over to other players and/or earlier athletic seasons?

-- Considering the fact that UNC was already on probation following its multiple infractions from several years earlier, why didn't the impermissible benefits received by McDonald and Hairston trigger immediate repercussions from the NCAA?

CHAPTER TWENTY - THREE

NATIONAL MEDIA ATTENTION; THE COST OF A SCANDAL

The different athletic/academic scandals at UNC had caused small national ripples at times over the previous three years, but never had any truly moved to the forefront of the national media. That finally showed signs of changing, however. The New York *Times* published an article on the scandal that appeared online late on December 31, 2013, and then in print on New Year's Day. *Business Week* followed with a series of articles that began on January 2. There was an in-depth CNN report by Sara Ganim on January 7. Incidentally, Ganim was the reporter who had uncovered many key details during the early stages of the Penn State case involving Jerry Sandusky. The New York *Post* contributed a piece on January 11, and then a crippling episode of ESPN's investigative show

"Outside the Lines" aired on January 14, 2014, blatantly calling out UNC for the apparent fraud that benefitted athletes, and the NCAA for refusing to take any action.

The implications of so much attention from national media sources meant that it might be extremely difficult for the NCAA to ignore the issues going forward. Why that had even transpired for so long was truly a mystery, especially when considering past similar cases. Several years earlier the NCAA had ruled that Florida State had been guilty of major violations in a widespread academic fraud case from 2006 and 2007. An online music class was apparently taught irregularly, a former learning specialist had typed portions of papers for three student-athletes, and answers were provided to an athlete for an online psychology course. The case involved 61 athletes, all of whose individual records were eventually expunged. Furthermore, a total of 12 wins by the school's football team were retroactively erased by the NCAA for the use of ineligible players. The number of classes and affected student-athletes in FSU's case paled in comparison to the AFAM fraud at UNC.

At the University of Georgia in 2003 a former player – Tony Cole – claimed that an assistant coach had paid some of his bills, done schoolwork for him, and taught a sham class on coaching. Cole said he never attended the class, but along with two other basketball players received an A. That seemed extremely similar to the AFAM scandal, except for the fact that it was only one class and three student-athletes at Georgia – compared to hundreds of courses and student-athletes at UNC. The Georgia basketball program self-banned itself from the 2003 postseason, but then the NCAA added further penalties: the loss of future scholarships, the vacating of numerous wins over a three-year period, and the expunging of players' records.

A scandal surfaced at the University of Minnesota in early 1999. A former basketball office manager said she had written papers for at least 20 men's basketball players over a period of several years. Two days after the story first ran, the NCAA suspended four current players. Following a full investigation a number of violations were uncovered, and the school was ultimately stripped of all postseason awards, titles, personal records, and statistics dating back to the 1993-94 season. Later, the Big Ten conference vacated the school's 1997 conference title, and the school also returned 90% of the profits earned by the team during various appearances in the NCAA tournament. There were stark similarities between Minnesota's and UNC's cases. But once again, the situation in Chapel Hill appeared to dwarf what had happened at the other school. If the same scrutiny were given to UNC as to Minnesota (a full-fledged, external investigation), the vacated results and titles would be much greater.

* * *

Often over the past several years fans of UNC had complained that the media and other factions were "out to get" the school, and were determined to have the basketball national championship banners removed. What those individuals likely did not realize was that the basketball team was a massive part of the school's image, and people often associated the success of those year-to-year teams with their overall perception of the university. In essence, when the team did well, in various areas the school also did well. For example, a March 19, 2009, article on wral.com was titled "Heels merchandise head and shoulders above rest." The article stated that the Tar Heel brand name was a money-maker, and had generated $25.9 million for the university, according to a then-recent analysis by *Forbes* magazine. Those sales had made UNC the most valuable men's basketball program in the country. As a result, it became clear that UNC and its leaders likely weren't just trying to protect the banners that hung in the rafters of the Dean Smith Center, but also the revenue that poured in due to those teams' successes.

Retailers in Chapel Hill spoke to wral.com about the ease of selling UNC-branded clothing, mugs, and other items. "I told somebody the other day there's only four things that people need. That's food, gas, shelter and Carolina souvenirs, and we happen to be in the latter part of that, so we're very fortunate," said Genny Wrenn, manager of a store on Franklin Street. Carolina Brewery manager Thomas Transue said his restaurant was usually packed during the NCAA Tournament, especially when UNC was playing. "There is such a strong background. We've had folks coming in for years for the Tar Heels," he said.

There were other measurable benefits to having a basketball program that accomplished great feats. Based on a December 19, 2012, article in the *News and Observer*, the prior year's profit from the school's basketball team had been $16.9 million. It had also ranked number one in a recent ESPN assessment of top 50 college basketball programs based on wins, championships, and lack of NCAA sanctions. During the 2012 fiscal year, donations to the school's Ram's Club, which funded student-athlete scholarships and capital projects, had increased to $33 million.

The positive effects of a strong public perception could spread to other areas of the university, as well. Statistics had long shown that freshman applications to a school often increased following a sports championship – of which UNC had won three since 1992. Based on data from the school's own uncnews.unc.edu site, the application rate continued to climb. The site reported that in the fall of 2013 the university enrolled nearly 4,000 first-year students from a record 30,836 applications. Furthermore, the school was 9th among leading private and public research universities for the level of federal funding devoted to research and development in all fields. It was also among the top 100 U.S. colleges and universities awarding undergraduate degrees to minority students, according to a 2011 issue of the magazine Diverse: Issues in Higher Education. The school ranked 2nd for graduating African-American students majoring in area, ethnic, cultural, gender, and group studies. Unfortunately, that last statistic might be viewed in a somewhat critical light going forward due to the extensive AFAM scandal.

How many of those donations, applications, honors and awards were connected to an image carved at least in part by athletes and their successes? That would be a matter of opinion, obviously, unless one could find specific quotes from people who stated they were influenced by such athletic accomplishments. The fact that UNC men's basketball merchandise was the top seller in the entire country, however, spoke to the mindset of influence and desired conformity. The fact that UNC sold merchandise, received applications, and were given grants was not just beneficial to it as a university and brand. It also conversely had a negative effect on other area schools – schools that were actually doing things the right way, instead of simply claiming to do so. Those schools that followed and played by the rules may have lost out on merchandise sales, and may have lost out on potential applications. And while less likely, it cannot be said for certain that they didn't lose out on grants and funding from certain entities, as well.

* * *

Based on the numerous instances of public documents having been withheld, misinformation uncovered, and "no comments" often given, UNC made a conscious choice as to how to approach its problems over the past several years. Those choices had come at a price – both in terms of reputation, but also one of monetary value. Some of the figures have been discussed earlier in the book, but when looked at as a whole they become even more daunting. An article appeared on the online site of *Synapse Magazine* in mid-November 2013 which gave an in-depth breakdown of some of the tolls incurred by UNC over the past three-plus years.

Titled "The Cost of a Scandal," the piece gathered its data from both publicly-released information as well as figures provided by the school itself. The total amount spent for the academic and athletic portions of the university's troubles reached nearly five million dollars. Almost $500,000 was spent on lawyers during the initial 2010 football revelations and the first round of academic issues that arose afterwards. That bill was picked up by two funds, the article reported. About $219,000 came from the UNC Foundation, a portion of the University's endowment that drew its funding entirely from private donations. Approximately $248,000 of those first legal fees came from the athletic budget, university spokeswoman Karen Moon said. The athletic budget typically did not set aside funds for unexpected expenses (such as legal fees), according to Martina Ballen, chief financial officer of the school's athletic department. She said extra revenue from men's basketball and football from that year helped offset the costs.

Other dollar amounts were related to employee payouts. When Butch Davis' contract was terminated by the university, the choice was made to pay him a severance package of $2.7

million even though wording in his contract suggested that he could have been fired with cause and paid nothing. Disgraced assistant coach John Blake resigned, yet the university paid him $74,500. Both of those monetary payouts came from the athletic budget.

Next would be the fees for various public relations experts. Those companies and/or individuals were hired at the urging of the school's Board of Trustees and the UNC System's Board of Governors. In former Chancellor Holden Thorp's own words, "Our board was uneasy about whether we were doing the best things we could in terms of public relations." That led to the hiring of at least three communication experts, with a combined bill of over $530,000. Sallie Shuping-Russell, secretary of the university's Board of Trustees, tried to justify the high costs. "It was no longer just about the athletics program," she said. "It became about the integrity of our school. We were dealing with a level of issues that we didn't have internal people to sufficiently handle. It wasn't like our internal team was just issuing the news – suddenly, we were the news." However, the hiring of the public relations experts didn't bring about transparency and the truth, but rather a well-crafted message that was passed off to the public. Many onlookers were intelligent enough to see the scandalous situations for what they truly were, and thus saw through the PR attempts.

The infamous Martin investigation cost the school over one million dollars, much of which was paid to the Baker Tilly firm. Even after spending all of that money for months of work, the company was still forced to recant one of its most vital findings when the local *News and Observer* newspaper showed it to be false. All of Baker Tilly's costs were also financed by the UNC Foundation. All told, about a third of the money spent during the two scandals came from that Foundation. It was a financial holding tank for the university that primarily funded scholarships, professorships, and fellowships, but in times of controversy the Foundation was said to be able to help with the load. An issue that remained unaddressed was whether the numerous alumni, outside affiliates, students, and faculty who had donated money were satisfied knowing that part of their contributions had gone not towards the advancement of education, but rather to help pay off the effects (and suspected cover-up) of scandals.

Hodding Carter, a UNC professor of leadership and public policy, told the magazine that far too often consultants were only hired to support the position of the administration. "If you're going to hire outside anything," he said, "you better be damn well sure that those outsiders are ruthless, unyielding in their demand for information and absolutely committed beyond their paycheck." Based on how much information on the scandals those outside entities either missed (or purposely overlooked), it certainly did not appear that they fit the stringent parameters of which Carter referred.

On the flip side of the coin was Jan Boxill. The faculty chairwoman of the university had come under heavy fire for her suspected role in tampering with reports in an effort to dissuade the NCAA from returning to campus. Not surprisingly, she toed the company line when it came to defending the use of extravagant outside sources, saying that external consultants were crucial for attempting to keep a unified faculty. "I think if we had the faculty running investigations, the situation would have been more contentious and split," Boxill said. "It would have divided the faculty. We wanted to bring consensus." To that effect, near-total consensus was exactly what UNC's leadership got: other than Mary Willingham and Professor Jay Smith, virtually every other faculty member refused to speak out and stand up for what was moral and right.

With regards to the handling of public relations, Stanley Katz offered a different and more sobering viewpoint. A professor of public and international affairs at Princeton University, Katz gave his professional opinion that external help was inexcusable for public relations. "Universities ought to be able to handle their own public relations," he said. "If the university sees the problem as a public relations issue, then it isn't internalizing the fact that there is a problem with the way (the university) handles (itself)."

Former Chancellor Thorp indicated that the current situation in which the university found itself could have possibly been reached more cheaply and with less turbulence. Then, almost as a recurring punch line to an overused joke, he ended the article with the very same tired PR message that had been rolled out by university leaders for several years: "But it was a tough situation, and I think Carolina is in a good position to move forward."

* * *

The essential (and unanswered) questions:

-- Would the influx of national attention given to UNC's scandals finally cause the NCAA to take appropriate action?

-- Other schools had been punished by the NCAA for much lesser infractions. Why had they not shown public outrage over the preferential treatment that UNC seemed to be receiving?

-- How much money had UNC taken in – from merchandise sales, applications, and other sources – as a direct or indirect result from athletic successes that had possibly been built and achieved through fraudulent academic acts?

-- Why weren't alumni, outside affiliates, students, and faculty who had donated money to the UNC Foundation not showing public displeasure at the arguably moral misuse of their contributions?

CONCLUSION

After nearly four years of scandals there ultimately are very few definitive answers. Not because of a lack of evidence, but rather due to an obstinate lack of cooperation and openness by UNC. The university has held on tooth and nail to an ideal, all while trying to protect an image of past glories. As a result, the public has slowly formed a jaded view of an institution that had once appeared to have some leaders of virtue. What is left is a series of "what if" questions, the answers to which would likely have put an end to the scandal – one way or another – long beforehand. Those answers would have also allowed a process of healing to begin, as well as shown that the university valued character.

-- What if all of the emails and phone records of Julius Nyang'oro had been released and thoroughly dissected to determine the original birthplace of the AFAM scandal?

-- What if the list of basketball and football players whose grades were changed had been released, and the effects of those grades on their GPA (and eligibility) were clearly outlined?

-- Along those lines, what if the transcripts of former athletes had been closely inspected to see if academic fraud (from no matter what academic department) had indeed kept them eligible to participate?

-- What if the hiring practices of those closely tied to athletics were more closely and honestly examined, as well as the connections between UNC alumni and people providing impermissible benefits to athletes?

-- What if more members of the university's faculty had spoken up in defense of the school's academic reputation, and against the protection that was continually offered to the major revenue sports teams?

-- What if the students and alumni who had earned honest degrees had spoken up in outrage for the same reason – the defense of the school's academic, as opposed to athletic, reputation?

-- What if Chancellor Holden Thorp had refused the suggestions of the Board of Trustees and Board of Governors and decided against hiring a myriad of lawyers and public relations experts, and instead offered full transparency into the university's darkest corners of the past?

-- Along those lines, what if the school had not delayed and/or refused countless Freedom of Information Act requests from the media?

-- Essentially, what if those associated with the school had truly practiced what they professed to be the "Carolina Way," and chosen to come clean and start the healing process much sooner?

Sadly, the answer to the majority of those questions has become painfully obvious as each month and year has passed. Data and information strongly suggests that many players would have been retroactively ineligible, wins would have been vacated, and yes – those national championship banners which constituted so much of the school's national image and pride would have been null and void. Despite NCAA president Mark Emmert having said that universities must eradicate the "sports are king" mindset when he handed down Penn State's punishment in 2012, his bold sentiment has still not spread to encompass the University of North Carolina at Chapel Hill.

* * *

A quote used by some parents who strive to be solid role models goes as follows: "Your children will become what you are; so be what you want them to be." That statement is attributed to David Bly, a Minnesota politician and former member of the Minnesota House of Representatives, as well as a former teacher. They are strong words to live by, especially for adults who truly believe in positive modeling for the young. The words also provide an interesting case study for factions within UNC.

If past and present players, coaches, students, professors, staff members, administrators, and any others claiming to be associated with Chapel Hill had any desire to set an example for those who might look up to them, yet took a hard look at their own actions and true motives, what would they see? Would they see people they would want their children to become? Hundreds, if not thousands, have chosen to remain silent in the face of overwhelming evidence of athletic/academic fraud, all apparently in order to protect an image and brand name. Along the same lines, what would the adults associated with the NCAA see? Based on past collegiate cases of impropriety, they have picked and chosen when to enforce their standards with favoritism apparently a guiding principle. Despite what Mark

Emmert had proclaimed in the past, the NCAA had still allowed sports to be king in Chapel Hill.

The stark reality, however, is that it should have never been necessary to expect and require the NCAA to police and punish the activities that had taken place at UNC. If the "Carolina Way" truly stood for all of the honorable platitudes that the school, its workers, and its graduates would have the rest of the world believe, then adults would have stood up, admitted what had transpired in the past, and done the right thing. Because that was, after all, what the "Carolina Way" was supposed to mean.

The athletic/academic scandals within the halls of the campus buildings in Chapel Hill had long been the proverbial elephant in the room. Unfortunately, athletic glory had been shown to be countless times more valuable than integrity. From a center of higher learning, that is a sad testament not only to our society, but also to the morals and values of the adults associated with that school – adults whose charge was to set a solid example and foundation for the young. A degradation of morals and character had stepped to the forefront over the past few years, and is what the leadership of the university appears to now stand for and accept as right.

No matter what new information comes out, and whether the NCAA ever takes the correct action and fully investigates the fraud or not, the charade of morality will be over unless those adult factions actually own up to the errors of the past. The honor and integrity of doing things "the right way" have sadly been overtaken by pride and poor judgment. Until a true will to change is shown from the school itself, it will be negative traits that will define the university going forward. Until that honest repentance happens, the "Carolina Way" will remain a remnant of the past.

AUTHOR'S NOTE

When gathering data, researching articles and information, and then actually writing this book, a number of disturbing issues stood out. Most of them were likely obvious from the narrative: the lack of those in positions of leadership to tackle a blatant problem head-on; cheating done for some sort of institutional, personal, and/or financial gain; and so forth. By the end of the book, however, the aspect that was perhaps the most frustrating dealt with the abuse of our education system. Education has been such a hot topic for years – not just at select colleges and universities, but nationwide and on all levels from kindergarten on up. Teachers in primary and secondary schools remain underpaid and underappreciated, yet are held to high (and ever-changing) testing standards, most of which are widely criticized as being largely without merit when it comes to properly preparing our youth for adulthood and careers. That is, of course, a topic for an entirely different book. But what has been shown throughout this account at UNC is an utter lack of respect for the education process. The fraud, cheating, and cover-ups have essentially created a trickle-down effect from the university, to the students, to the public education system (high school on down), to the teachers who are trying diligently to prepare their students despite many obstacles, and even to parents who have questions and frustrations about their children's education and future well-being. In essence, not only were morals and values compromised at the University of North Carolina, but so too was the supposed purpose and mission of an institute of higher learning: to teach students. The result of the UNC scandal is one that reflects an overall de-emphasis on the value of an education in our country, and, as a parent, that is truly troubling and sad.

INDEX

Evans, Jack, 101, 117, 264, 265

Faculty Athletic Committee (FAC), 119, 244-247, 251, 258, 263-266, 268-270, 272, 273, 279

Gause, Lee, 323-325

Hairston, P.J., 51, 313-325, 337, 339, 340, 344-347

Hansbrough, Tami, 186-189, 192, 194, 198-204, 207, 209, 324

Hansbrough, Tyler, 95, 186, 187, 192, 194, 204, 212, 216

Hargrove, Wade, 66, 106, 109, 115, 144, 194, 288, 289

Herman, Amy, 242, 243, 251

Howard, Spencer, 323-325

Ille, Vince, 178, 181, 183, 242, 243, 340, 341

Infante, John, 216, 217

Kane, Dan, 61, 62, 72, 74, 75, 89, 90, 92, 93, 98, 100, 118, 123, 128, 134-136, 138-140, 176, 210, 215, 217, 245, 246, 266, 267, 279, 286, 287, 289-291, 294, 302, 303, 310, 328, 329, 332, 339, 340

Kupec, Matt, 185-192, 194, 197-205, 207, 209, 324

Levine, Madeline, 249, 250, 307

Little, Greg, 24, 27, 34, 41, 43, 44, 50-53, 58, 334

Martin, Jim (Martin Investigation; Martin Report), 168-171, 179, 185, 189, 196, 207, 213, 218, 223, 225-227, 229-232, 238, 239, 250, 253-279, 282, 286, 288, 292, 299, 304, 309, 331, 345, 354, 355

McAdoo, Michael, 29, 34, 59-65, 70, 71, 78, 79, 89, 90, 93, 94, 98, 106, 125, 211, 277, 278

McDonald, Leslie, 323, 324, 337, 340, 344, 345, 347

131, 142-144, 148, 171,
223, 224, 230, 233, 234,
266, 273, 281, 282, 328,
331, 356

Sosnik, Doug, 309

Southern Association of
Colleges and Schools (SACS),
280, 281, 310, 338

Swofford, John, 68, 81

Thomas, Haydn, 315-325,
344, 345

Thorp, Holden, 32, 39, 40, 45,
46, 59, 65-68, 74, 78,
79, 81, 84, 92, 107-109,
111-116, 120, 121, 124,
125, 128, 132, 145-147,
168, 170-172, 175, 176,
178, 179, 181, 183, 186-
189, 191, 193-200, 202,
204, 209, 213, 215, 218,
219, 223, 239, 249, 256,
259, 261, 264, 267, 279,
281, 287, 291, 292, 297,
300, 301, 303, 305, 306,
330, 331, 355, 357, 360

Townsend, Jennifer, 236, 237,
239, 250, 258

Walden, Wayne, 161-165,
176, 216, 220, 236, 239, 257,
258, 265

Wichard, Gary, 20, 22, 23, 25-
27, 38, 39, 42, 43, 59

Wiley, Jennifer, 32, 45, 51-54,
58-60, 82, 201, 208, 209, 240,
278, 333, 334

Williams, Roy, 108, 153, 157,
158, 161, 162, 164, 165,
216, 219, 220, 236, 237,
257, 261, 314, 317, 318,
321, 338, 343, 345, 346

Willingham, Mary, 234-241,
243, 250, 252, 258, 259,
282, 292-294, 309, 310,
331, 339, 356

Winston, Bob, 39, 40, 50, 66

Woodard, Harold, 176, 177,
183, 190, 191, 225